CITY SURVIVORS

Bringing up children in disadvantaged neighbourhoods

Anne Power

D0555492

WITHDRAWN
UTSA LIBRARIES

First published in Great Britain in 2007 by

The Policy Press
University of Bristol
Fourth Floor
Beacon House
Queen's Road
Bristol BS8 1QU
UK

Tel +44 (0)117 331 4054
Fax +44 (0)117 331 4093
e-mail tpp-info@bristol.ac.uk
www.policypress.org.uk

© Anne Power 2007

British Library Cataloguing in Publication Data
A catalogue record for this book is available from the British Library.

Library of Congress Cataloging-in-Publication Data
A catalog record for this book has been requested.

ISBN 978 1 84742 049 7 paperback
ISBN 978 1 84742 050 3 hardcover

The right of Anne Power to be identified as author of this work has been asserted by her in accordance with the 1988 Copyright, Designs and Patents Act.

All rights reserved: no part of this publication may be reproduced, stored in a retrieval system, or transmitted in any form or by any means, electronic, mechanical, photocopying, recording, or otherwise without the prior permission of The Policy Press.

The statements and opinions contained within this publication are solely those of the author and not of the University of Bristol, or The Policy Press. The University of Bristol and The Policy Press disclaim responsibility for any injury to persons or property resulting from any material published in this publication.

The Policy Press works to counter discrimination on grounds of gender, race, disability, age and sexuality.

Cover design by Qube Design Associates, Bristol.
Front cover kindly supplied by www.JohnBirdsall.co.uk (posed by models)
Printed and bound in Great Britain by Hobbs the Printers, Southampton.

Library
University of Texas
at San Antonio

Contents

Acknowledgements

The research for this book was funded by the Economic and Social Research Council and the Nuffield Foundation, supported by the Centre for Analysis of Social Exclusion at the London School of Economics and Political Science between 1998 and 2005.

We are indebted to the following researchers for their direct advice and examples in developing our work: Jacqueline Barnes, Penny Mansfield, David Piachaud, John Hills, Ray Pahl, William Julius Wilson, Jane Walfogel, Carol Propper and Simon Burgess. Their expertise in social studies and qualitative and quantitative research was invaluable.

Katharine Mumford, Helen Bowman, Helen Willmot, Rosie Davidson, Lalita McCleggan, Astrid Winkler and Bani Makkar carried out the interviews and advised on family and neighbourhood interactions. Nicola Harrison collated the data on the families. Alice Coulter, Laura Lane, Jane Dickson and Anna Tamas worked on many drafts of the stories. Caroline Paskell helped with editing and advice.

The families in the four areas shared their time, experience and ideas over seven years. Their generosity and openness laid firm foundations for our evidence. The book is dedicated to presenting their views on what would help families survive.

Acknowledgements

ONE

Introduction – city survivors

Bringing up children in unpopular neighbourhoods

City survivors is about bringing up children in troubled city neighbourhoods, seen through the eyes of parents, mainly mothers. Cities can be cruel places, particularly if you have children, if you are a mother and if you are on your own. Where you live is all important for survival. Neighbourhoods form the cradle of family life, the place where families are sheltered and linked in. The physical space is woven into the surroundings by threads of supervision, provision and connections to the wider opportunities of the city or town. But important as the wider city is, it is the neighbourhood that nourishes family life, the much smaller space where families organise their survival and progress. If the neighbourhood is insecure and uncared for, families will want to leave. Survival in cities means coping with pressures, changes, competition and the environment of built-up and heavily frequented areas. For families it means coping with home, money, children, school and neighbours in constrained and often insecure conditions. You survive in an area if you can cope with its problems.

It is hard for families on low incomes in poor areas to survive in cities. There is a constant exodus, as this London mother explained:

> "The inner city is too difficult with a child. It's noisy, dirty, dangerous. There's too much violence. We moved out for lots of reasons like the house and garden. But even if I could take this house and garden with me, I still wouldn't want to go back for those reasons."

Another mother, from a minority background, described her move to a new town:

> "When I got here, I felt as though a weight was lifting off my shoulders. Before it was like constant worry. People are much more friendly here and have time to say hello. Even so I like to keep the link [with my old neighbourhood] because of being black and my son needs his identity."

Once mothers have children, they seem to feel differently about the city, as this Lithuanian mother explained:

> "Until the day my baby was born, I was quite happy in my little flat near the centre with my husband. Then suddenly I looked at the world through different eyes, and realised how it would be for my baby – no outdoor space, lots of traffic, dangerous roads to cross and lots of pollution. It's a good place to live but very hard with a baby."

The outward movement of families with choice creates uncertainty and even more anxiety for those who stay. The spaces are filled by newcomers, sometimes families, but more often people without children, leading to reduced numbers of children in the neighbourhood.[1] So poorer urban neighbourhoods can become a kind of no-man's-land where families and individuals come and go, undermining informal social control, a sense of community and eventually family life itself.

A popular neighbourhood holds onto families by offering what they need. An unpopular neighbourhood holds families back by denying them the things they need. When a neighbourhood is run-down, poor and unpopular, it feels unsafe for children. So, naturally, families try to escape. But if they are vulnerable and made more so by their children's dependence, often they cannot move out. Lack of money, connections, security and ownership make it harder for poorer families to escape. A combination of poor conditions, low income and limited choice constrain their lives, affecting their children's perspectives. Better-off families escape this trap by living elsewhere or by paying for compensating activities and support that they can afford. So this book examines the evidence provided by parents that neighbourhoods matter to the future of cities, particularly to families.

City neighbourhoods are part of a large collective structure that individual families neither control nor shape beyond their own homes, so families choose their neighbourhood carefully if they can. Low-income families cannot choose and depend on the wider city to make the place where they live safe. This is why local government first emerged in the 19th century, to protect and ensure the survival of its more vulnerable citizens.[2] Only within this wider social frame can families survive in the city.

This book is based on yearly visits over seven years to 200 families living in four highly disadvantaged city neighbourhoods in England, 100 in East London and 100 in Northern inner- and outer-city areas. These families are struggling with much harsher neighbourhood conditions than most people can imagine and this directly affects their ability to cope. Twenty-four families from four low-income, unpopular neighbourhoods, six from each area, explain over time, from the inside, how neighbourhoods in and of themselves directly affect family survival.

The three recurring questions that this book tries to answer are:

- Do neighbourhood conditions of themselves make it difficult for families to bring up children in cities?

- Do the informal social links that families create provide protection, security, friendship, trust and mutual support in an atmosphere of rapid social change?
- How can the wider city meet family and community needs in poor areas, given the central role of families in the city as a whole?

Listening to families talking about life in their neighbourhoods came to feel like being part of their lives. Seeing the areas through their eyes, visiting their children's schools, bumping into their neighbours, meeting their relations and friends and watching places around them decay and be rebuilt, abused, neglected and cleaned up, made their stories come alive. Families told us things that would otherwise remain hidden from sight. Normally they have little voice in what happens and they most often go completely unheard. But they have a constant eye on their immediate surroundings because neighbourhoods have more direct impact on families with children than on anyone else.

Older people in poor neighbourhoods often stay indoors to avoid trouble, something that parents notice and worry about, but families have to use the streets and spaces of their neighbourhoods daily, for without social contact and support, they cannot survive and children cannot develop. Schools, health services, shops, open spaces and streets are their daily terrain. Families carry the most powerful sensors for the problems of poor areas, and they talk openly about their anxieties, so that something will be done. Their antennae are tuned to surviving in difficult conditions. Low-income mothers and children are heavily anchored where they live through lack of cash and the constraints of childcare; therefore their knowledge of and sensitivity to local problems are intense.

> "Now I'm a mother, I'm in the area. The area's a major part of your life. Your children mingle with parents and children in the area." (Fatima)

Mothers are critical to our understanding of neighbourhoods, as they carry the lion's share of childrearing and home organising responsibilities, often single-handed. As a way of surviving in troubled conditions they build strong community links through local social networks that support their families in the face of poor conditions. They have the greatest contact with local services because children need many of them. On the whole, they spend far more time than men with children in the neighbourhood. Households without children are generally far less tied in to their local area, often with less time or reason to be involved.

In the present study we interviewed the main carer in the family – typically the mother.[3] Yet mothers' views are not reflected in many of the public priorities that determine local services. For example, the reduction in frontline staff over the past 30 years affects families with children disproportionately by withdrawing control over neighbourhood conditions in the poorest urban areas. Many services are affected by this withdrawal: park-keeping, caretaking, maintenance, health visiting, general practice, home visiting and rent collection.[4]

The trust and open hospitality the families offered us over repeated visits made us realise just how important it was to them to tell their story. They did not want our work just to be a paper exercise, for they were conscious of the gap between 'how it really is' and how it appears from the Ivory Tower.

> "The University's too academic. It's not the real world." (Phoebe)

Parents needed to feel their time wasn't being wasted:

> "Why are these studies done? Is anything going to change because of it? If it's just more statistics on a graph, then why? If it will change things, great." (Joyce)

One mother asked whether exaggerating problems might help to win resources:

> "If I say crime's serious, will it help us?" (Delilah)

But sometimes mothers wanted to make the area appear less bad than it really was out of loyalty to their community:

> "I wouldn't want to report it to make the stats look more crime ridden." (Phoebe)

One of our parents was quite critical of our work because it didn't hit hard enough:

> "I'd like to give a tip ... I do feel it's a political tool.... The policy makers should look at the research properly, otherwise it's a wasted chance." (Adam)

Sometimes parents asked us not to write down what they confided to us, which we always respected. Others were, if anything, too open:

> "Good thing you're not the old Bill. I'd be banged up for years for fraud and everything." (Fanny)

Our 24 stories convey powerful messages from parents about the problems they want tackled, and the things that would help them. Linking our work to action became more pressing as time went on. For we picked up acute neighbourhood problems that were unfair to families. It was hard sometimes not to think of these city neighbourhoods as cruel places to bring up children.[5] Yet we could not become directly involved in people's difficulties, so we gave families local information and contacts whenever they asked about benefits, childcare, language classes or local meetings. And we put them in touch with local organisations that might help them if they were stuck over problems. Where a family seemed desperate, or where there seemed to be a need for special support, we made sure the family knew whom to contact. Only once were we directly worried about the safety of a mother and child. In that case we referred the mother to a local voluntary organisation that specialises in confidential family support. Many families had serious problems but almost all had someone they could rely on. The families came from many different backgrounds, reflecting as closely as possible the diversity of the local communities. They could not, however, reflect all the variety of individual lives.

Generalising about the problems of difficult areas, conveying the impression that all the families are in difficulty or that all low-income areas face similar problems would be blatantly wrong. Professional women with well-paid husbands – a small minority of our mothers – are far from lone, isolated mothers without back-up, work or qualifications – another small minority. Most families are in between. The attitudes of 'battle-worn' local residents whose families have lived in the same area for several generations, who feel it 'belongs' to them, contrast sharply with incomers from abroad who are anxious about their position but seize opportunities with new energy.

Different families have very different links to their neighbourhood. The age of children, the presence of a partner, racial awareness, relations with neighbours, the condition of a particular street or block, whether there are two incomes or none, all help to shape neighbourhood experiences in different ways for different families. The stories show how different families and neighbourhoods can be, and yet how dominant the pressures of poor neighbourhood conditions are on families. So although families' lives within these areas are sometimes worlds apart, they share the same neighbourhood spaces and see many things in common. They walk the same streets and their children go to the same schools. This shared neighbourhood experience leads to a deep understanding of the areas, their problems and assets.

One undervalued asset of low-income neighbourhoods is their social capital, reflecting the value residents attach to links with other residents, to the support offered by family and friends, to the familiarity, sense of security and mutual help that comes with frequent social contact. These areas are mines of social capital, in large measure created by the families who live there because they need it in order to survive.[6] They capture this idea most commonly in the term 'community spirit', which most families recognise and use. Social capital is a constant thread throughout this book.

North and South

The North of England and East London could not be more different and originally I thought that a major theme arising from the families would be the differences between these regions. The atmosphere of Northern cities is far from the buzz of the capital. Yet in reality, area problems, while distinct, do not divide neatly into North and South. Factors such as the degree to which the area is: near to the city centre; ethnically mixed; dominated by council housing; near to good public transport or main roads – these are sometimes more dominant. How serious crime is, how government action is hitting the ground, how communities are changing – these are all things that shape families' experiences across the four areas. So although we centre our work in two distinct parts of the country – East London and the North – and although the families root their experiences in their own area, not elsewhere, these experiences have more similarities than differences – namely acute, visible and measurable area disadvantage.

The two East London areas were both traditionally white working-class areas, dominated by large council estates, until the 1980s. The inner area, on the edge of the city, was the original stomping ground of the pre-war Fascists, and retained a reputation for toughness and crime. In the 1980s, a big turnover of people led to a rapid increase in minority ethnic groups and by the late 1990s nearly three-quarters of children in local schools were from a minority ethnic background. The high blocks of flats that dominate the area are run-down, poor and 'rough'. There are few parks, several busy roads and a crowded atmosphere, but the location is popular and 'yuppies' are pushing up the price of Right-to-Buy flats that go up for sale.

The outer London area in the heart of the old docks has much more space, even feels somewhat empty and therefore more threatening with more low-rise blocks and many more houses, dissected by a heavily congested dual carriageway out of London. As a traditional dock area, it had always housed a mixed community but when the docks closed in the late 1960s, an exodus began and large numbers of newcomers filled the spaces. Extreme politics flourished in the fast-changing community and it was one of the few areas of East London to elect a British National Party councillor in 2002. The local council plans to demolish much of the area and build new, expensive housing in its stead to create a 'more mixed community'.

The Northern inner area spreads up a steep hill out of the city centre and is a mixture of old, stone terraces, with some large and potentially attractive houses. There are blocks of modern council flats, small housing association developments and traditional Yorkshire terraced streets. At its heart is a small green, with bus stops, surrounded by run-down and boarded-up shops. Older men of different nationalities gather on the pavements in traditional robes passing the time. The whole area was dominated by an atmosphere of decay and neglect when I first visited, yet among the four areas, it was potentially the most attractive and the most conveniently located. Already it was recovering and there were signs of young professionals finding the area appealing with its strong 'multicultural and traditional Yorkshire atmosphere'.

The Northern outer area comprises a single large, pre-war council estate, four miles from the city centre, on a frequent bus route. It is still predominantly white, housing overwhelmingly low-income families, many with roots in the estate spanning three or four generations, since the estate was first built. This fairly homogeneous community has a reputation for 'being rough' in the wider city and some property is hard to let in spite of shortages of affordable housing in the city. At the same time there are many Right-to-Buy sales of houses with gardens, reflecting the contrast between more secure, popular areas, and 'rougher' sections of the estate.

The Northern areas felt less pressured and more manageable than the East London areas. They had a distinct Northern character, less enclosed, greener, less tense. East London felt very much part of the big city; for all the neglect of run-down spaces, visible changes were much more in evidence in London than in the North. In spite of these differences, the four areas were all low down the urban hierarchy, housing overwhelmingly disadvantaged populations, which in three of the four areas were experiencing rapid ethnic change. No specific neighbourhood is identified, in order to preserve anonymity.

How do families survive in cities?

City survivors is organised around six main themes reflecting layers of local family life that emerged from different families' stories. The all-embracing outer layer is the ***neighbourhood*** itself, a physical space that frames family life, providing essential shelter and services. Second, the ***community*** is formed by social relations on which families rely, linking families to each other in a personal way based on whom they know. Third, ***family*** is the basic unit of organisation, shaping parents' survival instincts because of their primary responsibility for their children, and still by far the strongest and most dominant social support for most families. Fourth, ***parenting*** is the activity of bringing up children in difficult surroundings, helping their children to develop, but bringing families into direct contact with local problems and community change. Fifth, '***incomers***' form a distinct group from '***locals***' within each area, reflecting divisions in the community and tensions between families. Sixth, ***civic intervention*** by government and voluntary bodies such as churches needs to be closely attuned to community conditions in order to help. Four family stories, one from each area, make up the main body of each chapter, woven around these six themes.

The next chapter of the book looks at neighbourhoods as the basic building blocks of all cities and towns. There are many serious problems and a general atmosphere of decay and decline. But there are also many promising changes and historic assets. The two Northern families are very committed to their areas, one as a 'gentrifier', who chooses to live in a diverse inner-city area, the other as a long-standing 'born 'n' bred' old-guard resident. The London families cope with a much tougher environment and wonder if they can survive where they are. Even so, they are torn between strong local ties and the inescapable pressures to get out. All four families are worried for their children because local conditions seem beyond their control. Seen through families' eyes, these neighbourhoods are big and amorphous, particularly when there are direct threats to their children's safety. Overall, the neighbourhoods are difficult places for families, but the families find many things to defend, many positive assets they like.

Chapter Three explores communities within neighbourhoods – the smaller-scale, more informal social links that make life more secure, less threatening for families. The four families in this chapter find some community supports around them and they all believe that community spirit is vital for family survival. For communities are the 'heartbeat' of neighbourhoods. Without them, family life is too lonely, too fearful, too fragile. All four mothers have had terrible experiences – divorce, domestic violence, demolition, crime – that make them ask whether social conditions, council action and cities themselves may combine to destroy a sense of community within neighbourhoods, thereby threatening the survival of families in cities. Getting on together is not easy in these fast-changing, sometimes turbulent neighbourhoods, where family problems are compounded. The London families seem to have a tougher time identifying with their community than their Northern counterparts, and one London family left the area during the course of the study.

Chapter Four explores family life, which is the foundation of all social life and therefore of our ability to survive in communities and neighbourhoods. The four families in this chapter experience strong pressures from surrounding problems. Each mother, in different ways, has her fill of family troubles as well. Helping their children grow up happily is the major preoccupation of the mothers. Their stories show, without saying this explicitly, how small a role most fathers play in directly caring for the children. Family care, in the main, is a role most mothers accept unquestioningly. Working mothers feel torn between their children's need for their time and their need for more money. Three of the four mothers work, yet even so, family life is at the centre of their thinking. One of the London families moved away during the course of the study and a Northern mother desperately wants to do the same.

The second half of the book explores how, in spite of this inward focus, families are forced to depend on their surroundings and cope with the external pressures on their lives in order for their children to survive. Chapter Five looks at the active role parents play in teaching their children to reach out from the family towards the wider world in order to survive. This is the essence of all parental responsibility. In these neighbourhoods, parenting responds to a fear of surrounding dangers that constrains the essential maturing and distancing process of growing up. Parents invest heavily in protecting their children from terrifying threats and actual dangers. The four mothers in this chapter explain just how serious these threats are – one mother's son is on the run from the police for a serious offence; another mother witnessed a possibly fatal wounding to steal a few pounds; a third copes with family and neighbourhood problems by keeping large dogs, which in turn upset neighbours; a fourth suffers from such severe depression that her husband gave up work to care for her.

The parenting experience combines all the problems of neighbourhoods, communities and families in one intense activity – bringing up children in troubled areas. The risk of their own children getting involved directly, and being influenced indirectly by happenings around them, is both real and undermining to parents. The need to control and restrain their children from 'joining in', moving out of sight, mixing with certain other local children or in most ways leading a normal outgoing childhood gets more extreme as the children get older. Most parents express confidence in themselves as parents and in their children, but parenting is a severely constrained responsibility in these neighbourhoods. One London parent wants to move because of demolition and the other wants to stay; one of the Northern mothers was forced to move even though she did not want to, and the other is more or less happy where she is.

Chapter Six is about families from a minority ethnic background who move into these neighbourhoods and about the barriers they face in trying to integrate their families into the community. The four families in this chapter come from very different backgrounds – South America, the Middle East, East Africa and India. Two families, both in East London, fail to qualify for Income Support because they do not have legal status in the UK. Both are vulnerable and isolated. Another mother grew up in the UK, is married to a local, and gets on with her neighbours, but nonetheless leads a rather lonely life, lacking basic information and support networks because she is an 'outsider'. The fourth mother is on her own with a large family, is entirely dependent on benefits, lives in overcrowded council housing, is not able to work because of childcare and is not able to master the language, even though she wants to, because she does not know any English people. For their children, these mothers put up with isolation, poverty, humiliation and an environment they do not like much.

All four mothers hanker after the more supportive, more community-oriented environment they knew as children. But all see more prospects for their children today. The biggest threat they encounter is not hostility from the existing community, but the instability and uncertainties of the neighbourhoods where they live. They share this problem with 'more local' families, worrying about too many 'outsiders' moving in, but they can see no solutions because they literally have no voice and do not participate in the community. None of them is involved in any local activity, apart from taking children to schools and immediate family, none of them expect to leave their neighbourhood, although two want to.

Chapter Seven is about the gap between what families need and how city structures support their inhabitants. In theory at least, city governments try to equalise conditions on the grounds of fairness and cohesion. Low-income families in return provide many essential services to the city, as restaurant workers, drivers, school assistants, IT and childcare workers, cleaners, security assistants and carers of every kind, all vital functions within the city. The four families in this chapter argue the overriding case for community-level involvement to shape interventions more closely to family survival. External interventions are often insensitive to community networks and the informal supports they provide, whereas community-level activity values the normally uncounted benefits of families in city neighbourhoods.

The four families in the chapter all care deeply about their community: two are formally engaged in local programmes; two are long-standing, well-connected members of large, extended families and therefore enjoy strong informal community supports. The two mothers in London, one a true native, the other a long-standing outsider, see their families and communities affected by the pace of change, by uncertain community relations. One adjusts to incoming families and directly wants to help them; another feels 'her' community has been destroyed by strangers. An active, unemployed father in the North explains his frustrations with his community and with public services, but also demonstrates his self-created role of 'community guardian' and strongly supports the local school, local youth and a local newspaper. One mother with severe family health problems feels so supported and encouraged by family, community and public services that she shows confidence, 'bounce' and real caring for the community in spite of carrying huge personal responsibilities. The London family who feel that their community has been destroyed by strangers want to leave but the others want to stay.

The second half of the book illustrates how sensitive families are to the constant inflow of strangers because of the uncertainties this creates around bringing up children. Ethnic and cultural differences increase the fragility of social relations on which families depend. The neighbourhood environment and the lack of control or influence that parents feel make them heavily dependent on external supports. The uncontrolled external pressures of change run counter to the informal local networks that make cities more family friendly.

Cities can be cruel

The families live with problems that sometimes seem unbearable, with too little protection or support. Conditions can be so uncontrolled and undermanaged that residents are cheated of the most basic agreed provision. Many forms of social action, beyond the powers of any individual, family or small community, can help counter this. Social policy was born of repeated decisions to take collective action to tackle problems individuals could not solve alone, affecting how people live together.[7] Our universal basic services are the result. The neighbourhoods our families live in are social policy 'hot houses', because of their problems and needs. There is a lot happening in these areas.[8] Yet families cope daily with problems that threaten to overwhelm them; and they put up with services that are constantly on the brink of being swamped by the sheer scale of need. The connection between the needs of particular people in a place, and the wider policies that forge those conditions, is only observable close up. The patterns of need that parents relay offer profound insights into what cities as a whole need if families are to survive within them.

Cities often seem cruel to families. Yet, simultaneously, cities are made up of people who care about their communities, want to do the best for their families and children, try to progress in their personal lives and want to get on with families of different origins. Alarm at the pace of change is tempered by an awareness that 'this is the way the world is going'. Community is an essential antidote to the problems of neighbourhood but it relies on 'friendly contact' between people who may not know each other very well yet who share common spaces and 'look out for each other's children'.

Therefore, families turn from their problematic neighbourhoods towards their neighbours who help them build a sense of community. Bringing up children to cope with the world around them involves many people beyond the immediate family, not least the newcomers who find it hard to get their bearings in such a whirlwind. Families therefore act as a barometer of local problems and hope for a different future. Families need some combination of community-level structures and wider support, some mechanism for detecting and solving problems, some investment in building and protecting community links as well as building and improving houses and social facilities. Young people in these areas epitomise the gap between family, community and the city, belonging nowhere and yet everywhere.[9]

How the long-run study of 200 families became the life stories of 24 families

Between 1998 and 2004, we collected around 60,000 answers to over 300 questions during a sequence of five visits to the same representative 200 families from the same areas, selected to reflect the areas' population; nearly half are lone parents; half are in work; and nearly half are from a minority ethnic background.[10] The questions covered family relations, community networks, race relations, schools, policing, work, childcare, regeneration, demolition, gentrification, housing, transport, traffic, parks, play areas, young people, the local environment, crime, disorder, bullying, gangs, drugs and, above all, change. At every visit, we asked about change within the families as well as in their area:

- Did change help or hinder their progress?
- Did they want to stay or move?
- Were they happy in their areas?
- What was good or bad in their lives and their communities?

- How much did neighbourhood conditions affect their families?

With this rich source of direct evidence, we decided to base this book about neighbourhood problems and family life on what parents themselves said. We refer to other studies that relate to and support what the families recount, but the book relies on direct rather than academic accounts and explanations. Using parents' own words in the stories gives an in-depth picture of what is happening. Individual stories show how places affect people over time as well as people shaping places. The observations recorded as we walked round the areas, sat in people's houses, used local entrances, lifts, corridors and gardens, called in at local shops, schools, cafes and community centres, alongside interviews with the local families, lend essential detail to the stories. The four areas where the families live are part of a much bigger national picture of high-poverty areas.[11] On most counts the areas have much more serious social, economic and environmental problems than the national average.

City survivors draws on three layers of evidence: evidence gathered from 200 families over the six years between 1998 and 2004;[12] detailed life stories of 24 families selected to reflect the broader group of 200 families; and wider changes in the four areas under study between 1998 and 2004. The cross-cutting evidence from all the families provides a common backdrop for different family stories, while each family's story helps us to understand the internal conflicts and contradictions within families, communities and neighbourhoods; the broader study of 200 families provides evidence to support what individual families say, which we cite using percentages in the explanatory texts between the stories.

Over six years of visiting families, the range of topics gradually expanded. Some topics such as schools, community, neighbourhood change and crime recurred; others such as specific regeneration initiatives or policy ideas such as social exclusion emerged during the interviews over time. Meanwhile, families were constantly evolving, adding and losing members, moving, finding work, shifting priorities, taking up new opportunities. The interaction of all these different internal and external factors is played out in the lives of the families we visited, showing in depth how families from the four areas live through changes in urban neighbourhood life.

This book is based on personal experience of policies rather than on policies as articulated by decision makers and implementers. Studies focusing on the latter perspective can be found in publications such as *Poverty Street*.[13] The stories in this book have a clear purpose in showing how wider city decisions and structures impact at ground level.[14] Many ethnographic studies reveal the evolution of experience directly from the ground, complementing broader, more statistically based evidence, as *City survivors* aims to do.

Six interviewees per area who had responded to all five rounds of the study were chosen from a longer shortlist of 50 to reflect the range of family circumstances in each area. For each chosen parent, the interview records provided basic biographical details and major family events over six years, such as a birth or starting school. Conditions and changes within the home and immediate area, such as the state of the housing or the block, unusual family circumstances and significant external changes that affected the immediate neighbourhood were recorded at each interview and drawn on in the accounts. Family circumstances and events formed the backbone of each family's story.

By tracking changes in the family and the neighbourhood, we built up an understanding of how particular families interacted with neighbourhood conditions. Time-specific events were recorded in sequence in the stories but much that families explain is built up slowly over time, delineating a picture that becomes clearer with each visit on particular themes such as community and parenting, or particular issues such as schools, security and open space. Thus, although family lives are chronological, their views on particular issues are a kind of kaleidoscope over time.

The six main themes of the book emerged from the 24 stories. All families spoke about their neighbourhood, community and family as the factors most directly affecting them; they explained their parenting role, the impact of newcomers and their need for local support as the factors shaping their ability to cope. But as their stories became more familiar, so particular family lives fitted particular themes, and it was possible to identify one family from each area to reflect more directly each of the six themes. The themes themselves were intertwined, for example neighbourhood and family life or community spirit and parenting; so each family story both illustrates the theme of that chapter and links different themes together, underpinning the overall argument of *City survivors* that neighbourhood conditions do affect family life. Families often have views that reinforce several themes and these are highlighted in other chapters too. The commentary between stories in each chapter draws on evidence from the wider group of families.

Each story makes clear the sequence of main events for the family in question, while consolidating that family's wider views on the theme of that chapter. All the responses from a particular parent on the key issues were grouped together in order to consolidate the parent's experience of local conditions over time in relation to the themes. Parents' views could change frequently, even within one interview, and these different impressions and experiences are presented as well as the more composite picture. We make clear when particular developments happened. In this way it is possible to understand change over time without hampering the stories with too much detail. Thus, although the main family and area developments relate to particular dates and stages in people's lives, many parents only reveal their real views as they develop trust and confidence over the course of several visits. Some families did not disclose detailed personal information and we respected that. Some details would betray family identity and we modified those. Therefore evidence is not entirely even between stories. Appendix 1 explains the study methods in detail, Appendices 2a and 2b present information on the 24 families whose stories we tell and Appendix 3 sets out the themes and topics round by round.

Conclusion

City survivors exposes neighbourhood problems in the raw that most parents would not want their children to grow up with. In spite of this there are mixed views among the parents about the prospects for their areas and most have higher hopes for their children's future than their own. A majority are torn between wanting to stay and wanting to leave their neighbourhoods. *City survivors* explores the major role low-income families play in creating a sense of community and 'taming' the city in some of the most difficult urban areas; it illustrates the need for families to be caring, low-cost service deliverers as well as users; and it looks at the potential to upgrade poor neighbourhoods without displacing existing residents.

City survivors explores three possible reasons for the persistence of neighbourhood conditions that undermine family survival:

- First, cities need low-income workers, many of whom are women who over time have children, but their contribution to the economy and services is given such a low value that they cannot afford better conditions. Nor do they have sufficient status or even recognition in the wider city to command better conditions. Therefore low-income families trapped in poor conditions are an inevitable outcome.
- Second, society does not recognise the lack of control low-income families have over their collective conditions. So society as a whole fails to compensate for this deficit. Therefore poorer neighbourhoods continue to lack the means of control over local conditions while family resources in these areas remain far below average.
- Third, the significance of community links and social networks is hard to pinpoint or measure and is therefore frequently ignored as a result; interventions often disrupt these local relations and many wider pressures make them more fragile. Given that local community networks can be extremely valuable in overcoming family problems, new ways of matching more closely community needs with external support need to be found.

The 24 families in *City survivors* try to give an explanation from a bottom-up perspective of why poor conditions persist. Will the top-down structures of complex cities bend to pick up the signals coming from the ground?

Notes

[1] Halsey with Webb, 2000, p 2; GLA, 2005.

[2] Briggs, 1968.

[3] Mumford and Power, 2003.

[4] Mumford, 2001; Power, 2004a.

[5] Farrington and Loeber, 1998.

[6] Willmot and Power, 2007.

[7] Alcock et al, 2003.

[8] Paskell and Power, 2005.

[9] Kotlowitz, 1992; Home Office, 2001; Ramphele, 2002.

[10] Bowman, 2001; Mumford, 2001.

[11] Lupton, 2003a, p 3.

[12] See Appendix 1 for methods on attrition and replacement.

[13] Lupton, 2003a; Mumford and Power, 2003.

[14] John Reader in his book *Cities* (2005) and Jared Diamond in his book *Collapse* (2005) used this case-by-case approach to convey important messages about cities and survival. These two books were particularly useful in inspiring the story-based approach.

TWO

Neighbourhoods matter – is it the people or the place?

Families tell us that their neighbourhood – the place – matters so much to them because of its people. All four neighbourhoods that our families live in are difficult for them; they all attract more than their share of newcomers, people on low incomes, families without visible fathers. The collection of families, other households and services that are drawn into these areas turn physical spaces into social entities. In this chapter, we look at places through family eyes.

A neighbourhood is a local area within a city or town, recognised by the people who live there as a distinct place, with its own character and approximate boundaries. Neighbourhoods are often separated from adjoining areas by roads, railway lines and open spaces. They acquire a distinct physical and social character through many layers of activity and change. Neighbourhoods are small enough for people to walk across easily, but big enough for a school, church, pub or shop to serve.[1]

Each family has its own starting point, the home, with a clear 'mind map' of where they live, and although many aspects of modern urban life reach far beyond the immediate neighbourhood, such as work, relatives, wider friendships, cultural networks and modern channels of communication, nonetheless neighbourhoods provide an organising base and springboard for these wider connections, particularly for families. The street, the block, the estate, the shops, buses, schools, doctors, play areas and parks all impinge directly on family lives. Neighbourhoods make up the city, particularly from the vantage point of families with young children.

Zoe's story – coping in spite of everything

Zoe lives in a council flat in the East End of London. She grew up just over the borough border, where her mother still lives. She thinks it is better than her area, particularly the schools. Her area is beset with problems that the tenants cannot sort out themselves – drugs, lack of play space, a dangerous railway line nearby. When we first visited, Zoe was very unhappy with where she lived, although she said, "They're trying". She was there by chance, having moved in with her brother and kept the flat when he moved in with a mate.

The block was run by a management cooperative organised by residents, so "repairs get done quicker than they used to. One night I had flooding and they checked it straight away. We have a really good caretaker; you always know when he's off because the others don't keep it so clean. But they've done this block up; they've put central heating in. I can always go to the tenants' committee [to sort things out]".

Zoe lived alone with her four-year-old son and found it hard to get to know people. She often got depressed. But she thought, "the block helps people feel less cut off. I think if you live in a house you feel cut off. Here it's like a big open area. Everyone knows one another". Even so, she took time to feel comfortable with her neighbours: "It's only over the last year I've really got to know my neighbours, even though I've been here 10 years". She was anxious to meet people facing similar problems and the health visitor suggested a local parents' support group: "I joined Meeting Point – I thought it would be a good way to meet more people. I talk about everything that's bothering me. You find out how other mothers are coping with similar problems".

Zoe said she was "mixed race", and did not want to be classed as black or white. She accused her boyfriend of being racist because "he tries to tell me I'm black. But I'm not, I'm mixed. My mum's white, my dad's black. It's a mixed community really, mixed race, black, white, Irish, Indian ... you all try to get on.... You still get a bit of racism.... There's still a lot of racism in the police – but I think the kids get on OK. When they're playing outside, you rarely hear any racist comments".

"Just right there, next to the flats"

Zoe had lots of problems with her son: "If you're a single mum you haven't got the time to take him to the park. He can play along the balcony but the neighbours don't like that. I had a falling out with one who got fed up with kids running along ... it got to the point where we were arguing in school. Simon can be a bit rough with her children – and one of them is sick and has a catheter. But things have calmed down. We talked about it and she apologised".

Zoe was unsure how to discipline Simon: "My mum wants me to bring him up the same way she brought me up, slapping him. I used to slap Simon but I found it didn't get anywhere. Now I sit him down on his chair to calm him down. One friend f's and blind's at her children but it doesn't get her anywhere. Another drags her son up the stairs and pushes him into the room. We've all got our ways". Zoe found it hard to stop him following others: "When he's naughty I've got to stand my ground. I've got to be hard on him because he takes the 'p' out of me.... My neighbour's children are so rude, he's started copying them. I don't like the attitude of kids in this area". Zoe decided to "put his name down at my mum's so he can go to school there".

Although Zoe favoured a school outside her area, her mother was ill when it came to choosing so she opted for the local school: "It was just right there, next to the flats". On our second visit, Zoe was worried about control at school: "Teachers should be a lot more alert in the playground, especially if all the children are like my Simon. You see the dinner ladies just standing there chatting". Simon came home one day with red blotches on his neck: "I went to school about it, but still haven't had a response". She felt aggrieved about this: "If I'd sent him to school with marks on him, they'd have had social services on my back right away.... Simon's teacher is strict, and he needs that. But I saw one teacher pull him by the wrist. I don't like the way this teacher handles him. Simon's a liar, so I don't know what to believe when he tells me about things that go on at school. But this teacher, I've seen for myself what she can be like".

Zoe always went on school outings because of her worries about Simon: "He gets a bit wild. When I pick him up, I wait to ask the teacher how he's been". Zoe was grateful to the school: "I get a bit tired. I don't know how these teachers cope with all these hyper children". Zoe picked up other people's children for cash in hand – it helped her "get trainers for him".

"Nowhere to play"

Zoe found being a parent in this area was "more difficult because of all the unworthy children ... so many children are running wild. I don't want my boy to grow up like that. Young mothers bring up their children to run riot". Yet she couldn't stop her own boy: "We've stopped going to a neighbour's because he jumps about too much there and she's got a lot of ornaments". She tried to be tough: "I put him to bed at 6.30 because he kicked someone and I didn't let him have the McDonald's I'd promised him. That's the strongest I've been. I wish I'd stuck to that". Zoe worried that "he'll end up inside – he's so easily led. His school has told me he's a follower".

Zoe thought that a lot of the trouble with kids was down to the lack of play space: "They've pulled all the swings down. The kids have nowhere to play. We tried to fight the council to stop them taking our play area away but they sold it to private buyers. They should be doing more for children, for example on that green there. But then you'd get old people moaning. You could have a time restriction like 8 o'clock. There's a community scheme that takes kids out for a couple of hours each week. But that's not enough for single mums; we need more help".

"Bins were being set alight"

When Simon was six years old he went through a phase of lighting matches: "He set light to my neighbour's curtains. That was another day I sent him to bed early. Also bins were being set alight by children. I went over the fire station and spoke to the commander. I had to push myself to do that. But I thought, next time it could be fatal. The commander said he'd go into the school, and the fireman would do something for the children in the block to show them how dangerous fire is; nothing's been done yet. It's really frightening; he's obsessed with fire.

We went to the local fire station with Meeting Point and now he wants to be a fireman. I've told him, if he gets into trouble with police, he can't".

A big magnet for kids was the railway line behind Zoe's block: "Children play on the track and cling to trains. Simon doesn't do that because I stopped him hanging out with rough boys. I found him where I told him not to go, so now he has to stay here".

"He stole oranges from a shop"

Some problems were caused by older kids: "Simon's got pressure in the block with black boys aged 13 to 15. He tries to avoid them. They stole his toy and it shook him. He hangs out with a group of boys but when he uses the word 'gang', I tell him, 'No, you're not in a gang', because I don't like that word. There's loads of black teenagers hanging around, smoking weed 'til the early hours. Some white people are aggressive to them and they don't move, but I've asked them to move on and they have". Zoe thinks how you treat them makes the difference.

Zoe was furious when Simon shoplifted: "He stole oranges from a shop with his cousins; I was carrying too much to go back, so I threw the oranges away. When he stole bubble gum in one shop and a sweet in another, I tried to get the bloke in the shop to tell him off. He just laughed. But to me it was nicking".

Zoe was keen on more security because "teenagers hanging around make you feel frightened.... It's getting worse, there's been so many shootings in the area lately. There's talk about a security guard for the block but I don't know if it's idle talk. We recently had druggies pass out on the stairs. They go round leaving their needles on the steps where the children are. A friend's child had a needle in his pocket. If they've really got to do this, do it in their own home, don't bring it out on the street".

"After all, we've got to live round here"

On our fourth visit, Zoe told us that local action could make a difference. She was quite keen on getting involved: "I know I've got it in me to speak out and get involved. One of the young blokes on the committee asked if he could nominate me. They want some younger people. I'm not that young, I'm 36, but I'm going to a meeting to see what it's about, and if so, let my name be put forward. We could have a say a bit more. After all, we've got to live round here".

Zoe was manageress of a shop before she had Simon. But she was scared to go back to work because she felt it was safer to manage on benefits but "know where you are" than to earn more but "risk getting into arrears". Zoe thought money was a major stumbling block in raising children: "You can do a lot more things with money. Getting children into groups like karate, ice-skating, it all boils down to money". She'd like to do a childcare course so she could work with children, which she did unofficially anyway. She would put her efforts into "providing a play area for the children and some sort of youth club".

By our fifth visit, Simon was 10 years old. Zoe's biggest fear was Simon "not being able to get a job when he leaves school because of his lack of learning ability. They should've picked up on my son not being able to read or write before now". She felt that his chances were much slimmer here than elsewhere. So, in spite of getting involved, finding friends, wanting to be on the tenants' committee and doing childcare training so that she could contribute to the area, Zoe hoped to move out before Simon started secondary school: "Everyone eventually wants to move out of here". But Zoe was still in her block with Simon at the same school at our last visit.

People and place go together

Neighbourhood reputation is often closely tied to its location, its history, its housing structure and economic rationale. Intrinsic problems, linked to where places are, how they were built and their core function in the city shape neighbourhoods. The four areas in *City survivors* have a long history of industrial exploitation followed by acute decline. Council estates were built to rehouse families from older slum areas, concentrating poverty and problems in ways that were never planned, undermining community ties through instability and targeted access for vulnerable people.[2] Most families in these areas – over 80% in London, 70% in the North – rent from the council or a housing association, or occasionally a private landlord. Most of our families are too poor to buy or are too afraid to buy where they live. The entrenched physical separations of council estates, together with the lower incomes of most social housing tenants, create poor conditions that determine who lives there.

Mothers, alone, like Zoe, are managing precarious conditions with poor housing, few play areas, limited resources and an unsafe environment. Nearly half of the mothers we interviewed (44%) are on their own and the neighbourhoods where they live all but encase their lives, since they cannot pay for activities that are not local and cheap; they cannot travel far and rarely go away; they opt for the local school because that links them to other parents and children. For disadvantaged mothers particularly, the neighbourhood is like a battleground between negative pressures and their attempt to make things work for their children, building home, friends and activities locally to create a better life.

For low-income families, the neighbourhood environment is crucially important because of inability to pay for ways out. Lack of proper information and influence over how decisions are made or how money is allocated prevented Zoe and her fellow residents from saving their play space. Parents often feel powerless. They see needs, try to bridge the gaps, but face barriers that drown out their voices. Over 60% feel they have never influenced anything in their area. Conditions shape local services to reflect the status of the people who live there. It is a circular problem, as Phoebe, a mother described in Chapter Two, sees:

> "The appearance of the area is very bad and sad. It reinforces the opinion [that] it's a dump – because it is a dump. They don't want to improve it so they trash it. I blame the council a lot because they take the attitude that we're only gutter sweeps … that we deserve less services. If you don't get treated with good-quality services, why should you care?"

Neighbourhoods frame people's lives, providing a bundle of services that people need, and an environment on which families depend. They also provide a vital anchor to individual lives, the 'container' within which different social groups develop contact with each other; the 'bridge' that should make possible the transition from mother and baby, through mother and child, to youth and the wider world. If a family is on a low income and the neighbourhood they live in is precarious and fast changing, then the movement from childhood to adulthood within the neighbourhood carries many additional risks, as Zoe's story showed.

Neighbourhoods help to shape people's lives because they do more than house people. They form a base for wider activities, providing many of the social services that link individuals with each other, giving rise to a sense of community. Thus neighbourhoods provide a basic line of support to families. Neighbourhoods form the most immediate environment for children to socialise outside the family, to build confidence and develop coping skills. Some parents struggle with this because of the risks of children getting drawn into mischief, but other mothers feel that making friends with local children is their best protection.

Parents need to protect their children, anchor them close to home, yet encourage them to become independent. For this the neighbourhood needs to feel secure, yet these neighbourhoods often feel threatening. Many parents live in fear of their children getting involved in crime, particularly drugs. They may also be afraid for themselves. Neighbourhood conditions signal how to behave, particularly to young people.

Neighbourhood regeneration is particularly important as decisions about the future of particular areas will shape family life through many disrupted childhoods. Parts of the East End and inner Northern areas are in the throes of major demolition, displacing many of our families. The upheavals of regeneration sometimes help but sometimes harm residents. Parents usually like their neighbourhood and 70% are satisfied with it as a place to live, yet want to escape its troubles. High-cost housing, which is being injected into poorer areas of the East End of London, does not immediately solve neighbourhood problems for low-income families. Indeed, as neighbourhoods are upgraded and property prices rise, local people often lose out.

People show the value they attach to neighbourhoods by paying much more for a home in a 'good neighbourhood'.[3] Most often, families in better areas buy their own homes, rather than rent them. This is especially true of families with children, who are often the keenest to move out of a neighbourhood because they want to be near good schools. Better areas will have more expensive houses, precisely because the neighbourhood conditions have tangible value, particularly for families. People compete to get into them, pushing up prices. Mothers recognise the difference money makes to neighbourhood conditions. In other words, people and place interact directly. Our next story shows how disadvantaged these neighbourhoods are, compared with other areas of the city.

Marissa's story – choosing the inner city

Marissa and her family had only just moved to Yorkshire when we first visited them. Marissa's husband worked from home as a freelance writer and Marissa was a social worker. They moved North from London with their baby and small boy because "my husband's originally from the North" and they wanted to get out of London. They liked the "strong sense of community": "We've only been here six months and we're already involved". They went to Yorkshire because friends had moved there and they had links with the local church. They saw a large, old, run-down terraced house going cheap in an estate agency: "We decided to move here in spite of the agent's best attempts to put us off". He tried to sell them a more expensive house. They got a much more spacious home than they could afford in London, a "beautiful bargain". There were lots of things they liked about the area: "there are lots of facilities, and freedom for the kids. I like the fact that it's multicultural. There's a more child-friendly attitude, certainly than in London. Also it feels less urban".

"It feels somewhat threatening"

Marissa thought that people outside saw the area as "completely desperate, crime-ridden, awful". Marissa was reluctant to condemn the area but did say "you're more aware of potential crimes and drugs; it's a background that's not ideal". She agreed with other 'locals' that drugs gave the area a bad name and caused trouble: "If drug dealing and using was reduced, then violent crime would go down. You do see people hanging around on street corners. This feels somewhat threatening". But Marissa was surprised and pleased how quickly she could reach better areas on foot.

By our second visit, Marissa was feeling far more wary: "The car's been broken into and the shed's been broken into. The post office at the top had an armed hold-up and the post office was shot out and a friend's brother was beaten up and killed". Later Marissa told us that her husband's work bag was stolen from the pavement by their house while his back was turned. Marissa tried to distinguish between small areas within the neighbourhood, as many mothers did, carefully mapping in her mind where it was OK to walk. "Some parts of the area do feel less safe. Apart from my fear, I don't feel particularly threatened, except in some streets". Marissa was thankful that "this street is particularly quiet and peaceful, a bit different from the rest of the area". Marissa was concerned at how the neighbourhood was affecting her family: "I don't want to pass on my sense of fear to my children. I want them to feel confident. It's definitely not getting worse; it's probably getting better".

Marissa thought that knowing and trusting people helped: "It increases our sense of safety, physically and emotionally. It helps you relate to people more openly and work together for things to get better in the community". For Marissa that was the point: "It needs people who live here to have an input.... If you want to feel at home you need to feel confident here, as much as anyone else. A lot of people I know do walk around more than when I was in London, so that has increased my confidence".

"It's poor but it's not hopelessly poor"

Both Marissa and her husband thought that community spirit "redeems an area that is poor and has problems with drugs". Community spirit "makes it an area with opportunities, that can change, not just because of middle-class people coming in, but because community spirit changes it to an area of hope, rather than hopelessness. So it's poor but it's not hopelessly poor". Being involved made Marissa part of the community but she worried that "people who are doing regeneration are middle-class people like me who've moved in the last 10 years, not people who it's intended to benefit. It would be better if they were involved [although] the committee do seem to be multicultural".

Being able to help shape the area's future mattered a lot to Marissa, "because this is where I live and particularly, given the area's reputation, it needs people who live here to be involved in changing our future ... I do feel it's my community and I'm part of it. Grassroots communication is what makes a difference so living in the area seems really positive to me.... A lot of friends live in walking distance, so it's easy to walk there with the kids. There's lots of support close by, lots of groups.... Events create a positive feeling about our community and demonstrate appreciation in the area of different cultures. They give people a sense of involvement and achievement – our own family too – because we can get involved ... because this is where I live".

Marissa liked programmes like Sure Start "because they organise events for under-fours". But she worried that it missed the most disadvantaged parents: "Some people who could benefit have never heard of it, which is a shame. If they don't connect with parents who don't come to meetings, it'll never truly work". She was also cautiously critical of such government-run programmes because "there are some committed people but they need to tick boxes and meet national targets ... maybe London is running the whole thing.... I'm suspicious of government initiatives, generally working to national targets. I'm not sure it leaves people free to influence particular needs. So it needs people who live there to have an input, to be involved in changing our future, given the area's reputation".

Marissa thought that poor areas were very separate from the mainstream: "A lot of people are unable to access services and are denied privileges and opportunities because of where they live, because of poverty and perhaps their education. This is an area where there's lots of social exclusion. It's evolved to be an area where there's a high level of crime and drug dealing and not a lot of business or enterprise, and historically, not a lot of good schools. So there's a cycle of poverty and deprivation that's been created and the reputation of the area increases that. Lots of cheap housing increases it too ... a lot of people who are poor and vulnerable move here, they get put here, so that increases the whole cycle". But she could see changes: "because house prices have started to go up, people are looking at the area differently.... Some houses that were burnt out have been bought up and turned into flats".

But Marissa was worried that regeneration and gentrification could undermine community spirit: "It may drive other people out of the area. These new people aren't going to be as committed to the area and it might displace problems". Marissa saw her family as different from other incomers because they wanted to be part of the area. They were there to help as well as to take advantage of its assets.

"An area with a lot of separate groups"

The family chose the area partly for its ethnic mix: "I like the fact that it's multicultural ... it's good for the kids to be with people of different cultures. It makes life more interesting and enjoyable for everybody". Marissa felt that cultures rubbed along quite well together: "There's no tension between young kids ... generally there's very good relations". But on our second visit, Marissa explained: "It seems a much more segregated area than where we lived in London. [In] the playgroups [in London] everyone was mixed; here they're all white. I haven't noticed a great deal of tension but also there's not easy integration.... In London people seem to mix across race and class barriers more than they do here. It does feel to me like an area with a lot of separate groups, 'just not mixing'".

Marissa noticed over five years of our visiting that "more asylum seekers have moved in; lots of Yemenis and Cameroonians and Somalis. Arabs and Afghans come too now. Although there's not a lot of antagonism, a lot of what's needed is trying to understand one another". This lack of understanding and familiarity was counterbalanced by a sort of opportunity that Marissa felt the area offered her children: "I think it's a great place for them to be, especially the multicultural things and learning about different faiths, so that balances out against the problems of the area".

"How will it affect my children?"

Marissa worried about local schools: "I think if we lived in an area where secondary schools were full of high-achieving students, then the possibility of them achieving higher is higher. Presumably [the local] comprehensive had to close because it's not a good school. If it's because English is a second language, that's very different from students being on drugs. I'm not sure secondary school experience in the area is positive; it's a potential obstacle".

Marissa hoped that the family could compensate for such problems: "I'm not sure how much school contributes to what they can achieve in life, or how much that depends on family? How will it affect my children?" She knew how many activities they were missing in the area: "Some parents have kids who have lots of opportunities mine won't have, school clubs and stuff like that. I don't really worry about it; basically I feel happy for them". Marissa became a parent governor and her husband joined the primary school's Parents' Association. So they were doing their best to help. But she didn't "feel hugely confident about the governing body. It feels inexperienced and unconfident".

"Things aren't fixed"

Marissa wanted to improve the area: "The parks need a lot of improvement to get rid of litter and used condoms and glass. Things aren't fixed". Marissa shared with neighbours a feeling of being trapped: "I don't have transport so I can't get to another park, or get out of the area.... Buses are much more hassly". She hoped things would get better: "All the activity makes you think you can influence things". If Marissa had influence, she knew what she would want: "lots of things for kids and teenagers to do". She felt somewhat powerless: "You end up thinking nothing you say'll make any difference, so I'm not entirely sure". Marissa, like Zoe, was torn; she had a nagging doubt about coping with neighbourhood problems. In the end it was what the neighbourhood offered to families, and particularly children, rather than simply what the neighbourhood was, that made the difference.

Environmental signals

Marissa's worries about neighbourhood conditions affecting her family grew over time. As children gradually break away from their mother's tight hold, the significance of the neighbourhood becomes more obvious and they begin to find their own way, through friends, school, activities outside the home and eventually work. This risky process begins as early as four years old, as Zoe's story showed. Sooner or later, mothers have to let their children try things out for themselves. Many are deeply afraid for their children and 80% find crime a serious problem. The search for independence by young people comes up sharply against neighbourhood conditions.

Neighbourhoods are the place where low-income families link into social institutions like schools. They want opportunities, so their children will succeed. A good education, skills and confidence are far more significant for the children's future than physical conditions. Ironically, it is parents' fears that lead them almost always to choose local schools, in spite of their often poor reputation. Mothers worry about their children travelling beyond their reach.

Staying nearby is one of the rules parents constantly instil into their children as they get older. This limits young people's horizons, while keeping them in constant contact with local troubles. Crime and drugs dominate parents' fears and cause withdrawal from the very supports that families seek. Of our parents, 60% say that crime makes their parenting more difficult. The problems of disorder and social breakdown, which all the areas experience, are often attributed to gangs of youths with nothing to do, making parents feel that they cannot control what happens.

Families are intensely tuned to their local environment, watching for signs of what is safe and what is not.[4] Marissa could 'tell' which streets were safe and which were not. Streets with a poor environment more often attract trouble, partly because they deter families with children; the lack of family activity on the street in turn makes streets less friendly, less familiar, more open to abuse. If families withdraw, trouble grows and conditions deteriorate even further. This often makes decayed neighbourhoods family unfriendly.

As a result, a family may be torn between local connections, good neighbours and familiarity on the one hand; and on the other hand the desire to be in a more spacious and peaceful area, where there are fewer risks because the local environment is more favourable, where children will stand more chance. Annie's family epitomises the tension between a strong sense of local belonging and deep alienation from neighbourhood conditions.

Annie's story – torn between local ties and the urge to escape

Annie is a lifelong East Ender. She and her husband have a close-knit extended family, mostly within the local area, and three girls, two teenagers and one younger. "There's seven of us brothers and sisters, and we've got lots of children between us, they're all over the area. Sometimes I might not go to my mum's in a week, but just knowing she's there, over the road, or my sister's round the corner, makes all the difference." She believes that "families make up neighbourhoods because they are the foundation stone of communities". Annie describes herself as Black British and her husband is of mixed race, so they are not the stereotype of 'traditional' East Enders.

Annie felt very lucky in her marriage: "We had Vicky when Neil and I were 19, just a pair of kids. We are still together, it's worked out lovely". But Annie's husband wanted to move and this created tension. Annie did not want to "because there are people here who care, and people who are working to make the community better, like his mum. I'm so proud of her.

But if all your experiences are bad, I suppose you're going to have a grim outlook and just think it's low. I wouldn't agree with the fact it's low".

"Because of the new faces in the area, I don't feel safe"

In spite of Annie's connections, she worried a lot about raising her children in the area: "My daughter tells me what's going on at school and sometimes I'm horrified, children even smoking drugs". Deep down she liked living where she did, but even Annie had her doubts: "If I could take them somewhere else and bring them up, I would". She felt torn between her local extended family and wanting somewhere better. She thought parents' feelings about where they live affected their children's sense of security: "If you feel happy with where you live and what you do, you'll pass it on to your children. So I do try all the time to be a good parent. It's paramount to me that I raise the children well".

Annie's sense of security was undermined by constant inflows of new people and outflows of familiar faces: "There are just so many strangers", and this, she felt, could undermine a whole community, as happened where they lived before: "new people came in and it wasn't nice". Now it was happening again: "families that were here have moved out and there's lots of new families. People that I've known have moved out because families want better for their children, or their families have moved away and they've followed them. You're not always sure where the new people are coming from, but definitely refugees. You're forever seeing new faces round here. Because of the new faces in the area I don't feel safe".

Annie and her husband owned their terraced house, but "you have no control outside your own home, kids vandalising and breaking into cars. That isn't outsiders, it's being done by those already here. It really gets me down when I see stolen cars smashed to pieces. That's when I really want to move away". Annie's attitude was strongly shaped by her environment: "They used to have a park-keeper. I don't see the park-keeper there now, so I have to tell the older kids to be really careful. The parks are really terrible round here. They're awful, lots of dog mess, the equipment is old and dangerous, the swings are all broken. I don't let my youngest out of my sight. I'm too frightened to let her out to play. If there was an after-school club, then I'd be OK. But just to let her out the front door, there's no way. She's six and it shouldn't be like that".

"You shouldn't be forced to move out"

Annie's feelings about the neighbourhood shifted depending on what happened on the street. At our third visit, she told us: "It's a constant tug-of-war between the area going down and small gains. There are days when I get up and feel more positive about the area. But there are days when there's all rubbish on the floor, and you see children throwing fireworks and I'm with my eight-year-old. I want somewhere nice for her to grow up. If kids live in an area where there's a lack of facilities, then yes it will affect them". Annie saw it as part of a wider problem of poverty: "If the money isn't there, then the facilities aren't there and the people who live there will suffer, particularly young people. We need more facilities because it makes you feel more valued". Annie thought that there was hope for the area, in spite of "crime, drugs and the fact that it's just sad. If money's put here and people invest in the area and in the people as well, it could bring it up a lot more. Now there's talk about doing up the area. That's good and it makes me want to stay. I want to stay because my family and my identity is here. I do worry about us all getting separated. Some people don't have family around them any more, they just have to rely on people in the community to help them out. My children do feel safe, but I'm more anxious than they are".

By our third visit, regeneration had advanced in the area: "Over here we're cut off; over there is where it's all happening. You look over the garden fences and it's really nice over there". Annie did not know what was happening to her area yet: "A lot of people have been uneased because you're not sure what's going to happen, you're always left wondering.... We were told these houses were part of the regeneration, so we were thinking we might have to move. We didn't want to but that's what I understood of it. They were going to knock these houses down. And now we're being told they're going to stay for the moment. Eventually we are going to want to move on but not before our time. You shouldn't be forced to move out. There's lots of speculation and feeling unsure". But Annie's expectations changed when "me and my mum went to an exhibition to look at the plans. Some of the people who are doing it were there [to talk to]". This made Annie want to stay: "With the regeneration it's getting better, there's a lot more bustle, a lot more going on ... so now people have to look after it".

By our fourth visit, things were definitely getting better: "Recently they built a really nice play area for the children and that's made a big difference to the families here. Every morning I walk past and see lots of parents in there with children, whereas before people would just walk through the park and not stop – a big green space and no one using it. It was a shame. It's really nice to see families there and nice for me, because I can sit down on a bench while my youngest plays after school. It's good for her because I don't let her out. Chantelle said to me, 'Mum, can we go in there before it gets all broken?'". Chantelle, eight years old at the time, had damaged expectations, which Annie tried to counter.

"It's difficult blending in"

Annie, like Marissa and Zoe, thought that being involved helped: "You get to meet lots of nice people and the experience is good. There's security in a close-knit community, knowing people's faces". Familiarity was crucially important: "Now there's a lot of youngsters that look shady". But there were also lots who played together well: "It's nice to see children playing out, instead of being stuck indoors playing computer games. There's lots of children about and my door's forever knocking, it reminds me of when I was younger, it's good to see. It's good for the children as well, they get to know we're all as good as each other". Annie liked children from different ethnic backgrounds mixing together, under her watchful eye: "I grew up in a white street and I was ashamed of my own house and tried to fit in with white people, but we're all different and have to agree to disagree".

Annie sometimes felt that the area was out of control: "Recently there was a letter through the door saying a young girl was attacked around the corner. It happened at 8.30 in the evening. And the man in the close here was attacked coming home from the pub". Incidents like these made Annie worry, particularly for her older girls. Annie was also worried about changes among the residents: "When we first moved here it was mainly white. I ain't got a problem with it, but now it's mainly black people, so much so that in the shop there are sections of different food. That's nice, like accepting that we're here. But, when we had a fair recently, there were lots of strangers around. So some people are moving away. I think when I was growing up it was better because people knew a lot of people and your parents looked out for your neighbours as well as you. Local people who've been here quite a few years tend to stick together, and with the new families, it's difficult blending in, it takes time.... Those of us who've found some way of communicating and getting together as friends live together fine but some people can feel really isolated". So Annie worried about the exclusion of newcomers as well as their destabilising impact on the community.

"There's a really good feel in the school"

Annie thought that schools helped bring people together: "Anything that's happening in the community where people can actually talk and communicate together, things like schools, after-school clubs, youth clubs, special events, projects that bring families together, all help". Annie went to a parenting group attached to the school: "You go in there loaded and come out feeling good. It's nice to go in there and someone says, 'It's alright, we all feel like this, it's normal'". This group organised outings and had quite a strong social focus. The parents who went loved it, but Annie said some were too shy to come. Annie thought there needed to be lots of parenting groups.

Annie worked in the primary school, helping in a literacy club: "I was only supposed to fill in for six weeks but I did so well that they asked me to stay on. There's a really good feel in the school, lots of togetherness.... The children I've worked with didn't have confidence and do now. It opens opportunities and lifts their self-esteem. It has a knock-on effect on their families too ... a lot of the children are down as having problems, but when you get to know them, they're lovely". Annie's job helped her to start a university degree and she was doing really well, but study pressures got too much: "I was just drowning in the middle of everything, with reading club at school and three kids and husband, so I just had to put everything on hold and say, 'What's most important? My family', so I thought, 'This is where I need to be right now'. It was a big decision, giving up. I was washing up one evening, trying to think of the next line of an essay, and realised Chantelle was sitting on the bed, doing nothing – that was it. They depend on you". She hoped one day to go back to studying.

"Here you need to be tough"

Annie's older children went to the local secondary school, which "doesn't have a very good reputation in terms of discipline ... but special measures are in place. Before there was a lot of turbulence; it was going under". They chose the troubled school, like many other parents, because it was local: "I didn't want to send her out of the area. I wanted a church school but didn't want her travelling on the bus". This led them to abandon the idea of a high-performing church school further out and keep their daughters close to home. Annie was reassured by the fact that the government had stepped in, and the school was improving: "Now there's strong leadership in the school. Some parents don't like it, but here you need to be tough". The school's familiarity was accompanied by worries about peer pressure: "I do worry for my kids. I think every parent worries, most anyway!" Yet Annie confined them to the neighbourhood about which she felt so insecure.

Annie put her faith in her children's future. She hoped they would not "get in with the wrong crowd", since "you'd be in a minority if you hadn't dabbled in drugs here". But "you can be a strong person. You can stand back and say, 'No, this isn't for me'. As far as I know the eldest doesn't get involved, but I'm not with her all the time.... They're teenagers now. Whether I like it or not, they're growing up and they've got to go out there and find out for themselves. That's difficult and I can only help, give them all the information and then they've got to make the choice themselves. I'm there for them, not necessarily to find solutions to their problems but help them. "We want our children to have better than we had. Both of us really encourage them. I want them to be happy and healthy and reach their potential".

"I sweep up outside"

Annie's family coped with neighbourhood uncertainties by trying to make things work, very much like Zoe and Marissa. She thought that you could improve things in small ways: "Anything you're involved with you influence, whether you know it or not. I've been keeping up the garden for the good of the whole community. It's really important what you do yourself. Your children look up to you as a role model, so you have to think about how you go about your life. I sweep up outside. I buy from local shops". So Annie maintained a positive outlook through small actions to enhance the area.

Annie wanted neighbourhood management to solve problems quickly: "The streets used to be cleaner, it gets me down because the bins are overflowing and people throw chip papers on the floor.... It would be nice to see more policemen on foot, you always see them in cars, but they were there for me the other day". Annie thought that neighbourhoods were about more than physical conditions: "You can make something look smashing but it's about people and attitudes and community spirit. It's about a lot more than the area looking nice". Even so, "when something looks nice, it makes you smile".

Survival of the fittest

Mothers with roots in an area, like Annie, felt that as the area declined, their lives were dragged down by it, in spite of their efforts. The extreme social need is a product of most housing in the area being for rent from the council and therefore offered as a priority to highly needy families. Although council tenants generally move less often than average, in extremely poor areas turnover is above average. This led Annie and others to feel that there were 'too many strangers' and yearn for somewhere more rooted; they knew they could not turn the clock back to when the area was less transient.

Transience is a product of many economic, social and environmental factors combining in a place that is convenient for its low value and easy access.[5] Rented housing for poorer newcomers is invariably concentrated in poorer areas of cities. Marissa explained this connection, borne out by worldwide housing studies.[6] This reinforces the sense of lack of control over conditions. As poor areas evolve, their history generates a powerful influence not just on who lives there but on how they live. Parents often, therefore, feel embattled.

The process of outward sifting, driven by better housing outside older city neighbourhoods, results in a constant erosion of social networks. Thus, the fight for better neighbourhood conditions and greater opportunity is constantly eroded by an outward exodus, and a weakened sense of belonging. Area conditions drive people to look for ways of escaping, either into their homes or out of the area, fuelling the instability. Longer-established residents may fight for and defend improvements, but as they move away, there is less and less local capacity. Newcomers have less familiarity, less confidence or clout in the eyes of long-standing residents or established local services. They keep a low profile.

Turnover creates space in unpopular areas for people to move into, yet many city families opt out. So young, low-income families and other newcomers become concentrated there. This shapes services and conditions in a way that polarises neighbourhoods into alarming places. Minority ethnic communities are increasingly concentrated in low-income areas because they have disproportionately lower incomes and are often more recent arrivals.[7] In London nearly half of the families we talked to are from minority ethnic backgrounds, some, like Annie, long established. One Northern area is still overwhelmingly white but Marissa's area is very mixed and fast changing. Families like Annie's struggle in neighbourhoods that play host to newcomers with complex needs. So neighbourhood instability is closely tied to their intrinsic characteristics.[8]

Poorer areas such as these often attract people with serious problems, and a significant minority of the families we interviewed – about one-fifth – have experienced major setbacks in their lives that make survival a struggle, and the neighbourhoods more precarious. People who start from an unequal position in society end up in places that 'pull them down', so it really is chicken and egg, since neighbourhood conditions shape who lives where. Families recognise this harsh social reality – poor places, poor people, poor prospects go hand in hand:

> "This is a forgotten little land." (Joyce)

On the other hand, many parents, like Marissa, Annie and Zoe, believe that:

> "Everywhere's what you make it." (Zoe)

Unequal neighbourhood conditions give people unequal chances, but these inequalities are partly offset by the families' own efforts to compensate by clinging to the idea of community, as Annie's story showed. No one could epitomise this philosophy more directly than Peter, who positively loves his neighbourhood in spite of its problems because he has a rooted sense of belonging and is determined to "stick it out" and "make it work" through a strong partnership with his wife, and an optimistic view of self-help.

Peter's story – a neighbourhood that works

Peter lives in the outer Northern estate, is married and has two children who were seven and 10 when we first met. Peter could not work because of a work injury and played a strong parenting role. He was very happy with where he lived: "It's lovely round here, I'll be living here as long as I'm alive". Peter's relatives were mainly local, his wife's were in Lancashire, where she would prefer to live: "If we had money, we'd move tomorrow".

Peter had always lived in this part of the city. He was indomitably optimistic about his neighbourhood despite its reputation. But he knew there were problems: "It's a good area that could improve. It's beginning to get run down". Since he was a lad "it's gone a bit downhill, people dumping stuff down the beck. We did play in it when we were kids, now it's full of rubbish". But Peter was a strong community man: "I get on well with people and talk to anyone". He explained problems such as the rubbish as happening because "there's a lack of playgrounds".

"When they own it, they look after it more"

Peter knew the area's character: "There's good people here, it's just little pockets. [Some streets] are dens of iniquity. The majority are alright". But he thought things were gradually getting better; after all, he said, he progressed a long way past his father: "When I finished school in 1952, and all was rationed, I started selling papers and people would come and buy them. I earned more that way in a day than my dad did with overtime as a road digger in a week, and today there's more prospects".

Peter's wife, Margaret, still felt an outsider, despite being married to a local: "Ten years I've lived here, and I'm just getting to the point where I can rely on someone up the street. 'We keep ourselves to ourselves', we were told from the outset". The beck was a social divider: "At the school they think we're snobs because we live over the water". Even so, Margaret found lots of good things in the area: "You're near enough if you want to go to the countryside; the shops are close at hand. I like the open area at the back, we'd've moved otherwise".

The family had fought to protect their open space: "We had a battle to keep the green behind our house but we have. The kids like it – the wildlife. We get foxes and bats". The couple bought their house from the council. Peter thought Right-to-Buy helped: "It takes the strain off the council and off ratepayers. Often it lifts people up because when they own it they look after it more. Maintenance is hard though, we need a new roof. But if things get really bad, at least you've got an asset you can use".

The family were hard up because Peter lost his job after his injury. He hated forced retirement and had been trying to get his job back, or any job, but he'd not been allowed to return to work. Peter knew his rights. He was fighting for compensation for his accident and to return to work. So far he had not received an acceptable offer from his employers. His wife worked part time in a launderette, which Peter did not really agree with: "there's enough to be done at home". But Margaret explained why: "Peter was told not to work. That means we don't have enough money for holidays any more". Luckily they could often go down to her sister's caravan, Peter explained, "to give her sister a break, their father's lost the use of his legs" and they helped look after him.

"We've had alarms fitted"

The couple talked about trouble in the area: "We've had alarms fitted and we've bricked up the bottom half of the back window. The kids burn out cars on the green. The police should get around a bit more". Peter thought the police were making more effort: "There's been a slight improvement, mainly from police coming quickly when cars are abandoned to stop them being burned out. There's been four taken, but two were saved from burning. It won't stop the stealing. But when people phone and the lads see a response and people trying to stop them, they might stop … burning them".

But Margaret was not so optimistic for her children "because of society. I don't like the scruffiness and the crime, the joyriders and the cars being dumped. It's not so bad since they built houses at the bottom. Before it was open, an unsupervised space where trouble could occur". Both of them worried about drugs and early sex, but they were not sure the estate was worse than anywhere else: "It's everywhere and in every class. Sometimes I think the privileged areas are worse off. I just hope [our children] don't get involved". Peter added: "I hope they won't be un-enterprising and that they take opportunities and that they will have a good life, that's all".

Peter and his wife worried about young people in the area: "There's been a problem with bullying at the youth club. There doesn't seem to be much for kids to do or much for them to be. They're just going to hang round on the streets – they've got to do something here. They used to have a track on the field for mountain bikes and for some reason they stopped it, which I think was a very bad move. They used to play up there for hours, quite happily, and it was good to see them; I don't know if someone complained". He knew they needed to keep young people busy because some parents were not coping: "At the end of the day you have to concentrate on the youngsters, to help them forgot the parents they've got".

"We bring it on ourselves"

Peter thought the council should help more: "They've got to persevere when they build these places. The flats they took down, it's made more greenery but it may be wise to put some play things there for youngsters. You do need the cooperation of the parents as well, you need something that would tie the parents more together, but it's getting someone to lead it. I tried ... but it was difficult. It's a lot easier when children can play out. We've got all this grass and woodland and they have nothing to do. The sports centre's not used as much as it could be; it's expensive, too much for people". Peter wanted the council and the community to do something: "They don't keep things up, nothing's done – they've got furniture dumped but they don't take it away. We bring it on ourselves because we don't make the council do it, it might mean paying more rates. But at the moment they just want to conserve money, not cure things. So we've got to do it ourselves".

Peter believed in self-help to tackle neighbourhood problems. He organised get-togethers in their back garden. His wife explained: "three weeks ago we invited all the neighbours in. I know some but not others, Peter knows everyone. It's a better place to live if you pull together, if you've got friends to chat to, if you're looking out for one another's kids and that". Peter agreed: "I get on very well with the neighbours round here. They know they can come to me if they need me and I can go to them. I don't see any problems; there are some fall-outs now and again but it all gets sorted out when you invite them to the next get-together. It's friendly and caring here, we look out for each other".

On the other hand, 'garden crime' occurred: "We had a table stolen, we found it in the road, then it got taken again and the bird table. I didn't report it, it doesn't bother me so much. I buy it all from car boot sales so we don't lose much". At our last visit, Peter had joined the neighbourhood watch: "We started it a month ago, it's brought us closer together, keeping an eye on each other's property".

"They're in a bad area and they're making a go of it"

The couple worried about schools but preferred to keep their children local, like Annie, Zoe and Marissa: "They underachieve compared with children at other schools. Parents have moved their children and they've come on in leaps and bounds. School's an unsettled place at the moment, there's talk of closing down the primary school but ours have both been keen and happy, so we haven't moved them. Does it matter if they're not reading at nine? By 15 they're all the same! They both love school; no problems getting them there. They've got lots of friends and are holding their own". Being nearby was more reassuring than a better school further afield.

They did worry about secondary school and looked elsewhere. But during our third visit, they explained their choice. At first Margaret thought: "There are too many coloureds. [Peter] would say I'm being racist but there are only three white girls in her class". She did not like her children being in the minority. But she explained: "We went to the open day and it far outshone the others. We were impressed. The teachers seem more interested in the child. They have more going on". Peter added: "It's a mixed school with a lot of Asians. In general they seem to get on well. She's been there two years and she's just adjusting to different forms of religion but she does like it there … they had a talent contest and the acts were brilliant. The head is doing very well to bring the cultures together. They're in a bad area and they're making a go of it". Muslim families from nearer the city centre sent their girls there because it was an all-girls' school.

But just before our fourth visit, a nasty incident happened on the bus involving boys unconnected with the school. After the incident, their older daughter had to be met from school: "She can't come on the bus because a group of youngsters were taking the emergency hammers and trying to set fire to the seats. They should've been removed from the bus". Their daughter felt very threatened, but "it happened outside school time so they're not concerned. I don't know the answer for outside school. They used to look out for us outside school". Peter and his wife were very shaken. "We've brought them up to respect adults."

"They spend most of their time near where they live"

Peter believed that his neighbourhood would pull through its "troubled patch": "There's one or two vandals and hooligans now and again. If you say something, they do respond, if you're civil, concerned but not aggressive". He thought that community efforts and trust between neighbours helped: "Trust is important, because without that you couldn't walk down the street. We do have little bits of trouble, but not as bad as it was. I feel extremely safe, I'm quite big!" Peter thought that the neighbourhood anchored families "because they spend most of their time near where they live and they depend a lot on local services". This was why the neighbourhood for all its problems was the centre of their universe, the place where they really "want to be".

Conclusion

Children root parents where they live and parents therefore need to protect their children within the local environment, which becomes engraved in people's sense of place. Thus people and place are interwoven. The four families in this chapter show how strongly their neighbourhoods affect them. The problems seem remarkably similar between the two white families in the North and two black or mixed-race families in the South, although the London environment feels more extreme and pressured. Parents cope by constantly looking for positive signs. Families find confidence in the people they know around them as well as improvements to the place. In the next chapter, we look at why community matters to families, and whether it compensates for neighbourhood conditions.

Notes

[1] Peter Hall's evidence to the Urban Task Force: Hall,1999.

[2] Bowman, 2001; Mumford, 2001; Lupton, 2003a.

[3] Cheshire and Sheppard, 2004.

[4] Gehl, 1996.

[5] Power, 1997; Bramley et al, 2000; Glaser et al, 2000.

[6] UNCHS, 1996, 2001.

[7] Lupton and Power, 2004.

[8] Proceedings from a workshop organised by HM Treasury and CASE, 1999.

THREE

Community matters – survival and instincts in social animals

Human beings are social animals, needing other human beings to survive. We live in communities. Community is a common, even overused, word meaning groupings of people around a common purpose, belief, social structure or geographical base. It implies common interests and values that bind people together. Here community is taken to mean what families say it means: the social links between people that attach them to a particular place and to the people that they know and identify with.[1] Community as people is distinct from neighbourhood as place and yet, as we showed in Chapter Two, is intertwined with it through local social connections. Families are closely tied to their community because parents with children develop an overpowering social instinct, closely linked to basic survival.[2] This makes them search for and help create a sense of 'community' as well as a sense of 'place', as Phoebe's story illustrates.

Phoebe's story – creating a sense of community

Phoebe "grew up in the South – in a dead-end street in the country. My experience was the 11-plus and then an all-girls' grammar school. I hated it and left at 16. My parents didn't go to university so that wouldn't have been a route I'd have taken. It's not done me any harm, learning how to use things and make things work".

Phoebe worked her way around Europe, busking. She lived in a self-sufficient community for two years, took courses in carpentry and jewellery, worked in Scotland on her own smallholding, then on a building site for a year in Yorkshire while she did environmental training and then returned to Scotland where she had her first son, Ben. Then she did A-levels, had her second boy back in Yorkshire, and went on to university in the city.

When we first met Phoebe she was 42 years old and her boys were aged nine and four. She was two years into her degree, which she finished the following year. She was living in a council flat in a run-down block, pending demolition. Phoebe had hard times in her previous flat: "The block didn't have security doors. I wouldn't go back there. It was a sink place. I was being sunk as a single parent and pregnant again. I was homeless before that and in bed and breakfast". She'd previously been evicted from a private flat. Now she was in an area she liked and her block was going to be demolished. Only three of the 15 flats were still occupied and her windows were covered in plastic sheeting after youths broke them. "I've found that because it's got that reputation, it kind of self-perpetuates, it reinforces itself. We get treated as if we were mental cases, especially in these blocks – but everyone who lives here are stable, sound people."

"Throwing away a resource"

Phoebe was positive about the area: "It's very friendly and people recognise me. I feel I belong here and am accepted. It's unpretentious. There's a lot of communication between parents. There is community spirit because that's why you live here. It becomes home and familiar and you've got things in common with other people.... Together is stronger than separate, which is why the tenants' association has potential to be a good thing". But she was sceptical about communities' ability to run things: "The people without power become less powerful, and the people with power become wealthy".

Phoebe was upset by the proposed demolition for many reasons: "Having to move out has put a damper on everything. I would love to get involved. I'm torn between staying loyal and local, and trying to better ourselves, to get away from where life is a struggle and the streets are all littered". She believed it required stability to sort things out: "The area will only improve if people stay and improve it. There's a drain because people feel disheartened and move away".

Phoebe felt that the council's response to her worries had not helped: "I went to Housing and asked when we would have to move. He said July, but he just picked it out of the air. He said he didn't know any more than that. I've not asked about going out of the city. It's a bit scary because I wouldn't know people and we've lived here for 10 years. It's familiar and I liked it ... but the block is getting emptier and crying out to be vandalised". All this was going on during her exams.

Phoebe saw demolition as often unnecessary: "They put all that money in and they say new people don't want to live here. I think demolition is a big mistake because it feels like the council's throwing away a resource. They had to go for demolition because they were empty. But they were empty because they were run down. Going about it the way it has been done seems awful. They made decisions without seriously consulting the tenants or local people. They seem to think local people made decisions by not living there, but there were reasons for that, like disrepair".

Demolition made the area "a phase in my life. For my children, it's their childhood memories, and I feel a bit sad about that. Theirs are going to be 'don't go there, don't do that'". Phoebe's boys worried about playing out: "They want me to be with them, they're a bit afraid, they're nervous of going outside". She did not use parks because "the park doesn't seem to be run, and there are no parks local to here, just tarmac".

The council's 'hard' attitude to displacing the community had left Phoebe troubled about the future. She half wanted to move away from problems. But she also felt this was betraying everything she'd worked for in the community: "It would be nice to get a job and move somewhere stable and pleasant where I could feel that what I was doing wasn't going to be demolished. I don't want to put any effort into [this place], which isn't good. I like to improve things". Demolition had undermined her confidence: "Moving affects everything. There are so many things I would like to do to contribute to the community but I can't. There's no point being on a committee if we're moving".

"The people that make policies have no idea what life's like"

Phoebe found managing on a low income with two children while studying full time hard. She felt under intense pressure and was scathing about new policies towards lone mothers: "All this blarney about single parents going back to work is just rubbish because it's built on flimsy foundations. It's hard enough giving your time to your children and then studying and working and applying for funding and then you're relying on someone else in a similar situation to help you care for your kids. I'm sure the people that make the policies have no idea what life is like. I'm sure they have stable situations with someone at home. If there's no back-up and nothing reliable, there's massive tension. I've been living like that for a long time, struggling to better myself from NVQs to A-levels to university". Phoebe was glad that the father of one of her boys, Luke, lived nearby and took both of her boys some weekends, even though her other son, Ben, was not his son. He occasionally picked them up from school if she was stuck.

Phoebe felt that the local environment affected the community. She despaired of people's attitude towards it but tried to understand: "It's got this hopelessness in how people don't care about the area, dropping litter and smashing things". Sometimes she felt: "it's getting better but it's difficult to say why. I'm in contact with people who are involved, touched by this energy". But sometimes she felt overwhelmed by problems: "There's more rubbish around and rats as well as pigeons ... there's some kind of mental thing that no matter what you give people, they trash it. If they had some kind of pride and didn't litter the place or dump mattresses on any bit of grass, people would want to improve things, like in residential posher areas. But here the houses are smaller and meaner with no gardens or trees. People seem to like to live in squalor. They moan about it but they create it". Phoebe went around picking up litter and so did some of her neighbours, including the only other tenant still in her block.

"Everything's made up of small things"

Phoebe made many contributions: "We planted fruit trees on communal land, below the school near the allotments. No one really knew what we were doing, even though they had been leafleted. Kids helped. It was a small thing, a couple of days' work". But Phoebe believed that this "almost invisible" action did make a difference: "Nothing is sustainable except for trees" and "everything's made up of small things". Phoebe hoped that when she was forced to move, she'd get some land: "If I can find a place with a garden on ground level, I'd like to have some'ut outside or an allotment". By our second interview she had an allotment, but it had problems too: "The other day I found a needle. It was in the middle of the allotment, so they must have been in the allotment. There is a notice on the gate about the law".

Phoebe also helped local children, developing a kids' club as a community enterprise: "My son was one of the first to be in the after-school club and he's been there from the beginning. It's beset by difficulties". Phoebe needed it for her children, so she was upset when things went wrong: "It has reached crisis point. There's no management, so the parents who depend on it stepped in". But managing an enterprise without experience or money or back-up was difficult: "That's taking time. Funding is difficult to get. You have to apply hand-to-mouth. Therefore there's insecurity for the club. Other people have got the strings to pull and lots of money. We haven't got the time but also we don't know what's going on. I haven't always got time to go to external network meetings. We've got funding from New Deal but not for workers. The money is to help buy things we need. But it's no use if we've no workers for the club. It's going through constant crisis. One woman has left us in the lurch a bit; now I'm doing both jobs, organising and fundraising".

Without resources, the club could not succeed: "The club's the worst in the city. We had promises of money and we got the least of everything. Now I'm involved in the wider planning and steering group … I'm not going to abandon the after-school club. It would have folded if I hadn't given it that time". By the time Phoebe moved, "the after-school club was in a strong position, and was going to carry on. It moved to a more suitable room".

Phoebe was also involved with friends in developing a mutual aid network and on Sundays they did projects in the community – painting a house, tree planting or tidying a garden. In addition to such forms of mutual aid, Phoebe wanted to "do something with older kids, because there's nothing for them". She thought maybe setting up a garage and teaching them to fix cars would be good because they were always coming up and asking her lots of questions and offering to help when she was fixing her own car. Phoebe also wanted to "make a small nursery on demolished land" on a self-help basis but "I haven't got the time to follow it up because of moving away. I'm only a volunteer, not a childcare expert".

"Schools do far more than they have to"

Phoebe thought "the local school does the best it can, given all the difficulties. I'm really happy for them to be there. I don't want Ben to be a snob. I don't think it's the best school that could be found, but given the situation and circumstances of the area and different ethnic groups, they do quite well really, far more than they have to. The classes should be smaller.… The reality is these kids are starting from below the level of kids who already speak the language. They have to work even harder to get the same level". Phoebe's children had not experienced bullying, because "Ben kept his head down all the time and kept out of the way. Luke, the younger boy, has no trouble. He's naturally confident, rarely shy and quite willing to give things a go".

Phoebe was worried, however, that "Ben's not a very good pupil. I'm not sure how much is him or being exposed to naughtiness. I don't enjoy hearing about it". Phoebe was worried that the school didn't help enough: "They acknowledge there's problems, but don't want to do anything about it". She feared Ben could "slip through the net ... I think he's quite behind". On our third visit, after she had finished her degree, Phoebe felt more able to intervene: "I'm en route to getting some help. Now it's the end of my course, I feel I have more time to do it. I need to go and meet the teachers".

When they moved, by our fourth visit, his new teachers classified him as having 'special needs'. "He's clever but he doesn't get anything down on paper." Phoebe knew that her son needed her time: "Ben's not very confident. The more I spend time with him, the more outgoing he becomes, the more positive I feel for him". Phoebe depended on the school to provide her with progress reports and worksheets to do at home with him, "to give me structure, to see what he's able to do and help congratulate him. If we don't have that, things slide. I've got a sheet of tasks for him to do before SATs [Standard Assessment Tasks]". Ben did not have a place in the secondary school in their new area. Phoebe could not get him into her first choice school: "no chance because it's full". The next choice was "also oversubscribed. They will have to measure as the crow flies and I might appeal".

Phoebe's ideal activity with her children would be "just sitting around and we never do it!" Phoebe was sure that they "don't have enough time together. I want that to change. I've just spent so much time putting myself through different education stuff, I owe the kids a lot of time, and myself". She decided when she finished her degree that she should have a year off to devote to her children. But Phoebe found it very difficult to pay for the activities they wanted: "Ben's got swimming lessons; he's interested in karate too … but you have to be able to pay". He also played football after school, which cost £1; she struggled to find the cash.

Phoebe talked openly about her money problems: "I don't know what normal is … we haven't got a TV or carpet. Our shoes are full of holes and everything is second-hand. We're among the poor technically, although I don't feel poor. I don't spend very much because we don't consume very much". Phoebe told the story of a National Society for the Prevention of Cruelty to Children (NSPCC) appeal leaflet coming through the door. Ben asked if they could give something. Phoebe explained that they were the kind of family the NSPCC was trying to help!

"I'm forced to be an island"

Three years after we first met Phoebe, she had been given a nice house with a garden in another area, yet she remembered the neighbourhood and the community she left behind with real regret: "People went out of their way to be inclusive. People lived with different races and colours and cultures, so it was normal that someone might speak a different language or have a different religion". She asked whether she "might be idealising it". But in her new neighbourhood, for all its better conditions, "it's not me at all. I don't fit in". Phoebe felt constantly anxious: "There's always things troubling me" and sometimes she saw the doctor because she suffered from depression. She found it "helpful to talk through all the things" that troubled her.

Phoebe's new house was in a much more respectable area on an all-white estate, with "posh people over the hill". But she found it hard to settle and felt very isolated though she did talk "to the man next to me at the new allotment!" Her sense of loss was real: "I hate this area. I'm neither in the city nor out of it. I'm forced to be an island. I can't afford to move again and the children are settled in their schools, well not really". Phoebe was anxious to give her boys some stability, so she was thinking of buying her council house, notwithstanding her doubts about the area, because "it's an investment and it's got a garden. I'd never have bought the maisonette" because she couldn't grow things there and there was so much she and other residents could not control, even though Phoebe felt more at home there.

Phoebe worried that wider environmental and political issues might affect her sons' future: "I don't feel optimistic about what they're going to experience and what's happening globally, like global warming and oil; I have visions that when they're older they won't have the choice. There are people that have to live their lives under those threats now, and we're so lucky. I'm always saying to my kids how lucky we are in the world as a whole, you know, we're not at war". Phoebe hoped that her boys could have "as much experience of life as I had, through my parents leaving a poor background and making an effort to get somewhere better". She mainly wanted them to be happy, "to make the most of wherever they find themselves and be positive. I think they've got that from me".

A basic need for community

Phoebe understands the problems of community and wants to help solve them. But in the end she is forced to move on and, like so many vulnerable mothers with children, feels powerless in the process. Neighbourhood change erodes community feelings, yet Phoebe articulates passionately the need for community. She wants to belong where she lives, to support the community she is in and to reach out to the wider community as well.

Many think about community as a vanishing reality and an outmoded idea, in the same way as many people believe that modern social conditions undermine and destroy the family. Families have changed almost beyond recognition and so have communities.[3] Yet both survive, often intertwined, as antidotes to the harsh realities of changing urban neighbourhoods and as the strengtheners of smaller, more old-fashioned places. People often talk of a 'real sense of community' as well as regretting its loss.[4] Community retains a powerful hold on people's sense of what makes life work.

Nine out of 10 families say that 'community spirit' matters. Yet community implies trust, familiarity, confidence, small-scale and informal social networks, recognisable roots and a level of social and geographic stability that is undermined by neighbourhood problems and mobility. Parents want more community spaces and activities within the neighbourhood so that their children can play with other children and they can meet other parents in order to create a sense of community or belonging.

People may no longer know each other well enough to bond together, cooperate and organise their social lives in a collective and mutually supporting way. But community also means something smaller, and more elusive; familiar faces and local contact; someone to call on in an emergency; simple, friendly gestures; social links of the most basic kind. Community matters to families because it makes problems more manageable. Some mothers just believe in community because it surrounds them where they are and it makes life work.

Mothers need local social contact while caring for small children, to share the burden, particularly mothers with jobs. To ensure mutual support, many mothers maintain frequent contact with relatives and close friends; at least half have relatives within the area. In the large Northern estate in the present study, 78% do. The most immediate community is often the extended family; over two-thirds have contact with their own mothers at least fortnightly and over a third daily. Only a small minority of our mothers feel completely isolated or isolate themselves from their surroundings.

Community matters more in low-income areas because families have less cash to buy support, need local back-up in emergencies and place a high value on local social contact because wider networks beyond the immediate community are harder to reach and maintain on a low income. Families talk about their isolation when community links are missing; Phoebe feels very cut off in the new area where she knows no one.

For professional working mothers who have nannies, nurseries, paid activities and expensive childcare, it is different. These mothers literally pass on, at high cost, much of the responsibility for their children and much of the sharing that low-income mothers rely on.[5] Poorer mothers cannot do this. Family members, particularly the mothers' own mothers, become very important to a sense of community. Relatives – not just grandparents, but siblings, cousins and occasionally partners too – all help when children arrive.

Communities need families as the basic building blocks of social relations, because families are more anchored than childless households, children are natural socialisers and mothers create social networks.[6] Families with children often gravitate together because children need other children to play with, and mothers like sharing with other mothers their experiences, ideas and childcare. This helps explain the gap between the significance of communities to families and to childless people. Just half of all households think community matters compared with nearly 90% in our families.[7]

Because difficult neighbourhoods are family unfriendly, as we showed in Chapter Two, community spirit acquires an intense function, protecting families from a negative environment. So community becomes a counterweight to neighbourhood problems. Knowing who your neighbours are helps to overcome real fear. Community requires shared physical space to grow in; without it, family life becomes miserable.

It is not mere romantic nostalgia that families regret the loss of community. It is well documented that social relations were less transient, family relations more stable and community bonds stronger, even a generation or two ago when families were larger and poorer, when modern amenities were not readily available and when work conditions were harsher.[8] Studies of happiness show how closely these family experiences reflect society's need for a sense of community belonging.[9] So families counter the negative impact of their surroundings by searching for more nebulous forms of support, which they generally refer to as 'community spirit'. This 'spirit' can be emergency back-up, familiar faces or common spaces. Community gives a sense of security and this is the positive 'people' side of places.

From the very earliest days of a child's life, smiles, known faces and voices shape a child's sense of security, development and happiness. This social instinct, as we mature, drives our sense of well-being; continual direct social contact is central to survival.[10] Mothers know this, seek it and secure it, even in the most adverse conditions. Bringing people together actively as parents is a powerful catalyst for positive feelings about an area. The same mothers who worry about community divisions praise local events, and express real happiness at the support they or their children receive within a community.[11] Bringing parents together builds social links. Mothers who lack local connections can become depressed as a result of their isolation. This undermines their sense of community.

Sola, in our next story, has family all around her, a strong sense of community and a commitment to strengthening it, yet because of tough life experiences, she often feels that "You're just on your own". Her story reflects the tension between her need for community and the harsh realities of the neighbourhood where she lives – very much like Phoebe.

Sola's story – working on behalf of the community

Sola described herself as "black with a totally mixed family". When we first met, her son was 16 and she had three adult daughters plus grandchildren. She had lived in her neighbourhood in East London for 19 years. Her husband of the last 15 years was a minister and "helps people who have problems. He brings peace into people's lives". She herself was very religious: "I go to church; that's the only thing that keeps me going, my faith. I pray every morning for God's protection". She empathised with everyone with whom she came into contact, her children and grandchildren, and by extension all young people: "There are so many hurting", but she found it hard to sort out everyone's troubles.

"I'm very fearful for my grandchildren"

Sola had one word for her neighbourhood: "problems". But she firmly believed that helping was the way forward: "If someone needs, I help". Sola helped her children "with the grandchildren, often, most days" because "I worry about my children, even though they're mostly grown up. I'm very fearful for my grandchildren".

When she split up with her first husband, she was forced to work nights to get by. "I had so much problems with my first husband." She believed she should not claim from the government and worked to pay her way. "I had to let my kids go with their father, otherwise they would have starved. I did have worries because they weren't living with me." Her son was the worst affected: "He was only four. Breaking up with my husband affected my son. I've had nothing but problems with him. You know how hard it is to bring up boys. It's making me ill. He mixes with people on drugs, the wrong crowd, he doesn't listen … I had a drugs problem with him and his friends. I had no problems with my three daughters".

Sola's son was expelled from school when he was 12 years old: "He had five years not at school.… After he was expelled he was outside a lot; he had a lot of freedom which he shouldn't have had." She tried to get him into a secondary school in the East End but as he had been expelled "they wouldn't offer him a place because the school he came from had a bad reputation. I always felt, if I wasn't in this area, I'd have had a better deal". Sola appealed to social services for help: "When you've got problems, social services should do more … they don't do nothing, you go to them as a young mother – you're just on your own. I can't believe they would let someone miss that much of their education". The local education authority offered a place in a unit: "They put him in special needs, but he didn't want to go because he felt stupid". Family problems made things worse: "broken families, that doesn't help. It's really hard. I can speak from experience".

"Being a boy is even harder than being a girl"

Sola did not want her son to go to the local college because of its bad reputation and "because he draws a certain type of friend". By our second visit he was at college in West London, doing building studies: "He only goes once or twice a week. I'm trying to get him a tutor because he's missed so much of his education, but it's hard". Her son's problems continued: "He's stopped a lot by the police in his car. He wants to make a complaint". At the same time, peer pressure was intense: "He has to have the latest clothes. There's a pressure all round to fit in. Being a boy is even harder than being a girl". She was worried about how he would cope on his own: "It will be hard for my son to get a flat and be more independent". He still kept the wrong company: "My son's friend wanted to kill him. Nothing came of it. I feel very sorry for young people. There's nothing going on to keep them out of trouble.... If you lose them to drugs and crime it's hopeless ... I feel I've got a lot to offer young people. There's a lot of suicide, drugs, crime. I've saved a lot of my children's friends from destruction".

By the third interview, things were a little better: "Thank God everything seems alright now, maybe not 100% but a lot better", compared with before. "My son was on crack. He's changed now, but while it was happening, he was robbing from the house." This was almost more than Sola could bear: "My son told me one time that he wanted to die. 'Thank God for a mother like you', he said, or he wouldn't be here today". Things gradually improved: "My son wasn't working before, now he's training" and still at college. He clearly cared about his mother: "Even though he is always out, on my birthday he treated me and took me out". Sola did not tell her mother, who also lived in the area, about her troubles although she saw her every other day, because "it wouldn't be fair. My dad's disabled".

Sola relied a lot on her daughter Sophie, who lived nearby; she could "talk to her in a crisis". Sophie told us how she tried to help her mother, even though she herself was "a tearaway when I was younger". Now she was fed up that her brother was giving her mother such a hard time. But Sola worried because "Sophie's son goes haywire when he's been away from me and with his mum for a few days". She often collected him from school to try and help. Sophie also explained the problems she had with her boy, a bit like Zoe. She was very grateful to her mother, as she found it hard on her own.

"If it's a good community spirit, things run smoothly"

Sola thought that community spirit mattered a lot "because I'm living in a community – everyone round here knows me. Even though I don't mix a lot, I'm a friendly, open person.... If it's a good community spirit, things run smoothly, it makes it more integrated. It's important to have it". But Sola was worried about the impact of run-down housing on community relations. Sola believed that the council put black people in the worst housing, so she saw community in segments; she belonged to "the black community", and she could understand white people's hostility to change. She was "willing to forgive" but thought "the racial concentration has got worse. You're already oppressed as a race. Don't oppress you more by putting you in bad housing".

Sola blamed the problems in the community on housing policy. "When it comes to crime, they concentrate a lot of people of the same type in one area.... There's a lot of sick people in the community – you have to be careful where you tread. You feel you should be entitled to a decent place to live in, not just the rejects, because it makes you feel you're not worth anything. I was trying to get away from it because there are no good prospects, especially for ethnic minorities, unless you've got a good job".

Sola worried about black children in schools, following her son's experience. She thought that "in secondary school they don't bother with black kids". As a result, she thought that her grandchildren's prospects were poor because "they don't get treated equally". She did not think that white people could understand: "nobody knows what it's like to be black if they're not black themselves. It's alright to say that black kids are making problems, but it's very hard. If they're treated badly, and do badly as a result, they're bound to cause problems". Phoebe expressed similar views about white children in her Northern community.

Sola did not feel that she had much influence in the area: "We can't because the big mouths have got all the say. I used to do voluntary work, cooking for the pensioners' club and go to committee meetings.... But I dropped out, I never had a proper say, so I thought, what's the point? But we've got ideas, things like creches, show movies, get youths off the streets, get things positive. There's so much you can do for the kids round here". She thought that "crime has brought people closer". Sola used to "help at my children's school and youth clubs when they were young" and she was in the church choir, which she really enjoyed. She also helped an old neighbour with her shopping.

"We're here to do good"

Sola was not as involved in the community as she wanted to be because she was so busy with family, work and informal care but she still wanted to visit "people in hospital who've got no one". Typically "I wake up at 7.30. I help an old lady, she's partially sighted. I bath her and clean her house. Then I come home and do my housework. I pick up my grandson from school sometimes. I go to work at 9.15 at night ... I help with childcare a lot". Sola worked as a night cleaner and did care work during the day. "We're not put here to waste time. We're here to do good. As long as I've got my strength, I'll bring my money in. I don't care what job I do. I wanted to be a scientist when I was at school and go to college but after a while I went and learnt hairdressing." On our third visit, Sola was worried about her care job because there were major cuts in the council and she had to reapply for her job, having been made redundant, but she got through this bad patch.

Sola had other work troubles: "At work I had an intruder. I work alone at night". Luckily the police "dealt with it well". This boosted her confidence in them after her son's problems. She thought, "they've got better. There's less harassment and more police ... I see two walking around together ... police–community relations have improved a lot ... and vandalism has been cut down a lot". Sola also noticed that neighbourhood wardens had been introduced locally. "I wouldn't mind being one."

But a violent fight reinforced Sola's worries about racial divisions. "Two children were playing at Sophie's, one white, one black. They had an argument and the white mother started hitting the little black boy. Then the women fought each other. One broke a bottle and attacked the other. Family members got involved on both sides and someone stabbed the boy's uncle and he's on life support. The white family has run away, they haven't been caught yet. So many police have been involved ... the flat has been cordoned off. It doesn't need to escalate like that. Children play. It makes you think, is it a nice world to bring your children into?"

"We're all one nation"

Sola wanted people to understand each other better: "It doesn't matter what nationality you are, we're all one nation. We can learn so much from other cultures. It's not fair to judge someone by their culture 'til you really know that person.... You just get one or two ignorant people that cause things to flare up. They need to be educated and do some travelling". Her own family is very mixed: "I've got a very interracial family. My cousins are all married to English girls". So it could work. She had a lot of sympathy for newcomers, trying to fit into a strange place without knowing the rules. "We all have to live. They're not trouble people, a lot of Africans and Kurdish people ... mixing among everyone." She knew there was "a little trouble, but it's mostly OK. I think it's got its problems, but it's still friendlier than other places, there's more community spirit."

If Sola was in charge, she would "focus on people with families because that's where life begins, we all need a good home life and family. There needs to be better housing for families.... For the last year or two, I've seen a lot of building going on, nice buildings going up. It looks like eventually it'll be a nice area.... The area's really getting built up a lot ... but it hasn't changed in drugs and violence ... I just hope it improves.... If it does improve, I might be changing my mind about moving because you do get settled in an area".

Many different communities

Sola's story illustrates why mothers try to create community around them. The grim experiences of her family are eased by a sense of belonging. She sees that social contact provides a bridge between different ethnic groups, between young and old, between long-standing and more recent families, between desperate boys and sympathetic adults.

Community is not a neat idea with clear boundaries, because there are many different communities within particular neighbourhoods and many families talk as much about community divisions as about community 'togetherness'. Some minority ethnic parents understand why white people feel displaced and how this can threaten a sense of community. In London, high property prices, pressures on councils to house those in greatest need and changing populations are causing major dislocations in local communities. Often mothers feel isolated by cultural and language barriers that cause many misunderstandings.

The sheer volume of strangers to a community is a threat to social links, as Annie explained in Chapter Two; confidence in the local community is weakened because by definition you cannot create a sense of community until people have time to settle and become familiar.[12] In a community with too many strangers from too many places, families feel ill at ease, unclear about who belongs and uncertain whether they do themselves. Particular groups, such as Yemenis or Somalis or Kurds, are singled out as 'having their own community'. As a result of community divisions, mothers from both minority ethnic and white backgrounds talk emphatically about there being "no spirit of community around here". Yet a striking aspect of fast-changing, ethnically mixed neighbourhoods is that social contact quickly develops between mothers who are strangers within these communities. Because they need it, they create it if they can. But contact is often fragile and parents notice the barriers to community.

The 'constant new faces' that Annie spoke about in Chapter Two make organised activity all the more important because the informal links that constitute community are inevitably undermined by the lack of familiar faces and the sense of insecurity. Mothers can find it hard to create bridges between their family and the diverse and unstable community around them. So they rely on long-established roots, most particularly close relatives. Without organised support, a changing environment works against families developing trusting relations beyond immediate family and friends. 'Outsiders' are more likely to become isolated, lonely and depressed within these communities; Chapter Six explores their weaker community links. When people cannot join in and are not part of the community, they miss that elusive quality of 'community spirit'.

Almost all mothers in the present study recognise some signs of community and two-thirds of parents think that different races get on fairly well together, bringing benefits particularly to their children. Of the parents living in the three ethnically mixed areas, 70% say that it is more positive to live in a racially mixed area. Even parents worried by community change often hold this view. Some community-minded parents argue that a sense of community can cross ethnic boundaries, in spite of community tensions. One East End father believes that community development will encourage stronger community identity, even though he recognises internal divisions and older people's insecurity at the pace of change:

> "The elderly in the population feel a bit threatened. Community ownership is the solution, not imposed solutions." (Alan)

However, supporters of mixed and integrated communities argue for clearer rules of entitlement and a more stable environment. Alan feels that his children's future is uncertain because of competition for community resources:

> "We have worries for the children, whether there's going to be housing for them when they get older. Secondary schools are a major worry. The eldest has been turned down by every school."

The next story is about Nadia, who returns to her community of origin after failing to settle in new, fast-changing communities in the East End. In her eyes:

> "It's just a pile of houses, not a community."

Nadia's story – community means belonging

Nadia is Irish; her husband is North African and a practising Muslim. They have two children who are being raised as Muslims. During our five visits, the family lived in three different areas, near the Docks, then near the East End of London, then Ireland. Nadia's story took her back to her roots, offering useful insights into what 'community' means.

Nadia went to college in Ireland, but failed her first-year exams and came to London where she met her husband, became pregnant and later worked as a school lunchtime supervisor. When we first met Nadia, she worked in the local adult education college and was doing an initial teaching course. Her husband worked up to 60 hours a week as a waiter in the West End of London.

Nadia and her family had lived in the Docks for three-and-a-half years. They moved "because they offered us a house. We were living in a small two-bed flat before that. We'd never been down round here before. It's not very built-up yet". But Nadia saw drawbacks: "The children still go to school in our old neighbourhood. It's about four miles, and the traffic's really bad" but the school was friendly and they all hankered after moving back.

The new area was quite dirty, even though it was supposed to be a high-quality mixed neighbourhood: "People dump rubbish over the wall. The bushes are full of rats. The contractor cleans the ones that face the road, but not the ones behind. It's nice to have greenery, but not so thick that it's full of rats. Everyone dumps their rubbish in a place which is hidden from the road". The hospital also had a bad reputation as dirty, inefficient, and delivering a poor service: "They were rude. I missed my last appointment because I had no confidence in them". A local child was said to have died after incorrect treatment. It was the only hospital of which we heard bad things.

The new development had quickly acquired a bad reputation, like the wider area: "You hear so much about drugs and thieves, you worry about bringing children up here. There's no shops you can walk to, there's noise from the planes, and the smell from the factories is very bad". The area felt "quite isolated, not much going on, not really a place where lots of people want to come and live. It's quite friendly, but dirty from pollution, traffic, factories – and busy, because of all the traffic going through, not because of lots going on. My husband is the only thing keeping me in London. He works shifts and comes home late at night; it would be better to be living more central". A new underground station meant quick journeys to the centre of London for his work, but his evenings were very long, so their old community still appealed.

"It's nice to belong to a community"

Nadia did not think there was much community spirit in her new neighbourhood, "not from my point of view" because it was too new and unsettled and "it's changed beyond all recognition.... People at the bottom of the pile have been dumped here; it used to be much better. It might be different for the people who live in those old houses and have lived there for years. My husband is not the sort of person to get involved in community things anyway. So it probably would be just me and the kids, which wouldn't be the same. I don't really see anyone except at work ... I do get to know local people through work". But Nadia would like to be involved in community events: "I wouldn't mind helping with Halloween or a Christmas party, that would be good. But I wouldn't want to be in charge, I've got enough on my plate".

Nadia knew hardly anyone in the area, "I would rather keep myself to myself ... I wouldn't fancy someone coming round every day at any time they wanted". But she would "like to find some more things for the children, music classes. The children want to learn, but there isn't anything in the area". She encouraged them to do after-school activities, like sport, computers and drama: "They're always busy. That's what I like about their school, they do loads of things; but more music would be good". Nadia did not let them play out: "I don't like them to go out of my sight ... I wouldn't let them go to the park on their own because that road is so busy to cross and it's quite an isolated park. I wouldn't go there by myself, even me". But the smaller parks in her area "are always nice and tidy and clean and well maintained".

"I haven't got any close friends"

Nadia's own childhood could not have been more different: "My own childhood was more relaxed, free; I could go for walks, see friends. We lived in a little village and knew everyone. My children are in the house most of the time. Their social time is much more organised. I supervise them. We don't know many people and have no family here. We never get involved in anything because we're not here much. I think it's nice to belong to a community and know you've got neighbours. It's good for the children as well to know people and be involved in different things. I haven't got any close friends here. I couldn't say that I can trust anyone in this area. Over the years with my husband, even close friends have let him down. It would be different if we had family and friends living round here".

By our second visit, her husband's brother lived with them and babysat occasionally, which helped. There were also some positive changes under way: "The new school's opened now. You see people going up and down to it and there seems to be a lot more people about". Nadia's adult education classes moved into the school, which she liked: "It's lovely, it's really nice, it's less isolated than before. It's in the middle of everything, a really friendly feel".

There were also bigger changes under way: "they're building so much, lots and lots of expensive houses and people moving in. New apartments start at £185,000 [in 1999] so what hope has anyone round here got of buying? It's good in some ways because it will probably improve the area to attract people into the apartments. But it will probably attract thieves too.... No children from the private houses go to the new school.... Things are changing really quickly – the new Centre, the bridge, new park. My husband can get to work in the West End in 20 minutes. They've also opened one more shop, it's useful and not on the main road, so my son can nip there. A lot of new people have moved in.... But I suppose all the underlying problems are still there – the crime, the drugs, a lot of people on Income Support and struggling. So although we have new things, people are still struggling".

"Learn to be more tolerant of one another"

Like most mothers in the area, Nadia worried about drugs: "I suppose I'm scared my children will be exposed to drugs at too young an age, and people on drugs are hanging around the area, with all the problems that brings, like crime. There also seems to be, it sounds awful to say, a lot more alcoholic people around. They sit on benches near my house. I was going to my car and a man came out of the bushes. I thought he was a burglar at first. Then I realised he was drunk and must have been going to the toilet or something ... I think drugs are a problem too. That bench out there, sometimes there's teenagers out there. They light a fire under the bench. I'm suspicious. I don't know anything about drugs. I never took them. Where I grew up no one did.... But I've been having problems with students taking drugs in break time. I'm so green, I didn't notice 'til someone told me". Nadia thought that adult education moving into the new school had helped as "it's a more controlled environment".

Nadia did not feel she could greatly influence what happened in the community: "I work with adults, but what real difference is that making?... There are tenants' associations, but I suppose I never wanted to stay in London ... I know they say that everyone has their say, but we haven't really got any. You can go along but I doubt it would be taken into account". Physical improvements failed to create a sense of community.

Nadia hankered after Ireland, but having married a North African, she worried about fitting in there: "It would feel a bit uncomfortable to live somewhere like that, so it's nice to be in an area that's mixed". Her children "play with the children in the black family here – they mix quite a lot at school ... I haven't experienced any bad things on that front. For me it's more positive because my husband's Algerian anyway. When we first moved here it was nearly all white people who lived here. I've noticed refugees moving in. Children are exposed to all different cultures and backgrounds. That way they should learn to be more tolerant of one another".

"There's a community here but I've never felt part of it"

The family did not really settle. Nadia felt "we're isolated here. There's a community here but I've never felt part of it". They wanted to escape the main road: "You get used to the planes but the traffic is very noisy. You can't keep the windows open when you're going to sleep. The whole house shakes when lorries go past". Her husband, sitting in at this point, added: "I can't sleep past 5am because that's when the traffic gets going again – even with double glazing".

By our third visit, the family had succeeded in moving back to their old area and Nadia felt a lot happier: "Everyone seems to know each other here, there's a community here". But it was far from trouble-free. If anything, there were more social pressures on the children: "There's a split between communities, a big Bengali community and a lot of gangs.... Teenagers who think they're fantastic and go around in gangs". The compensations were familiarity, proximity and informal links, which simply were not there in the new area: "Here I could go next door and I could leave my son there.... When I moved back here I let them pop to the shop or newsagents. But I worry about drugs. My older son had a lot of problems with a boy in his school. He brought cannabis in and tried to make him take it. Those boys vandalised my car". Her younger son was under similar peer pressure: "He tries to be like his friends". Nadia felt that there should be more policing: "There are no police in the area. There should be a lot more police walking around. It's a visual deterrent. You would drop dead in amazement if you saw a policeman!"

"We're on our own island"

Nadia felt that the area "is cut off in some ways. People from here say 'We're on our own island'", a phrase that Phoebe also used to describe her area. But it was a much more connected community than their last: "Where we were before was very isolated. They worked to make a village, but it isn't".

Having moved back to the community they liked, secondary school was their next big problem: "I was disgusted when I went around the secondary schools. We didn't apply for any in the area.... He got into a strict Christian school, but my children are Muslims, even though they're not practising. I always said I wouldn't be a hypocrite and get them baptised, just to get them into schools. But when we went around and my husband saw the schools, although he's a Muslim and doesn't want his children as Christians, he agreed". They decided to send their son outside the area: "The secondary school was much nicer, more serious about work, stricter than primary school.... Behaviour is better. He needed to become more organised and he can do that now".

By our fifth visit, Nadia's life had been transformed again by her decision to "move back to Ireland. My husband is staying in London because we need the money from his job while I'm studying". She decided to become a midwife and to study back home because it would solve the school problem for their second child. She was worried about her mother who was very ill. Also they could not see how they would ever be able to buy their own house in London. In her home village in Ireland they were able to buy based on her nursing grant and her husband's earnings. When Nadia moved back to Ireland, their son boarded at his secondary school, staying with his father at weekends and returning to Ireland for holidays.

"The community's going"

Nadia, looking back on East London, saw radical community changes under way. Their old area had been something of a let-down because "people had bought our maisonettes and were renting them out to students.... That makes a difference because the kids used to go out and play together, but it's just not like that any more. There's less of a community feel.... It's not so much for families any more.... It was a close community but a lot of council tenants bought and sold on to other people and most of them have now been bought to let.... You don't really get to know your neighbours like you did before; it's just not the same.... Obviously if someone's renting a maisonette out to six different people, it's not the same as if it's just one family. It's a shame that a lot of English people who were living in East London have all gone away and been replaced, because the community's going.... I think most people who could afford to, were trying to move out of the area, rather than do anything about it. This isn't necessarily good, but I'm one of them. I couldn't stick out being in London any more".

Neighbourhoods can "improve and become more socially mixed" and yet be harder for families with children: "They used to have a nice restaurant; people would go there for kids' birthdays. But they knocked that down to build flats. They seem to be building on every spare bit of land. There's nothing really child friendly. It's nice they're building new houses in the Docks. The council is trying. The council block we were in is being taken over by a housing association and hopefully they're going to do it up, because the majority of council housing is really bad. The council doesn't have enough money to fix up the blocks, everything's falling into disrepair. I'd put a lot more security into housing estates. I'd get a lot tougher with gangs and their parents. The problems aren't getting any better: gangs, crime, drugs".

Looking back, Nadia felt that "Schools were atrocious – the behaviour of children and how they deal with it. At my son's primary school, if a kid was told off, the parents came into the school and abused the teacher in front of the class. It happened quite a lot". She felt that this undermined teachers' authority and set a terrible example for children. She also worried about expectations: "My kids started homework in year five. That's too late to start. Maybe the school thought there were parents in that area who wouldn't be able to do that".

"Here everyone knows everyone"

In Ireland things are "completely different – wide open spaces, big gardens. People are much more house-conscious. Everyone does up their house nicely and cares about their garden, whereas in the East End most people couldn't be bothered.... Here everyone knows everyone. I was gone for 15 years but when I came back, everyone still knows who I am. There were financial barriers to moving back, especially trying to find a job in a small rural area, plus the fact that my husband has to stay in London, for financial reasons". Nadia's nursing training created financial pressures but it offered the prospect of a steady job. They were able to buy, which they "couldn't afford in London". Now they had "got the responsibility of a mortgage". So that forced them to live apart: "If you lose your job and you go on benefits, you get your rent paid but you wouldn't get your mortgage paid".

There were other things that were more difficult: "I live in a nationalist town. The police hesitate to come here because it's nationalist, or that's the excuse they use.... So there are problems here too with teenagers". But Nadia felt that she had made the right decision for her children: "I've moved back to give them better prospects.... It's really nice out in the countryside and there's a really nice community school.... Here drugs are a problem too, but not as bad. In East London they never really pushed the brighter ones. They never encouraged them to achieve their potential. They were just keeping them where they were so other kids could catch up". Nadia and her husband hoped their children would go to university, although cost made it difficult. Her older son wanted to be a journalist, but currently was aiming for a summer job in the supermarket. Her second child wanted to be a bone specialist since he broke his arm. Nadia's husband planned to "become self-employed, run his own cafe."

Nadia felt happier 'at home': "I wanted to be closer to my family, I wanted a better quality of life, better schools, and I needed to get away from the crime and teenagers in gangs. Because of the children, I'm happy. It's a small village in a valley beside the mountains and the forest. I didn't appreciate it when I was living here before, but now I do". Her sisters and brothers were still there, so she felt "it's my home, it's where I was born and brought up, with my family. What do I miss? Nothing at all, not really", apart from her husband.

Community anchors

Nadia's life was undermined by too little sense of community until she reached the point where she simply quit. She had a ready community to go back to, which underlined what she was missing.

Urban communities house many unsettled families like Nadia's and they need both formal and informal anchors to foster 'community spirit', this nebulous sense of belonging that families say they need. Institutions, such as schools, health centres, churches and friendly societies have long existed within urban communities, cementing social links while 'holding families up' by meeting their direct needs.[13] Local institutions provide social and physical structures that families recognise and rely on. These wider organisations with outside backing, resources and professional organisers, such as teachers, ministers, health and community workers, encourage community activities. They are popular because they make it easy for parents and children to get together and they are cheap. Over 80% of parents think that local organisations and activities make a difference.

Local projects and local community events are mainstays in meeting parents' needs, enhancing the sense of belonging merely by bringing people together. Outside interventions such as Sure Start, aimed at parents and young children in highly disadvantaged areas, enjoy unique praise because they support parents within the local community in very direct ways. One criticism from parents in the present study was that it only helped very young children. After that there was a vacuum. It also sometimes failed to reach the most vulnerable families, as Marissa pointed out in Chapter Two. In spite of this, Sure Start operates in all four areas, organising community events and enjoyable activities for families, focusing strongly on the local community, lending it a sense of worth. It also offers training for local parents so that they can actually do some of the jobs available in the community.

Local schools have become central in anchoring families and their children within diverse communities. The school brought Nadia back from the Docks to near the East End. Schools help parents overcome community barriers by literally gathering them in the same place daily. Because schools, like churches, bring the same people together regularly, the sense of familiarity and therefore community grows. Parents support the organising role of schools precisely because they do not feel able to do this unsupported, because of fragmented community relations. Schools in particular can help to smooth out many of the tensions that undermine community.[14] Parents praise the way schoolteachers broker community conflict. Being in a local school in a multiracial area helps to build contact between groups.

Most parents explicitly do not want schools to become segregated, a strong trend in three of the four areas in the present study. The desire for integration comes from parents of different ethnic backgrounds, because otherwise a sense of community may be undermined. Exclusive ethnic communities, particularly concentrated in specific schools, do not help children understand each other. Families, especially children, need to mix to get to know each other. We discuss problems of ethnic polarisation in Chapters Six and Seven.

Some families see large-scale, expensive regeneration by public bodies as destructive of community. Families whose homes are under threat of demolition experience heightened feelings about their community. Parents often express a fear of moving to where they do not know anyone, where they will have to make new contacts all over again. Demolition disrupts communities, because poorer people know they will be displaced and funding to improve conditions often displaces the activity local people most need:

"They just build on all the available land and don't provide anything for the children." (Zoe)

This makes some community representatives extremely suspicious of major regeneration on behalf of the community.

While the goal of regeneration schemes is precisely to change the character of the local community, the role of community leaders is to represent and reinforce the existing community. Yet the vast majority of parents in the present study feel that they have very little influence and less than half the parents think that official local meetings make a difference, whereas the vast majority think fun events do. Three of the fathers who play a major part in childcare are also active in community regeneration. They are highly critical of professional efforts at regeneration because they see a conflict of interests between the local community and the financial power that lies outside it.

It is in regeneration that the distinction between neighbourhood conditions and community becomes clear. Public interventions aim to improve poor neighbourhoods by trying to eradicate visible problems; but this cuts across families trying to create a sense of community by holding on to familiar places and people. Reconciling these countervailing needs of regeneration and community may be the biggest challenge facing low-income communities and government approaches to neighbourhood renewal; we return to this theme in Chapter Seven.

Community is undermined by over-rapid physical as well as social change. Traffic is one of the biggest physical barriers to community, militating against safe use of streets, limiting access to parks and play areas that could encourage a sense of community. Faced with busy streets, children and mothers will simply not use parks. In the neighbourhoods in this study there are no 'home zones' restricting cars to walking pace, with pedestrian-friendly streets allowing parents with pushchairs to stand and chat. Accidents involving children are all too common in these neighbourhoods.[15]

Social contact is also undermined by unsupervised open space. Parents want well-kept parks where they can take their children to play alongside other families, yet parks within the areas under study are widely regarded as unsafe. Fifty-four per cent think that there is not enough supervision and half the mothers only let their children out into the garden or balcony. Avoiding open spaces, out of fear, increases vandalism, bullying, crime, drug abuse and general antisocial behaviour, which undermine the local sense of community. By removing supervision and regular maintenance from parks and streets, depriving urban families of open spaces where their children can let off steam and develop informal contact with other children, public bodies have undermined one of the critical forms of informal supervision.[16]

The world over, mothers, sometimes aided by fathers but often alone, find ways of creating and recreating small-scale community links within fast-changing, pressured environments.[17] Almost all families recognise the significance of community, whether they experience it or not. Becky, a local 'outsider' to the Northern estate in which she lived, shows how difficult it can be to fit into an established community. She works hard at 'fitting in' and gradually builds links within her local community.

Becky's story – communities need links

Becky had just moved from a nearby area to the large Northern estate when we met her. She had three boys, aged nine, six and four. She had just split up with her husband and chose this estate "because of the available housing and because it's still quite local for the children's school. I knew I'd get a house here because other people see it as a dumping ground.... The woman in the housing office nearly fell over when I put this as my priority. She said: 'Not many, well nobody, chooses it'". Friends told her: "I'm not going to visit you when you move down there", so she was under pressure not to. But Becky found: "it's got a reputation but it's got a lot to offer as well".

Becky's children were in a very different world from that of her own childhood. "There [in the neighbourhood of her own childhood] it was your average family, 2.2 children, two parents, a car. Most children achieved at school, everyone had a holiday. The housing was better than here – two bathrooms, but what was the point of that? It was quiet, not much vandalism or much crime. Everyone was law-abiding, I only remember the fish and chip shop getting burgled. Church was a big thing, but not in my family. They were all university lecturers or policemen or owned fish and chip shops!" In fact, Becky's own background was quite troubled. She worked with young people because she "got thrown out of home at 17 and thought I could relate to young people, you know, drugs, trouble, all that stuff, like loads of other people do".

Becky worried about the clash between her family values and the norms of the area in which she now lived: "My children are being brought up in a different type of area and they see different things from what I saw. They've seen people having rows in the street, women fighting. It's the norm for the kids to have a friend to stay because ma's in a cell. You can only protect them from it for so long, then you have to throw them in and hope it turns out OK. It doesn't stop the way I bring up my children but it's outside influences. It's the norm for others to steal but I try to show mine it's not the way to live. I'd love one of them to go to university and get a career and keep out of trouble". Becky added: "I just want to live peacefully because I've got the children to look after". But she lived in the thick of social problems and was "sick of stuff getting nicked, it's your neighbours doing it and you can't do owt about it".

"There's as much bad feeling as good"

Becky found it easier to communicate with children and young people than adults. She was working in a girls' youth club when we first visited but Becky found the community centre a bit "closed. I'd say on council estates there's an element of mistrust, a 'we keep ourselves to ourselves' sort of thing.... It's the family-group thing where they've got their own little territory. It's where people who go there feel safe – like when they had courses, it was just the people who were already there, they didn't make anyone else feel welcome. There's as much bad feeling as good".

Becky did not know many people because she had just moved in and she found it quite a closed community, as Peter's wife, described in Chapter Two, found the area in which she lived: "They don't seem to want to get involved, they're quite private. I invited the neighbours to a little housewarming but they didn't come. I don't think people round here want anybody other than a relative or close friend". She wanted to trust her neighbours "if they're willing to trust me and invite me into their houses".

Becky suffered from depression. "I sometimes find it difficult to motivate myself and do all the things I have to do. I suppose you get what you give." But there was nobody she could talk to when things troubled her. "I try not to let it bother me." Two years later, we asked her whether there were people whom she could trust: "Quite a few really, I do trust my neighbours". Gradually she found her way into the community: "I'm more accepted than I used to be, even though I don't really have any friends around here".

"You can feel the friction between people"

Becky worked evenings and was nervous when walking back: "At night it's really scary. I have to walk home and I hate it, especially past the shop, which has closed down, it's pitch black". She did not let girls walk home alone after the club: "When you walk through the estate at night, you can feel friction between people, someone calling someone else. I have to try not to let it bother me. I fear for my safety, so I let them get on with it ... I wouldn't get involved in disputes". The real problems were concentrated in certain streets: "You can walk down some parts of a street and it doesn't feel right, with neighbours shouting at each other and fighting. Nobody wants to live there, my kids don't like it". Becky felt that stronger community spirit would help: "The whole estate would end up with a more positive image if people got on better".

At our second visit, Becky was bothered by the turnover of residents: "People have moved in and then moved straight out again. I don't know why empty housing should bother me, but it doesn't make it look attractive to the people coming onto the estate". Becky hated the run-down environment: "There's loads of litter everywhere and rubbish all over the place. But saying that, I regularly see the lads out litterpicking and the main road is kept smart – it's just litter, rubbish and dogs that let it down".

At our third visit, Becky was pleased that "they've been cleaning up the gardens lately" but thought that the area had "always been ropey" and wondered whether it was really worth trying to improve things. She was waiting for better heating but "nothing's actually happened.

Sometimes you think, surely some of them should be knocked down and better ones built, rather than putting money into old damp houses without heating". She knew demolition caused problems in the estate, "more burglaries because of easier access, but it got rid of homes that were undesirable. I suppose it'd make the estate better if there weren't rows of boarded-up houses, and it saves the council money".

Becky had to give up her youth work job because of problems with her Working Families' Tax Credit, but at our fifth visit, she had a better-paid, full-time social survey job on a local estate and as a result came to feel more confident in the area and in herself.

"I think everyone feels powerless"

Local acceptance was crucial to the family's survival on the estate. Becky took the children to the parks to integrate them into the estate: "It's not a nice park but we use it. It's the only place they can meet other little 'uns 'cos they don't go to the local school. It's got a broken climbing frame, which is a death trap because it's got no rails … and there are no proper surfaces … last time we went up there, there were kids making petrol bombs and throwing them at us. It was two older lads, age 10 and 11, getting a younger lad of about seven to throw them. They should be cleaned up more often because there's lots of glass. It should be made safer. They've taken the swings down, so they could do with more equipment. They did repair the climbing frame but it took a year". One of Becky's main ambitions was to see safer play areas for local children.

The main road stopped Becky from letting her children play out: "I worry about them stepping into the road and getting hit … it's just the nature of where the house is. I have let John out a little bit, but he's not allowed further than the bus shelter … he's got a friend there. He wanted to go to the beck with his friends but I go with them … I say I have to be there for the little 'uns so as not to undermine him. I wouldn't let them go to the park or the basketball court on their own because they haven't grown up around here, so their faces aren't known – they haven't got groups of friends". Becky worried a lot about their safety "from crossing the road to violence … my youngest picked up a syringe from the grass on the corner".

It was hard to improve things: "You've got a group of people who want the area to be better, that are fed up of being victims of crime, and the other half who are involved in it". She felt that "people have a tendency to put up with things" to avoid conflict, as she herself did: "I think everyone feels powerless and at the end of the day they just want to live happily. I don't think people round here would do anything as a group to change the area". Becky experienced crime herself when her bike was stolen from her shed. Later she got a new bike, but did not use it "because of the traffic". More upsetting was the loss of their two guinea pigs: "Someone stole them from the back garden!"

"Play a part in the community"

Becky gradually felt more accepted in the area and did things to help. She ran a stall at the 'village fair': "it makes a difference because it gives you an opportunity to play a part in the community, get to meet other local people and bring people together. And there are people who help each other out quite a bit. They take parcels in next door. I lent a hand to a woman over the road and to my neighbours on the other side. I sorted out some kids' clothes for someone over the back and I asked the chap next door to get a rottweiler out of my garden".

Becky strongly believed that no one should be excluded: "There aren't different sorts of people, everyone's the same and should be included". She thought it unfair that some girls, "the non-school-attenders, aren't welcomed in any youth groups. I thought that was the whole point of the youth service, to work with socially excluded young people; being supportive to one person might make all the difference. It's awful that nobody wants them. You could say next door has a gang, they're nice boys and girls who hang around together, they're a gang, a group of friends".

"There's a lot of things I could do with them if I had the money"

Becky's children went to school outside the area, so she found it difficult getting them there and meeting them at the end of the day. Going to a different school meant that they did not have friends on the estate, so children "don't call for them". But "it's too disruptive to change schools, especially with my middle son who has difficulties. He's in a world of his own a lot of the time". She was happy when he got "one to one with a classroom assistant once a week without me asking". Becky explained how he loved his first teacher because "she was like a mum. I know the school don't get enough resources. It's not the school, but he's not getting enough help. It doesn't seem like they're learning as much as other children at other schools".

Becky noticed that some parents moved their children from her children's primary school to the estate school, which had a better reputation. So she was "trailing the children to over there while they're trailing theirs here". The Ofsted report was not great, which Becky thought "isn't very fair. All of the teachers have been very committed; they're good teachers. But the pressure of inspections is too much".

When Becky was "stuck helping her son with his maths, he said 'you're my mum, you're supposed to know everything'. I'm not bothered that a child at another school might be on a higher reading book, as long as he's doing work that's set and doing it well.... To be fair, he's done well, but sometimes hides his homework. Also they've started football practice, though you have to pay £1 for it. There's lots of things I could do with them if I had the money". Paying for activities created real problems for Becky, like Phoebe and Zoe.

Becky thought that she and her ex-husband were "better parents than we had. We encourage them a lot more". They tried to bury their differences for the kids, and when Becky was stuck for babysitting or picking up the kids from school she could "always count on him to help, so he does have his good points". She and her ex-husband "have always rewarded [the children] and their good behaviour, encouraging their positive behaviours with praise, especially Neville, who doesn't fit in at all anywhere". Their father wanted to be more involved in the children's lives but Becky found this difficult. By the fifth interview her oldest had moved to his father's. "I'm not happy about it, I wish he'd leave us all alone. I can't say what will happen."

There were dilemmas over secondary school: "I can put my son down for City Secondary. I don't want him to go where they go from here because of what you hear. My next-door neighbour's son goes there and he's always telling me terrible things about the school-bus trips. I've sort of grown up with City as my local school and my nephew went there from a special school and he's at university". Becky, her ex-husband and her son were very impressed with the school when they visited: "We really want him to go there because they have so many resources. I'm looking forward to him learning more and succeeding.... All that new information at his fingertips, it'll be great; I love it. The teachers are all young and enthusiastic". By the time her oldest boy was ready for secondary school, the primary school was improving: "They've got a young new head and the teachers have a lot of enthusiasm for the school and pupils ... there seem to be more classroom assistants".

"They get more of a sense of belonging"

Becky's community was troubled. But "places go through bad bits and then get better again. You can tell it's got worse when you're in your garden, it's different. On a night, it's quite noisy. Pretty decent families are moving out of the street. It's not good for the street, it used to be pretty smart and now it's scruffy. It starts a chain. These changes are not good, but change is change. Community wardens are new and they make a difference because they cycle about in summer. People know who they are, they chat to them in the street, they're less of a threat than a policeman on the beat, they are a link really, aren't they?"

Becky liked her house, garden and immediate area: "It's quiet here and peaceful and secluded. In my garden I could be anywhere". So Becky decided to apply for the Right-to-Buy. However, she was upset when her application to the council for heaters was turned down because of her Right-to-Buy application. Her aim was "to live more cheaply, not to sell it".

Becky hoped "to get more involved in local provision, groups and stuff" as a way of getting to know more people. She would like to join an environmental group. "All activities are important because it's giving kids opportunities to experience things they might not otherwise experience. Plus they get more of a sense of belonging."

Becky, Nadia, Sola and Phoebe all felt that belonging within a community met a basic need. Their local community was their main social protection. Finding support from neighbours, friends and family was a lifeline because their families could not survive in isolation. To a limited extent, Becky appeared to be succeeding, whereas Nadia escaped back to Ireland. Phoebe was forced by council demolition to move from the community she felt she belonged to and Sola struggled to help everyone in her community "for her grandchildren's sake".

The idea of community in the areas where it is most tenaciously sought after is undermined by uncontrolled conditions and over-rapid transitions that harm invisible social links. People with the least resources, most pressures and disorderly conditions around them have to rise to the challenge of change, cohabitation, tolerance and understanding. Parents are driven by the need to create a sense of control around them and to keep their children away from bad neighbourhood influences. This is one reason why families distinguish between neighbourhood conditions and community spirit, for community spirit compensates families for neighbourhood problems. Community spirit, they argue, helps hold people together. The next chapter explores family life under pressures of neighbourhood problems and communities in transition.

Notes

[1] Power and Willmot, 2007.

[2] Wilson, 1999.

[3] Walker, 2005.

[4] Beck, 2005.

[5] Winkler, 2005.

[6] Moser and Peake, 1987.

[7] Mumford and Power, 2003.

[8] Young and Willmott, 1957.

[9] Layard, 2005.

[10] Wilson, 1999, p 12.

[11] Layard, 2005.

[12] Putnam, 2000; Putnam et al, 2003.

[13] Thompson, 1990.

[14] Home Office, 2001.

[15] *National Travel Survey* (2000-2005).

[16] Worpole and Knox, 2007.

[17] Bartlett, 1999.

FOUR

Families matter – mothers carry the weight

Families form the most basic social unit within communities, even though families with children now form a minority of all households.[1] The ties created by family relationships have proved stronger and more lasting than other relationships because they develop over the long, formative childhood years, and the mutual dependence they reflect ensures survival in difficult conditions. This makes mothers in particular prioritise their children over other ties and leads to most adults retaining links with family members throughout their lives. Parents feel they are investing in the future by investing in their children.[2]

Although fathers play a crucial role in families, the dominant role of women in families is a universal pattern based on their traditional homemaking, childrearing and informal community roles. These roles are changing, but far more slowly and partially than was forecast.[3] They derive from the biological imperative that makes women the bearers and early nurturers of children, creating an emotional bond that is hard to override. That bond is forged long before birth and continues in most cases throughout childrearing.

Fatima's story – family relations can break down

Fatima lives in a Northern inner-city neighbourhood. Her family comes from India and she is a devout Muslim although she does not use the mosque. She prays and reads to her children in Urdu. Her husband is also Muslim. He buys lottery tickets every week even though Fatima explains, "we're not allowed to buy them in our religion".

Fatima had two small children when we first visited her and a third baby two years later. Her parents and sisters lived in the same road as her. "My mum moved to this area because there weren't many Asian women where we used to live. She doesn't speak English and dad's brothers live here, people she can communicate with."

Fatima saw herself as a completely different generation from her parents: "They're a bit old-fashioned. We're the modern ones. My partner's helpful but a bit clumsy". Her parents thought she "was becoming a white girl" as a teenager so they sent her to India at the age of 16 and she missed her GCSEs. For Fatima, her family was important but troubling; over the course of our visits she explained how family problems could swamp you.

The neighbourhood dominated Fatima's life. She did not see much future in the area: "I feel as if it's got worse and you don't want to stay in a dump. I feel sometimes there's no future for the children here.... This is their world and I don't want this to be their world". Families were inevitably linked into their surroundings: "The area's a major part of your life ... your children mingle with other children and parents in the area. If they stay in this area, they'll struggle. No matter how you protect them, you can't stop them from becoming involved". Fatima was worried that her children "might think that's life. The children do understand that their mummy won't let them do things that other children do. You have to educate your children and talk to them, so they stay away from all these things".

"I don't like the way children are being brought up"

Fatima thought life for her family would be easier in a better area: "There are other areas where you open your door and it's quiet and peaceful. I know what the problems are for the parents and I just want to get away". Fatima articulated how much her family life was affected by the area: "I'd rather live in a shoebox in a nice place than a lovely house in a bad place". Fatima did not like the local atmosphere: "When I walk up to get bread and milk, there's often young children on the street, looking to fight and argue. Things that go on are unbelievable, screaming, shouting. Everything's outside: fights, snogging, topless sunbathing, swearing, prostitution. I don't like the way the children are being brought up, playing in the streets past midnight. It's the small children getting involved".

Fatima's housing association house was in a little street with a small garden: "The house is alright ... one English family at the top are really nice". But there were many troubles: "lots of fighting going on over children". Fatima wanted to buy a house: "You feel more secure if you buy. You can do what you like with it if it's yours. We've been looking at houses, trying to get some money together ... but so many people were interested, prices doubled ... we've given up really".

Schools were a major motive for moving: "If I could just find something cheap around that area ... there are such nice schools there". She wanted to swap her housing association house for a council property: "I wouldn't mind paying council rent, because then I might be able to buy". But she failed to secure a transfer, so eventually tried to rent privately to get out of the area. Housing Benefit was a big barrier: "I've been trying to get a two-bed flat. I've rung everybody but I can't get anything because I'm on Income Support. The council have a bad reputation of not paying, and it takes months to sort out. If I was working, I would move. I would spend the whole wage if I had to and just leave myself £100 a week and scrounge the rest".

"We ended up going to my mum's for food"

At our second visit, Fatima had split up with her husband: "I threw him out". She was pregnant when it happened and had her third baby a few months later. She explained just what a struggle it was now: "It makes being a parent really hard. My sisters are busy with their own lives and education. I can't do lots of things. I can't find anywhere for them to go to school. It really gets you down because I really need a break and there's nowhere for me to take them. My sister came round for a break from her exams so I asked her to babysit because I needed a break".

Lack of money dominated Fatima's worries. She was hard-up before her husband left, he "wasn't really earning enough … we ended up going to my mum's for food. I don't know what other people do but we end up at my mum's". Fatima explained that she would not work cash-in-hand because of the principles her father instilled in them all: "My dad's very straight, he always said: 'If you claim you don't work. You should work and you shouldn't be on benefit'. He's on Income Support all the time now, he's had three heart attacks. But my sisters all work to support themselves". Although she did not believe in cheating the system, she still "wished there was something I could do cash-in-hand.… It's very difficult in this area; it comes down to poverty again. If we had money we would not be here. We'd be off doing other things".

By our third visit Fatima had fallen out with her parents: "I can't stand them … I need to move away". Her mother did not help any more and this obviously hurt. Her sisters still babysat and she called on them often although they sometimes wanted to be paid.

Fatima saw poverty as a major cause of social exclusion: "I mean in this area why are children playing in the streets? You need money to do things, to go out. When they say, 'Mummy, can I have this?' you need money … I mean the wealthy ones, they can pay tax, fine, but living in an area like this and paying tax as well – there should be something to do with working and having to pay tax and struggling. I know a lot of people in this area don't work for this reason, because you have to pay tax and rent … Working Families' Tax Credit is good but I had to pay so much rent, there was no difference really. Some people really struggle because they aren't strong enough, and don't know how to organise or plan … because the money you have isn't much and you just get so behind. You spend and you're left with nothing".

Before Fatima's husband left, they barely scraped by on about £150 a week. Now it was even harder. Once she was "down to £20 to last me for the week". She often had "to scrounge off my sisters". She had to take petrol money in exchange for lifts, but they "give me a fiver for it. They help me all the time. They're my family so they don't charge me interest!" But they did expect her to pay them back: "My sister lent me £70 and she's like, 'you've never paid me back'". By the third visit, things were looking a little better with her husband. He visited regularly and Fatima was debating whether she might actually be better living with him again.

On the fourth visit, Fatima was very pleased that she had managed to obtain a store card: "It means you can buy things when you've got no money at all and then you can save up and pay it off. The only problem is that in my religion you have to pay off the lump sum because we can't pay or receive interest. I've written to the bank to say I don't want to pay or receive interest. But if they want to take it off me, I can't help that".

"They're always trying to help parents"

Fatima thought highly of the nursery workers: "they're always trying to meet the needs of the area and help the parents". She liked the fact that "they tell you ... what they've done in the day". Fatima decided to train as a nursery worker and worked for four years in a children's centre. She also did supply work in the school nursery, but had to give this up when her second baby was born. She had reservations anyway about being a children's worker: "When you have your own children, you're with them all the time, and then you have to be with other people's children all day. You have to be flexible and wear crappy clothing basically, in case they spill things".

Fatima decided to try office work: "I'm doing this course to try to get a job ... I wouldn't have even thought about it if I hadn't done that little course last year and the tutor said to me I was really good and could go on". She had reached NVQ Level 3 by our third visit.

"These people don't have anywhere to take their children"

Fatima explained how the neglect of the area affected her family life. She picked up litter to try to keep the street clean. "There's a car smashed up outside and we phoned the police but nothing's happened. There's a park round the corner with a climbing frame and some old swings. But there was a fire and it's all burned. It's not been renewed. There's glass and mess. You can't take your children to play with sofas and fridges and chairs in it; that's spoilt it." Fatima took her children out of the area: "I went to college and was working so I've got a car and can take my children where I want to. I've tried my best and done it differently. Other families have got no car and no support ... but we go swimming twice a week. We go out for picnics. You know, these people don't have anywhere to take their children".

Fatima was conscious of the decline of the area: "Oh my God, it feels like another country. I've seen the houses getting older and things getting broken and tatty. If it had a fresh look it would be better. But there is hope; you can't live without hope". Fatima felt that her immediate area was better than others: "Round here it's safe".

Fatima felt that she had little influence: "there isn't any opportunity. They probably wouldn't agree with me because they like their children going out and I don't want children on the streets, so there'd be conflict there. Don't they know they're ruining their area?" But she thought that if they "had meetings and worked as a team to tackle it, then the children would help too".

"There's no future for the children here"

Local schools were a problem: "I don't want to send my children here. The children are wild, swearing and aggressive". She did not mind sending them to a Christian school and her favourite was a Church of England school. But she worried that if she applied for more popular schools outside the area, her children might not get in, so "I've just been putting it off. I haven't filled in the application form. I'll put the church school down. If I got a place there, I'd move as soon as I got my wages, I'll look for a property. I think it's depressing, thinking 'where will my child go?'" Fatima was bullied as a child. "All my family were bullied. It will go on in other schools, but not as much as it does in this area." Nonetheless, talking to a friend about these problems persuaded her that "there are schools where you can have a nice time. So I think it is still possible to have a nice life in this day and age."

She liked where the school was because "it's different, they're working and most here are unemployed. I feel left behind. There's no future for the children here even though I've got my family". She realised how hard it was to handle these decisions alone. "If I'd known I was going to be single, I could have prepared for it. But as it is, I've been left with nothing."

"How can you survive when the shops can't survive?"

Bad behaviour and small-scale crime really dragged Fatima down: "The area was bad last summer, with all the noise and shouting. Milk bottles have been stolen from the front door. My sister caught a boy from up the road doing it, but it didn't stop. I didn't say anything because his mum's always shouting and it would just become a bigger issue". Fatima's worries were compounded by concerns over policing: "I've not seen any policemen walking around, only in cars ... there's a lot of vandalism and issues in this area, so they'll have to be trained and caring, otherwise they'll cause even more strife".

Fatima knew about drug problems: "Right at the bottom of the street, there's always kids, black, white, Asian, they all deal it. This area's known for drugs and murdering. People say to me, 'Do you like the area? Aren't you scared? There's drugs, murders, rapes'". She was most afraid of these things for her children: "You don't want them to go astray ... and get into drugs. I've heard of women going down to London to do prostitution, claiming Income Support, one of them goes while the other looks after the children". This atmosphere worried Fatima a lot: "The children are wild around here".

Fatima was shocked by the experience of a local shopkeeper she knew: "Joan's shop got smashed by a car a few times. I think she had seen something happening and reported it to the police, so they were letting her know they knew. She's put up some bollards, she keeps fighting on. She's a strong woman. Shops have closed down because there were so many robberies during the day. How can you survive when the shops can't survive? And it's local people doing it".

Like Annie, Fatima was unsettled by new faces in the area: "It's not a bad thing, but you feel a bit insecure. Why have they come to this country? … If they were abused, will they abuse others?" Fatima felt that different groups, such as black and Asian groups, "don't communicate with each other. They don't have a link, there's no togetherness. They don't like each other really, and I suppose the children see that". She learnt that "if they're neighbours and get on really well, it's different. One good thing about this street is that the black children are young, six- and seven-year-olds, and they've grown up knowing me and they're not disrespectful and not swearing because they know you. My black neighbour's really nice and helpful. Usually I just say hello and that's it, apart from the woman across the road who's on her own. I take her shopping and to the doctor's.… Community spirit matters because I live here in this atmosphere and it affects me".

"Focus on the children to give them a better future"

Fatima liked activities that bring people together: "They had a multicultural festival in the park last summer, it was really good. My kids loved it.… Everyone in the area goes. There was Arabic dancing, black and Asian people and no trouble.… It's really multicultural with families and people living together, and it's nice, walking around, you bump into someone and they're nice to you.… People in the area don't smile much, but sometimes they're friendly. I think these festivals and things are good; everybody gets together and there's no fights. It's peaceful. It's really good, it makes you feel like one community, all friends. It's a nice feeling … it helps to share cultures and traditions".

Fatima was full of praise for those working in the community: "There's lots around trying to help people … groups do make a difference … I would like to be involved … I want to do something where I help people … you'd need something for all people really". If Fatima was in charge, she would organise "classes for parents in parenting skills. Focus on the children, to give them a better future, because they are the future. We've had half our lives".

Cities need families

Families respond to the pressures they face by trying to create a positive, reinforcing home environment for their children in troubled neighbourhoods, as Fatima does. But family life is more difficult when the environment within which it functions is troubled, and family problems can be internal as well as external. Fatima's story highlights the instabilities and conflicts that families face in their homes as well as in their communities.

Family life and circumstances are intertwined with community and neighbourhood, as Fatima's struggle to survive shows. The pressures from her surroundings feel stronger when things are going wrong within the family. Her personal difficulties may in part reflect the pressure she feels from the environment but also the poverty that confines her family to a bad area. Low-income families cannot pay to escape from neighbourhood problems. She is dreading sending her child to school, because in her area there are few good ones:

> "Schooling – I'm really stressed out about it. What shall I do? How are you supposed to send your children where you want to? Other people say, 'Why do you want to send your children to others areas?' I really want them to go outside but I doubt they'll give me a place, not a child from here."

Harsh family and neighbourhood conditions restrict a family's mobility, thereby shaping that family's opportunities. The most needy families tend to get trapped and have to accept decaying conditions. Unpopular neighbourhoods have depopulated over long periods in the 20th century, often losing families and developing family-unfriendly environments. One of our London interviewers made the following comment in 2002:

> "This block really seems hell to live in. The family is living in fear."

These neighbourhoods do not feel hospitable to family life. Yet urban neighbourhoods need families to replenish youthful energy. In areas with inadequate facilities, children often get blamed for creating trouble. This reflects a basic failure to meet family and community needs – supervised play spaces and parks, traffic-calmed streets, local meeting points, after-school activities and local sport clubs.[4] Children are noisy, demanding and, when deprived of constructive activity and space to let off steam, often destructive. Children need safe space outside the home, as well as within it, but most parents try to restrain their children, limit their freedom and keep them close because of the dangers they sense around them. The families' active concern about neighbourhood conditions makes them worry about other children whose families don't seem to care as much.

Families act as social anchors because children are instinctive socialisers, generating community contact, the very thing that helps parents. Children help to build contact between people of different ages, races and incomes. So urban neighbourhoods need to hold on to and protect families, with their complicated backgrounds and different cultures. if places are to work as communities, and hold people together across racial groups, generations and types of household.[5]

Families provide an anchor for local social conditions, as we showed in the last chapter. The presence of families, even in the most dislocated neighbourhoods, has a humanising influence.[6] Families help local services to survive because they actively need and support them even if their quality is poor. Fatima could not imagine surviving without local shops, and Becky, in Chapter Three, said how much less safe she felt when her local shop closed.

Parents and children also provide vigilance over streets and open spaces because they actively use these spaces more than other adults. Mothers through their constant active presence offer informal eyes and ears, which in turn help to make areas safer. Their need for security makes them hold on to the positive links and influences they find. Women play a dominant and strongly social role in families and communities, which clearly helps hold conditions and relationships together. It is a positive means of city survival. Many like Fatima maintain some order outside their front door and in their street.

Families adopt a vigilant, protective, defensive stance when their children are threatened. Father carers have similarly protective attitudes to mothers, even though it is mostly mothers who play that role. Only half the parents in the present study who feel the areas are generally alright to live in (a big majority) think they are good for bringing up children. Only 40% of London parents feel satisfied with where they live as a place to bring up their children, although many feel their fears are common to other areas too.

Joyce's story shows how much a family's life can be affected by neighbourhood problems interacting with the family's own internal problems. Joyce, like Fatima, finds ways to cope but, like Nadia in Chapter Three, eventually moves back home to be near her family.

Joyce's story – family roots are hard to break

Joyce's family tumbled into a spiral of housing and social problems. But Joyce worked remorselessly to hold things together. She was 46 years old when we met her, and had two boys and a girl aged 19, 12 and eight. She was raised in the North, but moved to London when she married. She was now on her own with her children, in East London because that's where she had met her husband. Alcoholism and serious violence forced her to leave him, so for a while life became precarious for the family.

"I just started shouting, 'Get me out of here'"

"After I split from my husband, I was put in a safe house.... You could refuse the first offer of housing if your grounds were reasonable.... I got an offer of an upstairs maisonette. It was awful ... really hard to lug the buggy upstairs ... tiny bedrooms ... the bathroom was totally filthy. The council expected me to move in by Monday but I couldn't move into that filth with my children.... So then they offered me a maisonette ... ground floor with a garden. It was all boarded up but I accepted it without seeing inside ... It was an absolute wreck. There was serious water penetration. The beds and TVs in the boys' rooms got regularly drenched. I discovered the wall in one bedroom literally bulging with water." Joyce was so frightened "I just started shouting, 'Get me out of here'". The manager refused to move her, but she managed to see his 'next in line' who sent a surveyor the next day: "It turned out there was a problem with the whole block and a lot of properties needed to be done that would cost millions. They eventually got the money through SRB [Single Regeneration Budget], but in the meantime they agreed to move me".

The first offer was a maisonette backing onto the dual carriageway. "They said I hadn't the right to a garden and they didn't have to give me like for like. They said if I turned this down, my next offer could be a tower block and I'd have to accept. I fought and fought. I wouldn't back down. I got offered this maisonette with a garden instead." It is across the dual carriageway from most facilities: "This is a little forgotten land, this side of the road. Since the docks died, that's it". Her doctor thought that traffic pollution was damaging her chest, but she was pleased with the house: "I love my little house and garden; I don't love where I live, being in this area, or some of my neighbours".

"A lot of the time it's OK"

Joyce thought that a lot depended on your attitude, and believed that the area was on the up: "Life's what you make it, I think.... The area's changing for the better.... It's not deprived but still lacking some things. When my mum came and visited, she said the area was so much better, you wouldn't think this was a run-down, deprived area. It's amazing what's here". In spite of improvements, "residents still believe they have no hope, no future. People can't trade on it being deprived any more although they still try. The cosmetics of the area are looking better; you can walk around and see how nice it looks. They've done the maisonettes up at the end of the road. People actually quite like living down there now".

However, by our third visit, the improvements were being undermined by "the dual carriageway getting widened.... Houses are being knocked down. They say it isn't going to happen for another five years but it's already started! I'd like to know I can call on someone in confidence and they wouldn't slag me off". 'Demolition blight' had already set in. In Chapter Two Annie explained a similar situation.

"We can all give and receive different things from each other"

Joyce noticed considerable ethnic changes in the area since she lived there: "There seem to be a lot more black people now. People have commented that every time a place comes vacant, a black family moves in, especially a lot of Nigerians ... I don't understand the allocations system. I know that deals are done with certain housing officers. Someone I know asked to be moved and the housing officer said, 'Make it worth my while'. He said 'no' and she said, 'Well, you'll never get out of this block'".

Joyce did not mind the changes as long as people got on, but she was troubled by tensions: "I think a lot of the time it's OK. It's only when you get someone who's a bit racist or bigoted and an innocent remark can spark it off. The white family upstairs think they've got this God-given right to do what they like. A lot is done deliberately. For example, they water their window-box on the balcony and it comes down into the gardens below. And they wash down their landing and then sweep the water off the landing into the gardens. I get a lot of stuff thrown into my garden by them: orange peel, cigarette ends, broken cups. If they know it's annoying you, they do it all the more. So what's the point? But a tennis racket came in one day when we were sitting out there and I thought, 'No, it's got to stop', so I challenged them".

"Next door are Nigerian. This family threw the water when the Nigerian dad was all dressed up for church and it soaked him." Joyce had total sympathy for the Nigerian family, but thought: "they play on it; they feel people do things because they're black. This Nigerian dad does have an attitude problem. He thinks the world owes him a living. His son is the same, he has a look of contempt. He won't even look at you. It's horrible. His wife's not so bad. It's good to see Nigerians on their special church days in their special costumes, though it can be very loud late at night when they're talking in the garden".

Generally, Joyce believed that living in a multiracial area was a good thing: "I think living in a racially mixed area is more positive because it makes you more flexible and understanding. Yes, they are a different culture but as long as they're not really intruding into your life, does it matter? That's what my attitude is to a lot of things". Joyce was keen to pick out the advantages of mixing: "There are so many different things you can see, and just learn about their cultures, sample all their foods if you're lucky enough to have an Indian friend like I have".

"I don't know about there being bad things about living together; we've all got different things in our lives, different values, standards and dress sense. I know a lot of white people are offended by the smells. The lady next door cooks a horrendous fish stew. But I wouldn't want to say anything bad. We can all give and receive different things from each other." But some things emphasised divisions: "A lot of graffiti used to say 'Pakis go home'. Now signs say, 'Pakis rule, white trash' – causing tension".

"Don't say anything because they'll have you next"

Local gangs were a big problem for Joyce's sons: "There are groups of kids around, all arguing and shouting". Her son added: "they have knives and drugs". Joyce confirmed this: "Yes, they do. Children go out and have to be the boss man. They have to have their own territories". There was a violent incident in her block: "A girl upstairs was throwing chips at this group of other girls. This girl was on the floor, being kicked by a black girl who was shouting, 'it's my manor, it's my manor'. They actually broke this girl's leg; she's now on crutches. It was shocking to see her boyfriend and mate just standing there doing nothing. They believe you don't get involved, otherwise it just escalates. My son says to me, 'If we're out and anything happens, don't say anything because they'll have you next'. It's frightening and not rare. It happens a lot. They congregate round the off-licence because all sorts of things go on there. So I stay in at night time and I don't encourage my kids to go out. I like to know where my children are". Joyce did not think it was "a safe environment. I feel safer walking at night when I'm with the kids. I won't go through the subway, even when I'm with them. When I have to walk at night, I don't like it".

Young people in groups were threatening: "The worst thing is the gangs. The blacks against the Asians and the white kids riding round on scooters. My son, who's 14 now, asked me, when he goes to football and there are gangs, and they've gone to stand round him, could he carry a knife? I said, 'No, it's an offensive weapon'". Joyce thought the biggest danger was retaliating or joining in: "My boy's been taught not to fight back. I've taught him never to take on gangs. He was confronted by a gang when he was 11 and he ran into a petrol station; the police were called. He was friendly with this horror of a boy and that got him into difficulties". Joyce thought that the police could be more active: "A lot of the time, the police turn a blind eye, then they pounce. The off-licence was renowned for selling drugs. Every now and again the police take stuff away and give a warning but it carries on".

"Parents want the best for their kids and fight for them"

Joyce had been active in the community but ended up disillusioned, although they won some battles. She was a resident representative on the local tenants' board, which led to her becoming a borough-wide tenants' representative, however "All that sort of fizzled out. It's like everything with the council, it's stage-managed, it looked good. But I haven't been to a meeting since their launch. They do all these things on the surface but that's where it seems to have ended".

However, Joyce still felt it had been worthwhile: "We've done a lot; we attracted money from the government and many improvements were funded that way". The new secondary school boosted parents' confidence and she managed to move her son there: "There's been a lot of pressure to get in. A lot of children from round here have got in, but only by going to appeal.... It proves the point that parents want the best for their kids, and fight for them. It's nice that they won, because sometimes they don't get there".

Joyce thought that families often set children a bad example: "I would say the estate has lots of families in it like that. They stay here near their drunk dad, that's the payoff, family and kinship". Her children's father had a bad impact on them. Her oldest son disappeared. Joyce searched for him, advertised in the papers and listed him as missing; after six months he returned. He'd been staying with his father in an abandoned building elsewhere in the East End. The father became a "derelict down-and-out".

Joyce took her son back gladly. While he was at home with her, they had long, heart-searching chats. Her son had had to cope with his father's collapsing health, and then the father had died. The other children were very upset by this, particularly the middle one, who felt he had missed the chance to see his father again or go to his funeral, which Joyce's oldest boy handled completely alone. After a few months, he decided to move out again, having found work and re-established rapport with Joyce and his siblings, and found somewhere to live. He rang home occasionally. He was managing and Joyce was pleased. He had made himself independent and also tried to help his brother.

"I do sometimes worry if they think I've abandoned them"

Joyce hankered after the North, where her parents, who were now infirm, and sister still lived. The only thing that held her back was the job she loved. Joyce worked in community education and was really pleased when she moved into the new secondary school where Nadia worked. Joyce also found it a positive place to work, but she had little time left for the children: "I have pangs of guilt as a working mum. I do sometimes worry if they think I've abandoned them. I do like having more time with them … going out for a meal".

By our fourth visit, Joyce's worries about her children, the area, the road-widening and her parents' illnesses, crystallised: "My mum and dad have had bad health recently and I don't think they would move here. So I'll move up there". Michael was now aged 16, and her girl was 12. Our fifth visit was to her new, privately rented house "back home" and she had no regrets. She did not want to end up on a large estate again, which was all she was offered by the council. "I love it, I'd like to stay." She managed to find work in a voluntary organisation and helped with her sister's children. Joyce was earning less than she was in London, and paying market rent, but she did extra hours at a shop "as and when work comes up".

"The youngest found it difficult to adapt and she's such a flexible child. She has all white friends up here. She found this difficult as there's no ethnic mix." The new school she went to was "smaller, more disciplined" than the school in London. There were more serious problems for Michael: "He threw tantrums and said I'd ruined his life, asking why we had to come up here. Ryan stayed in London". Michael rang him occasionally and often talked about joining him. Work was harder to find in the North. "In London he used to coach football and also worked at Gap." Joyce could not see how he was going to get that kind of work in the North. She thought: "reality might hit him one day. He wants the highest money and the fewest hours, in his dreams!"

"I've come back home where I'm needed"

Joyce felt that she had made the right decision to move back to the North: "I'm enjoying it, it's where I want to be. The determining factor was my mum's health". Joyce and her sister clubbed together to give their parents a week's holiday in Majorca. She was glad to be nearby to help. "I'm feeling a bit safer, more secure. I don't hear the kids outside doing whatever. It might be naive, but I don't see or hear anything like I used to in London. I do miss some of the people but I was glad to leave some of the neighbours. I've come back home where I'm needed. In some ways it's like I've never been away. In others, so much has changed."

Families need wider support

Joyce's family life is troubled – she survived homelessness, domestic violence, alcoholism, a runaway son, the threat of demolition due to a road-widening, a disillusioning community leadership role, violent gang incidents, racial conflict, insecurity at night and sick parents. Some of these pressures come from the neighbourhood and the city, but others reflect her own family troubles. Yet Joyce moves back North, finds a new home, new job, new school, with a quiet confidence that she has done the right thing. Her parents, her children and her sister are her 'lifelines' and she wants to help them. She finds her new community more peaceful and therefore more homely than the East End. Her regrets are for her children who struggle to adjust: her 12-year-old misses the diversity of old school friends; her younger son struggles to find a niche in a Northern city; her eldest stays behind in London and she misses him.

Relatives often provide the strongest support in times of need and one of Joyce's motives for moving back up North was to be nearer her family, not just to help them, but to be part of their lives again and share childcare with her sister. It requires more than one pair of hands to bring up children and insufficient family support or the breakdown of family relations make it a real struggle for mothers like Joyce and Fatima.[7]

Without wider families, life becomes more precarious, more isolated, harsher and more socially dislocated. Many of our mothers depend on their mothers in the same way as their children now depend on them.[8] Grandparents often urge their grown-up children to stay close by or to move closer, and adult children are often torn between wanting grandparents' support but also clinging to their freedom. Zoe, as we saw in Chapter Two, wanted to move back nearer her mother in order to stand a chance of better schools for her chilren. But she also had disagreements with her mother over childrearing and they often fell out over discipline. Extended families are far from smooth, as Fatima's story in this chapter showed.

Mothers with children are physically more vulnerable than men, not only because they are, on average, weaker and smaller than men, but also because protection of their children so dominates their actions. This makes them more fearful of danger and more intensely vigilant on their behalf, constantly responsible for the family as a social unit rather than themselves as individuals. Mothers and children therefore evoke a sense of responsibility and protectiveness in the wider society.[9] Active working fathers make a big difference to family life, for both mothers and children, as Olivia's story later in this chapter will show. Families are poorer where there is no male 'breadwinner' to help, even modestly, as Fatima's story showed. Being the sole parent creates extra strain.

Fathers who no longer live in the family may sometimes be hard to reach, but they do matter to families and communities.[10] They offer security and stability, even though in nearly half of our families the father is not normally present. Boys particularly need a father figure as a role model and are affected by the loss of their father. Joyce worries that on her own she may fail to keep her boys on track. For Joyce, Fatima and other lone mothers, juggling the needs of their children, the shortage of money and poor neighbourhood conditions is a huge strain. When mothers opt to work, as Joyce does, then time pressures on the family are even greater. Inevitably, the mother can do less with her children and as a result worries more.

Families offer many rewards to parents; both Joyce and Fatima mentioned how they enjoyed spending free time with their children. Children provide fun, relaxation and a sense of worth. Children create a sense of pride in parents, being in themselves a reward for effort and responsibility.

Helping parents in difficult circumstances to make family life work helps society because functioning families are the support base for children and parents. Low-income families, particularly with lone mothers, and incoming families who move into the poorest areas, are often seen as a burden on society and a cause of problems. Yet their socialising role raises the question: what kind of places would urban neighbourhoods be without them? The next story shows the major contribution 'new' low-income families can make in low-income neighbourhoods, while underlining the urgency of making cities more family friendly.

Delilah's story – coping in small spaces

Delilah and her husband are from Nigeria. She went to East London from Africa nine years earlier because "this was where I knew somebody. I lived with a relative, then with a friend in this flat. He left and I took over the tenancy. The council decided to leave me here and I was happy.... It's a good and quiet place, one of the best places to live".

When we first visited, Delilah had four young daughters in a small two-bedroom council flat on the upper floor. The lift was too small to take Delilah with the buggy so she took the stairs. At our first visit, the oldest girl was five years old. By the fourth interview they had a fifth baby girl and the oldest was 10. The accommodation was very crowded and Delilah said that she "can't wait to move. I've done everything I can to move. They've told me I've got all girls, so I won't move from here, even though the room's not enough". Officially,[11] up to four girls under the age of 10 can sleep in a room; babies do not count. Delilah gave away their bikes and outdoor toys because they just would not fit inside the flat with the buggy. Her husband did not always stay with them because of lack of space.

"I like the support they give children"

Delilah felt "comfortable in my little area" and was on good terms with neighbours. "Crime is a problem but not serious. It's a very small area, so if it was happening more, you would hear about it more." She let the children play outside: "They can go downstairs on their own because I know the children they play with, their parents live down there and look out". Delilah felt that "everyone is friendly with each other … friends help each other out. For example, they took my children to school when I had the baby". So in some ways her family had a great situation, despite overcrowding.

Delilah's dominant concern was her children: "the school, their friends.… We hope they're happy and doing well". She said that the school was "excellent" and that her children were getting on "very well … that's why I'm afraid to move. I like the support they give. Everything has to build up from that, to provide a safe environment for children where they know they'll be heard". Delilah was very involved in the school and was a parent governor. "I chose St Mary's because I was attending the church. I noticed the behaviour of the children going to this school. And they have uniforms, which makes them look decent … I take an active interest in their education and upbringing. I'm a confident parent".

Delilah thought she could influence the school, "except over money. We've talked about security and that has been dealt with; they built very high gates and redirected access to the school to try and protect children from cars. We also want more facilities on the playground and to change the floor from tar to rubber, so they don't hurt themselves as much. They don't have an after-school club. That's what we're trying to do. Most governors haven't got young children so the after-school club wouldn't mean anything to them".

"It's just new faces to know"

Delilah was acutely aware of ethnic change: "mostly black people live here now. Before, you would see mostly middle-aged and elderly white". Delilah was conscious that "people keep coming and going, people from all walks of life, it's just new faces". Like Joyce, Delilah was puzzled over rehousing: "A couple of years ago, they were boarding up flats and rehousing people for regeneration. Then the council started putting refugees and ethnic minorities in". Delilah was "beginning to panic about what type of person might come next door. It could be someone from Sri Lanka. That's the kind of environment where you could have a problem". People with unfamiliar backgrounds undermined Delilah's confidence, despite her generally positive views.

Delilah was worried about the area becoming "more black". But she stressed that "everybody's fine, especially in church, we worship with them. Everyone's friendly with each other. You could still have some bits of arguments over children playing, then parents take it from there". She felt that her church contributed a lot: it "brings all types together, people from different races".

"Widening the gap between the poor and the rich"

Delilah had mixed feelings about regeneration, although she desperately wanted it to happen: "It's just widening the gap between the poor and the rich. The bad houses are still for people without money. If it gets more popular, then that's good for the area as long as it doesn't change the quietness we have". But she worried it might attract trouble: "Good things also come with bad. Recently I've seen vandalism and kids exchanging drugs. The police keep coming. How did this come to be? For a long time it wasn't like that. If the new cafes make this happen, then it's not good".

The neighbourhood environment was not family friendly: "There are good and bad sides. There are no facilities for the children, no parks or play centres or nurseries. The poor state of the houses. The place is neglected. Everything here is just the lowest grade, and very dirty". Like Becky in Chapter Three, she sometimes felt that "they should knock the whole place down and build another". Her small flat was very damp. Although there was "a fund to install heating in every flat, it could take 10 years. I haven't met anyone who's had heating installed yet. It's just one person who cleans the whole estate. If he gets ill, no one else cleans". Delilah talked to the estate officer but "nothing has been done"; she even consulted a solicitor about forcing improvements.

Delilah wondered why her area looked so bad: "Is it being neglected? Is it the people? Who put the people here? I'm trying to wonder why this place is so bad, is it because it's the East End? West London is a different area completely. Every corner they have leisure centres, parks. We all live in London. But the old view of people in the East End, the old stereotype, still hangs around. Some neighbourhoods are better in terms of their environment, litter etc., but estates are all the same".

"It's getting better but very slowly"

Delilah decided that her only way to gain any control over her future was to buy her flat so that they would eventually be able to sell it and move. This meant that she had to work, despite the new baby, for the mortgage payments.

A year later, on our fifth visit, Delilah was more hopeful about her block: "They seem to be trying to upgrade the flats and make it better for repairs. You can feel changes coming. It's getting better, but very slowly. My fear is it will take a long time". She'd been to some community meetings about the improvements. She stopped going as "it was a closed room with people smoking. That's not good for the children.... I didn't bring the smoking issue up because I'm worried they'd interpret my reasons wrongly. I'll try to go alone".

Delilah saw advantages and disadvantages for her family in the area: "I could still say I'd want to live round here again, because of access to the city. But the houses are discouraging me a lot". And Delilah sensed the threat of drug crime: "Drugs have overshadowed every other good thing that comes out of the area. The man who was shot in the car here lives in Tottenham and comes to deal here. Now the good name of the area is tarnished. I do worry about their future here, the lack of facilities, nothing for children to do", and no easy way of combining work, family responsibility and childcare.

"It's one of the best places to live but so neglected"

Delilah was positive about neighbourhood wardens, who had recently been introduced: "I think they do a very good job. I met a few and they're friendly ... it's better". But children were in all sorts of trouble: "There are children hanging around in groups setting cars on fire ... I just see these teenagers looking for something to do and then they get themselves involved in some mischief that could get out of hand sometimes. One evening they were playing with a car and set it on fire next to a building, from there it could get into something very nasty. They might be sitting round, thoughts going through their heads, then they decide on something they think is adventurous, but actually it's serious".

Delilah was highly critical of the park: "Just two slides and a swing, it's a very small, closed-up area. By the time you see four or five children, it's getting so crowded". The other park was further away: "We had a picnic there in the summer. We want to go and spend a lot of time there. Other boroughs have better play areas for children. The parks are not very good round here. We do like going but I've mentioned the problems". One of Delilah's top priorities would be "more secure play areas". Her children desperately needed space; downstairs was no substitute for a supervised park and playground. "It's one of the best places to live, but so neglected."

Delilah described a typical day as "running around, hectic, stressful. I get up, get the children ready for school, have breakfast, take them, come back, tidy up, cook. I'm forever working to keep up with payment, I can't work part time as I can't afford to". Delilah was a care worker but wanted to train as a social worker for her "personal development" as well as money. Childcare was a problem because of her working hours. The few nurseries were very expensive. Usually she relied on friends and neighbours to pick up her children but she wished the school offered more after-school activities.

"Your mind is more at ease"

Delilah really valued her husband's help, although he could not always be with them. She relied on him for "comfort" and "in emergencies". She was also very close to her mother in Nigeria and spoke to her twice a week. She really missed her extended family, and wondered if she should bring a relative over to help with childcare.

Delilah wanted to be involved in "a group that would bring things together and move things forward". She was afraid to move away because of "fear of the unknown, and because of the children". So she hoped for "a clean environment, more security, more play space" and a bigger flat, alongside "the good things in a racially mixed area, learning from other people's beliefs and values, cultures, lifestyle, religious background. We know a lot of people, so it makes for a good community. Your mind is at ease more for your children".

Making cities family friendly

Delilah's family seems content, but she and her husband are under immense pressure with their large family, small flat and shortage of money. Like almost all the families, Delilah worries about drugs and crime, the condition of open spaces and parks, the generalised threat of new faces, unfamiliar neighbours and poor conditions. Delilah, like Annie, is torn between moving and staying, believing in the area and yet sometimes wanting it torn down. Delilah knows from direct experience that other, better areas, offer more family-friendly environments. Families with more secure incomes can opt for more suburban, middle-class areas offering more space, security, stability and services. Inevitably, they make poorer areas with poorer quality services seem inferior by comparison.

Families with children face not just lack of care but objections from older people who prefer to live away from the noise and disturbance of young people; in crowded, built-up areas this is difficult. Yet the older people cannot survive without the younger generation to help them.[12] Several mothers, like Fatima, help their older neighbours. Interestingly, older women can also become something of a lifeline for young families moving in, holding out a helping hand to families, regardless of race. One older East End neighbour notices that one of our mothers, who is black, is struggling with her children and says:

> "If you're going anywhere and want to leave the baby, just tell us and we'll keep an eye on her."

Families and children benefit from contact with older people, and vice versa, because older residents exercise a kind of vigilance within the community that young mothers appreciate.

Brokering family needs in a way that helps older people to stay in an area is part of making communities work but too much noise because of too little space or activity for young people drives older people out. Then families lose vital supports and links to the older generation. So reconciling intergenerational needs requires careful design, special social and management skills that favour youth, family and older people provision. The way streets and spaces are laid out and managed can provide family-friendly public spaces that encourage both older people and young people to socialise. Home Zones, traffic calming and pocket parks show this.[13] Recognising the importance of intergenerational links and creating space for them to grow recreates some of the benefits of extended families, even when families themselves are fragmenting.

Teenagers have special needs, often falling between family and adulthood. They are no longer satisfied by their family alone but they have not yet 'found their feet' and in groups can appear a constant threat. They have outgrown the constraints of a small home and a disadvantaged area and are searching for new avenues to explore. The families we talk to worry constantly about these difficult youth transitions.[14] Parents highlight the lack of facilities for youth as the single biggest gap because they cannot cope as families if young people are not provided for beyond the home.

Young people often learn to 'hang out' on the street, under lamp posts, at bus stops, around shops and benches, in parks or on bare land, once they reach the age when the impulse to socialise with peers becomes overwhelming. The places mothers go with their younger children are often the same areas that older kids try to make their own. These areas become local landmarks of a kind, where young people pass time together and make their mark – through noise, graffiti and sometimes direct damage. Such abused hangout places give a threatening signal to residents, particularly older people, mothers and younger children. But young people need space, so neighbourhoods are constantly degraded by youthful exuberance, lack of organised activities or supervised spaces. Youth interacts powerfully with local conditions.[15]

Families often see troubled youth as an extension of their own family experience within the areas. Parents want somewhere that young people could go which would be supervised. This is the only way both to restrain bad behaviour and to encourage positive activity before trouble brews.[16] Organised, accessible and cheap activities for young people are a key to neighbourhoods and communities working better, and therefore families coping. Mothers say it would make the most difference to where they live, and it is the first thing they would change if they were in charge.

Families on low incomes rarely go on holiday or use expensive facilities, because of a shortage of cash. So they favour action-oriented local provision for young people, like sports clubs that are not too expensive.[17] Parents say that sport and being outdoors are their favourite activities with their children, but families cannot readily organise this without support, given the surrounding environment and the internal pressures, as Phoebe explained in Chapter Three.[18] Involving youth requires creativity and resources.

Family pressures may be intense, but the pressures from the environment – overcrowded housing, run-down blocks, poor schooling, disruptive neighbours, out-of-control young people, general poverty and conflict – make family problems harder to manage. Mothers cannot help but feel that the poor conditions surrounding them are at least partly to blame for "dragging the family down". If social links weaken as a result of too little organised support and too unpredictable an environment, then families simply will not survive and conditions that are making their lives so difficult will deteriorate even further.

Families bring qualities of youthfulness, vigour, care and commitment to the future, but they need the wider city to secure their environment.[19] Olivia's story illustrates the tension between families as a microcosm of need and neighbourhoods as the receptacle of family problems. Her family traumas show how central wider supports are to her survival.

Olivia's story – overcoming family history

Olivia had had a troubled past but now had a steady partner, Sam, and a little girl, Emily, with whom she lived, along with two large dogs, in a large Northern estate. She grew up in a "very rough area" of the city. Olivia says that "here it's very different from where I grew up. Nobody paid any attention to what children did there. Round here they do. The western half of the estate, near my brother, it's different. Round here there's proper discipline. It's quiet, the kids are polite. It's 10 or 15 minutes from the shopping centre". Other mothers, like Becky, said that their half of the estate was much calmer than Olivia's. But 'her side' of this large, low-income estate with a poor local image worked for Olivia.

Its 'community spirit' worked in unexpected ways: "In this street it's pretty good. The neighbours are good. We lost our dogs and the neighbour knocked when he found them". Her main hope over the next few years was "to go abroad together". But she also wanted "a new house, a new neighbour and more hours in the day! We have a problem with the neighbour who stands outside shouting at the dogs". But the dogs were a problem: "There's lots of strays, about 17 running around. I know the neighbour started reporting everybody about their dogs since his dog died. He's got worse since we got the bigger one".

"I was homeless myself"

Olivia left home when she was 17, and had Emily when she was 18: "I moved out of my dad's because there was no space". She lived throughout the city, including "with friends and on the street". Olivia got involved with a homeless project while on the streets: "I used to work with homeless people, doing voluntary work. I was homeless myself. Through [the project] we did peer education and I went to speak in other towns. I got right into it and went down to London and to Thailand for 11 days ... I stopped being involved to start working full time". Olivia still went to the project for help.

At our first visit Olivia worked 37 hours a week in a pizza cafe, earning £120 a week, and Sam did electrical work, earning £190 a week. The couple received Working Family Tax Credit of £50 a week and Child Benefit of £15 a week. By our fifth visit, Olivia had "become the breadwinner" and Sam a full-time student, with a bursary and fees paid. He got £500 a month including Child Tax Credit. He was "training to be an electrician". Olivia had no qualifications at all. After the pizza cafe, she worked full time in McDonald's, earning more, about £6.50 an hour. When Sam went to college full time, she got a cashier's job in a club, "working nights" to earn more.

"It's the child that matters, not where you live"

Emily was in full-time nursery school and Olivia was full of praise for the help they gave her. She thought the school was "brilliant, they're always trying new things. They've accommodated when I'm working". Olivia was sad that she only saw Emily four hours a day and on Sundays: "I'd love to see her more".

Olivia thought it was not the school or area that determined how you and your family did, but your attitude towards your child: "It's the child that matters, not where you live. Emily's smart. She'll do well. She's a quick learner". Olivia had had very little schooling of her own but was determined to "make a go of things". Leaving school at the age of 13 with no qualifications made Olivia claim: "I don't give a shit about education". In fact, she depended a lot on the school, and supported Sam's studies.

Olivia was "not very happy renting off the council because they don't fix things". She hoped to transfer to a bigger house, maybe away from the area: "I don't know, it's not a great area to live in. I think I get bored of areas. I've seen a really nice house, and we'd get an exchange straight away because of no rent arrears". Sam wanted to use the Right-to-Buy, but Olivia did not because "I want to buy a new one, not a used council house". They lived in a prefabricated, 1960s concrete-slab house. Some positive changes were under way: "they've painted the windows and the doors" and "they're starting to build more things, and they're bricking the houses" to make them look better. She, like other mothers, was bothered by people's transience: "there's a lot of coming and going in the street".

Olivia thought that crime "wasn't too bad, 'til the car went missing. It was found in the woods. We're getting a lot of kids stealing cars. I've seen them driving them around. The cars get burnt out in the woods". One unique bit of local 'demolition' was the council "knocking the woods down so the police can see in there from a helicopter", to control youthful car theft and other crime. People "are going round selling alarms" but Olivia did not worry because "we have the dogs". Like Becky, she worried about traffic: "it's very bad for cars – there's been some near fatal accidents". Car burning was a big problem and many residents felt threatened when they saw huge bursts of petrol flames at night. Peter mentioned this in Chapter Two. The area had no useable park due to poor supervision and maintenance.

"My mum didn't give a shit"

Olivia relied on Sam if something was troubling her. She found others "very friendly" but could only count on family for important things: "Sam's parents, my brothers and sisters help". In exchange, Olivia helped with "nephews and nieces and friends' kids and my partner's nephews and nieces. When I have a day off and my brother, sister or friend look frazzled, I help. Emily sees Sam's family all the time".

Olivia had "no contact" with her own parents and "never sees them" although they live nearby. There was sadness as well as anger behind Olivia's separation from her parents: "My mum didn't give a shit about us when we were growing up ... we children were just left to our own devices". Her mother was not around during her teenage years when she left home, as did other siblings. "We've had a lot of problems with my dad." He was violent and ended up in jail; the younger children ended up in care. It affected one sister particularly deeply. Social workers got involved but Olivia did not think they did any good and just made her sister feel worse. Her sister suffers from severe depression, but luckily found a caring partner, and her brothers and sisters rally around to help her. They live around the area and are very close to each other.

Olivia got involved in Sure Start early, through going with her sister who received huge support from them: "She had problems with social services so she went for the groups". She felt it was a pity that her sister only received Sure Start help after everything had gone wrong. "It's good for parents with young kids who need to get out to get some adult conversation. It helped Emily to play with other kids, it helped her to settle into nursery, it was a good environment. Sure Start do a whole diversity of groups. There's a toy library and you can borrow tables and chairs and things for 20p a week. It's good for parents on Income Support.... The project's well known with the parents. They put leaflets through the door all the time. They came round the other day, but Emily's too old now. My mate works for them, running the craft shop, and another mate works for complementary health."

"People just want kids out of the way"

Olivia really liked local events and community activities: "It's nice for Emily because she's not bored; school fairs and the NSPCC and church fetes and fun days and Sure Start days". However, Olivia did not go to a housing meeting about the area's future because "it's pointless getting into an argument with council people who have to go back to their bosses". She did not think many mothers would go because people who do often go to complain about children: "they wouldn't attend meetings about their kids damaging property. At the end of the day people just want kids out of the way. People expect them to be taped up and not making any noise".

Olivia got a lot of satisfaction out of Emily being well behaved: "I feel really good when she's good at school and polite, well behaved and saying thank you on the bus". She worried when there were problems: "Emily was picking on a little boy at school. I think she was just playing but he was scared to go to school. The school didn't tell me and the first I heard about it was when I saw the parent shouting at the teacher … as soon as I knew, I stopped it. I had a word and told her she'd get no sweets".

Olivia thought that "young people are not causing that much trouble". She thought "mostly young families" moving in was fine. "The teens are well behaved; 11- and 12-year-olds will write on walls and set fire to bins at the nursery though." Olivia did not think that the police were the main local controls: "If anything happens, you best sort it out yourself". Once they had problems with a gang: "A friend got punched so Sam went up and grabbed the biggest lad. Then they came down with stones, throwing them at the windows, so Sam went out with a baseball bat. There's been nothing since that".

Olivia worried for Emily's safety: "you can't keep them completely safe. I don't let her off on her own. She plays in the garden and we've good neighbours who look out for her". She listened out for threats: "We've heard about a local paedophile". Neighbours helped a lot "because you know your house isn't going to get done over while you're out. And the neighbours know we would do it for them.… We do it informally in this street".

"They make it very hard for mothers"

Olivia understood social exclusion: "It's a term used in homelessness, people excluded by society. It's a hard one. Some people like to be excluded from some things. Society does exclude, but some people choose it". Olivia herself did not always want contact: "Wherever you go, people are like 'hello' and I want to be left alone some of the time". But Olivia thought that a lot of people might be left out, particularly "young mums trying to access college with no childcare. With me it's hard to work and have Emily looked after. They make it very hard for mothers to access things, so you just end up not going. It's like technically you're not excluded, but really you are. The offer's there but it's not accessible".

Olivia's estate was nearly all white: "there are no mixed-race children in our street". But Emily had "two little boyfriends, one's black and one's Indian, they're in school.… They're lovely little boys.… There's no problem.… Changes don't bother me at all. Some are racist.… But generally it's OK". Olivia welcomed change and a more open future.

Olivia thought that community mattered: "it's there, it survives, people will watch out for each other". She thought that community spirit "is better now. It would be a bit dull if you didn't talk to your neighbours at all. Our neighbour died and I said to his wife, if she needs any help, just to bang on the wall.… Sometimes everybody gets out and plays having water fights". But she noticed that older people tended to "keep themselves to themselves". There were things about the area that helped too: "The playgroups, the community centre anybody can go to, mums and tots, dads and tots, parks, the shopping centre, the cafe, the college; the majority of the time they've got places for people to go, which is good. The community centre does a lot of things and the church does a lot of fetes". She believed it was "really positive to involve dads".

If Olivia was in charge of the area, she would concentrate on "something for kids, small ones and older ones, apart from fixing potholes". Olivia thinks that family background is something that you have got to ride over. Her 'feisty' attitude to life is driven by the ambition to create a family with a different future from her past. She will do anything to help her sister. Olivia feels lucky to have a "great kid", a devoted partner, and his extended family plus her own brothers and sisters to rely on nearby. Her parents hurt her deeply but other parts of the family and local services have helped fill the gaps.

This chapter shows how mothers facing serious internal and external pressures focus their main energies on their children, on helping them to grow up happy. This ties them into their relatives, friends and neighbourhood life. Their stories illustrate the double handicap they face – problems born of their family circumstances and problems pressing in on them from their surroundings.[20] Families can help make cities work, if their suggestions are heard.

Families have suggested that supervised open spaces, after-school clubs, active policing, basic investment in housing and streets, consistent caretaking, school–parent links, cheap childcare for young children, extensive low-cost youth and sports provision, family-friendly working policies and training opportunities would all help to make cities work. It is a long, but not impossible, list since some of these things happen in each area. More space and a more stable community are hard to secure in crowded and changing cities, but making neighbourhoods more family friendly in the ways these families suggest would anchor families in cities, thereby creating the security, stability and care that they need to survive.

Notes

[1] Summerfield and Gill, 2005.

[2] Allatt, 1993, pp 139-59.

[3] Moser, 1993; Bell and Ribbins, 1994, pp 227-62.

[4] DETR, 1999.

[5] Phillips, 2000, 2005.

[6] Briggs, 1968; GLA, 2004.

[7] ONS, 2005.

[8] *The Economist*, 2004.

[9] Newson and Newson, 1968.

[10] Wilson, 1996.

[11] The legal definition of overcrowding dates back to 1935 and counts children between the ages of one and 10 as half a person.

[12] Young and Lemos, 1997.

[13] Department of Transport, 2005; Gehl, 1996; Rogers and Power, 2000.

[14] Based on our research.

[15] Metropolitan Police, 2006.

[16] Dunleavy et al, 2007; Department for Education and Skills, 2005.

[17] Davidson and Power, 2007.

[18] Paskell, 2004.

[19] Power and Hougton, 2007.

[20] Power, 1992.

FIVE

Parenting matters – pushing for kids

Parenting is about protecting and nurturing children, creating a safe, secure home within which they can grow, learn and gradually find independence. But parenting is about much more than homemaking, educating and caring for children. It is about constantly orienting children towards adulthood in the wider society, training them to follow parental examples and values while adapting to and coping with surroundings that pose dangers and threats, as well as supports and opportunities. Parenting depends on a family's material as well as emotional resources and it is powerfully interwoven with social supports of an informal and formal nature. So the wider family, friends and schools all play important parts in helping parents.[1] Parenting is not left entirely to parents, because children grow up to become part of society, so how they are reared matters to society as a whole. Children mature through social contact, so finding niches within troubled neighbourhoods that will keep children safe while allowing them more independence as they grow up is a difficult balance for parents. Parents like Flowella want to escape this problem.

Flowella's story – moving away from trouble

Flowella has lived in the East End of London all her life. She is African-Caribbean by background. When we first met her, she had a seven-year-old daughter. "I had her quite young and my mum and dad died within a year of each other, so I had to grow her up a bit." She had split with the father because of alcohol and drug abuse: "The only obstacle I've come across this year is my daughter's father. He doesn't really play a particularly big part in her life. He's a drug addict. We found out he'd got a crack addiction. My daughter was having contact with him because he still lives with his parents, so I allowed her to go there. But of late he's become abusive to his parents. He drinks a lot.... And I felt really traumatised by that 'cos I thought, 'My child's been exposed to this' and I wasn't even aware of it. My daughter said 'He's always hiding drink under the table and nan finds it, or he hides it in cupboards and stuff'. We just found out last week he's in prison".

"What life have those children got?"

Flowella was critical of the way other children were brought up: "You can't really blame the children because a lot of their parents are on drugs. It's the background they come from so they don't know any different". During our second visit, Flowella's neighbour knocked on the door for change, "as high as a kite. She's got two children, got involved with a man who beat her children and abused her. The man doesn't actually live with them. I've seen a pusher give her drugs. The grandparents are no help. One's alcoholic, one smokes marijuana. What life have those children got? I won't let my child play with hers as she's racist.... No one in the block likes their children playing with this little girl. How can you get to the stage where you let something control your life?"

Excluding certain children was Flowella's instinctive response: "I can't lock my child away. So I only let her play with certain children, which is wrong, but it's my way of protecting her. I don't really mix. I don't focus around the area. I don't really keep her within the vicinity round here because of the way things are and the way people are. When it comes to school holidays, when she's at home, she goes to play schemes and stuff and she goes on trips away. If I can stay out of this area, I'll stay out of it. Once I'm home, I'll just stay in here".

Flowella thought that the whole environment was working against children: "There's not a lot for the kids round here to do. The children don't respect the improvements and they're really abusive. Any facilities ... are constantly vandalised by local youth. The kids are still very violent. They're only 10 or 11, throwing stones. My partner was driving on the dual carriageway and a seven- or eight-year-old boy threw a brick at his window ... it could've killed him. He told the police, but it's a regular thing, they'll throw stuff at the buses, all sorts of things".

"Children repeat what they hear at home"

Flowella thought that 'bad parents' influenced the whole neighbourhood: "I find the person who uses drugs has an effect on everyone. It affects their children's lives, their family. Their children then go on to affect other people's lives. If the child doesn't get the right amount of attention at home, they will come out of the home and do certain things that are not right, and go on to tease and taunt others. They know they aren't going to get corrected because no one is interested in what they've got to say. I think it's a big problem. It's sad really. They know they can swear or smash something and no one's going to take a blind bit of notice of them within the home. It doesn't matter if someone knocks on the door and complains. The parents are not going to respond in the way they should. I'm not holding the child responsible. I'm holding the adult responsible because children repeat what they hear at home. The parents aren't doing anything because they're too high. I think it's a problem for the area as a whole".

On our second visit, Flowella was still very worried about parents and kids: "You're still getting unruly children that are vandalising things, and you're still getting the parents that take drugs and it just repeats. I think it's getting worse. There's a bus stop at the end of my road here and you can guarantee that every week or every fortnight it's going to be smashed.... It's got worse in the sense of children smashing things. They're very young, so they're getting their influence from somewhere. They're drinking and smoking, they're smoking drugs. They've got no respect whatever. They'll go and torment the shopkeepers and throw things at them and call them names. It's the background they come from. These ones round here, they just don't give a damn".

Flowella sensed the whole environment running out of control: "Some bad news in September: the Post Office got blown up. They were doing joyrides, crashing into the shop and taking all the stuff, the off-licence and sweet shop as well. A friend of mine was walking home with her laundry bag and someone held her up by a knife and took her washing".

"They're nice underneath"

Flowella had deep sympathy for the children in the neighbourhood: "When you talk to some boisterous boys, you realise they're nice underneath. They're only like that because they're abused mentally and physically". Flowella helped in children's centres: "I've worked with children and I know what can make them stop this. I do voluntary work for a play scheme in Barking. My daughter and nephew come every day during the holidays. If there was more to do, they wouldn't be on the streets, behaving the way they do. There's nothing for the kids. There's no football pitch for the boys, that's why they're on the street, throwing stones. It's havoc; the children swearing, things getting broken into because they're bored. There's nothing for them round here. I definitely would concentrate on facilities and parks. Is it more important to instil something positive into them, so they can go out and get jobs and make themselves better people? Or is it more important to re-modernise a bloody house? I mean, come on now, they should get their priorities straight. Ice rink or bowling alley, just something round here so they can say, 'Oh yeah, we're gonna use this today'. There used to be a swimming pool by the park. All the kids used to use it".

Flowella wanted to respond to community needs: "Counselling groups for drug users; after-school activities, with secure supervision; use of land and space – all kinds of things for kids". Flowella really liked the local summer festival: "It's nice for the children 'cos there's lots of things they can do. The activities were only 20p or 25p, which was nice as it's within your budget … it was done within the local area. It's really nice to see.

"The teachers are all great"

Flowella knew that schools were important: "People say schools in East London are crap but it depends how you extend your child". Parents need to be more involved: "They wonder why their child's not reading and think it's up to the schools but they don't sit and read with them. A lot of children are abusive because they're not stimulated. A lot are illiterate. They reach adulthood and regret not having learnt, but they think it's too late". Flowella's daughter went to a local primary school and she had high praise for the teachers: "The new head has lots of schemes for dealing with children who are being disruptive, making them more involved in things, concentrating on their behaviour. And you see a change in the children. He's out there every single morning and afternoon to watch their behaviour". Flowella liked the school's new, strict uniform policy: "now uniform is compulsory but it used to be a fashion parade".

Flowella helped her daughter with her homework and "I call up other friends and relatives when there's a piece of homework I can't help her with. I'd say the school's fairly good because my daughter learns a lot from school. I help her a lot at home. If your child's doing so and so and you aren't carrying it on at home, then you'll get certain parents thinking, 'Oh they're not learning nothing' or 'they've been taught nothing'. But I feel her education here's fairly good. The teachers are all great in my opinion. It's more about the parents and how they support the school. My daughter gets home at 3.30. She does her homework, then we might visit someone or watch TV. My daughter reads".

Flowella wanted to be home for her child: "I've decided to stay at home and be here to collect her from school and be part of her life because I'm not with her dad. I thought it would be important for her to have a stable upbringing. I don't work full time, but in half-terms I do play schemes". Flowella wished she had had a better education herself: "I was a 'latch-key kid', lacked support and supervision, so I didn't take school seriously. There was no one really to push me, to make sure I'd done my homework and stuff like that".

"I don't want to be on Income Support. I want to work"

By our third visit, Flowella was worried about secondary school: "I'd like to give her a head start and be somewhere positive. I was planning to move in the next three years anyway, 'cos that's when my daughter will be going to secondary school and I don't really want her to go to the one here". Flowella was in the regeneration area and was expecting to be rehoused when her block was knocked down: "I think in a way it has benefited me making all these changes 'cos they'll have to move me to a location I want, where there's going to be more facilities for her to do things".

Flowella was ambitious for herself but her child came first: "Once she has started secondary school, I can start thinking about myself. I'm working towards going back to work part time so I can be there for her when she gets home. If I was in a full-time job and earning a decent wage, I definitely would take myself onto the road of getting my own property.... I would like to be out there earning so me and my daughter could go on holiday and better ourselves. I don't want to be on Income Support. I want to work ... to get all these qualifications and work with children with special needs".

Adult education in the new secondary school provided a great opportunity: "You walk in and there are lots of smiley faces and you just feel really comfortable and welcomed. They do lots of courses. They do so much and there are so many people from round here that feel they've got some sort of involvement. They can go and get some new skills and find themselves some new employment.... It's really good". Nadia and Joyce, who worked there, had similar praise.

But Flowella wondered whether it was worth working: "I want to be in a job that's going to pay me a fair wage to keep my head and my child's head above water, and I'm going to find something beneficial to myself, and rewarding. There are obstacles in having a child to bring up, so it is a case of childcare. Who do you trust? How do you pay? Also, the longer you leave it, the less confident you feel". Flowella hoped her courses would pay off: "Someone said they'd done classes so I went and found out what was available. I'm still doing the massage and I'm doing anatomy and physiology, looking to my exam now. By the time I go to college in September to do sign language, which lasts for two or three years anyway, I'll be qualified to go into a new job".

"They should get their priorities right"

Flowella was always extremely houseproud: "I love my flat. I would do more but there's no point because of the demolition. They're knocking down a lot of these houses, including my block. It's not my home. My flat's newly decorated. My brother said it doesn't look like a single parent's living room.... I've got a better chance to get a new property somewhere else if I went through the demolition than if I put in for transfer". She thought there were better schools and more jobs further in to the centre of London and demolition would get her away from "a very untidy place, a lot of vandalism, a drug zone; that's everyday life round here. I'd rather start afresh somewhere else, 'cos there's always going to be little Johnnies smashing things. There's always trouble in my block. There's just not enough supervision in the area. They should get their priorities right".

Flowella thought that regeneration was helping: "The only thing round here that brings us together is the new hotel. There's a nice bar. There's nothing positive apart from that. They've built some really nice properties round here. In the sense of people within it, it's deteriorating. I like to see new faces; a lot of people from the west are moving in. New building for high-income families is a good thing because it upgrades the area.... It's not even like being in the old docks. They've brought a different clientele, nice working-class business people. Those are the only positive things. I'll bring my friends and for once I don't feel embarrassed. Normally I feel quite embarrassed because you can tell they're sort of looking down and thinking, 'Who are they?' When you go to the other side of the station, where they haven't improved things yet, we're seeing all this vandalism, so that's what they need to tackle to make the area different. In the sense of marketing and property, it's getting better. In the sense of the people, it's getting worse".

"They've all moved out"

Flowella knew many people from living in the area so long: "I know everyone in every shop. If it was for me, I'd stay here but it's for my daughter's benefit, I want to move". She hankered after the old days: "None of my family live round here now, they've all moved out. People do look out for each other but it's not like it used to be. In winter I don't hardly see any neighbours. But in summer, out in the garden I do and I go into next door's house. There needs to be a few people within your setting, your community, that you can talk to or everyone would walk round with glum faces and it would make it difficult to work in those surroundings. You don't have to speak to everyone in your community, but I do speak to quite a lot of people because I've lived here so long, it's nice. But most people keep themselves to themselves now. If things were more inviting and I could take my daughter with me, I would feel more involved in the community. There's too many negative people round here. I don't feel too safe anymore". But, like Olivia in the Northern estate, she witnessed self-help policing: "The people round here, if they was robbed and they was aware of the people that'd robbed them, rather than phoning the police, they'd take it into their own hands and do something about it – use violence themselves".

"Children ain't got any ignorances installed in them"

Flowella liked the small signs of familiarity: "Just even saying so much as hello, it's really nice. People just talking to the neighbours. Neighbours in my block are very nosy, which is probably a good thing. They all seem to look out for each other". Flowella thought that schools help: "They're becoming more aware of people's ethnic backgrounds. This is good because they will understand why people wear certain clothes and why they eat certain foods and do certain things. There isn't any ignorance any more. Children ain't got any ignorances installed in them".

Flowella felt that white people were gradually accepting change: "They just turn a blind eye to racial difference because they have to; they'd be too outnumbered to say anything. I think they've become a little more educated. They don't use terms like 'coloured' any more. I used to find it quite insulting. They say 'black people' now.... A lot more Asian and African families, a lot more black families moving in, a lot more multicultural families. There are a lot more bi-racial relationships too. I don't find it a problem. It's positive in a way because it gets everyone to be aware of other people's cultures. Several years ago people didn't want to know about anyone else's culture. In schools they are introducing Indian and other festivals, so they're more aware of people's ethnic backgrounds".

In spite of progress, "there's still a big race thing round here even after all these years. People taking drugs and making racist remarks to my daughter are the negative things, especially with her being half Asian, with mixed parentage". Flowella's daughter experienced racial bullying at school: "It was getting out of order 'cos the kid was tripping her up in the playground and saying, 'You smelly Paki'. She cried because of the physical aspect, not because of what he was saying, 'cos he was punching her and tripping her over. She would tell people, 'My dad's Pakistani and I'm half black'. It's quite strange 'cos he happened to be a black child. I said to his mum, 'you of all people should know what it feels like to be bullied and don't tell me you haven't experienced it in your life. You need to discipline your child. You need to respect everyone's culture'. My child knows I'm not going to tolerate it. The school handled it really well … my daughter signed a statement [about the incident] and him as well". Flowella was happy that "at the school we had to define my daughter's ethnic origin. My child's been given a label now, 'mixed race'".

"You're on your own – no one to share it with"

Flowella struggled on her own: "Fewer people are getting married now. People have no values or respect. They go out as a couple but take it one stage further. Men have all these children and you're on your own, no one to share it with. It all comes down to you. Been single for years; I don't want to get into the relationship thing". This was despite having a new partner. Flowella felt confident as a parent, in spite of the problems she saw around her, but she realised that "my daughter could be dragged into violence and drugs". So she hoped that by moving somewhere where schools were better they would escape the neighbourhood pressures and secure their future.

Parents and children in troubled surroundings

Women play a dominant role in parenting. With or without a partner and whether or not they work, the mothers we talked to generally manage the home for the family, including shopping, cooking, cleaning, washing, ironing, tidying, taking children to and from school, play, bedtime, getting everyone up and so on. Much of this is socially determined. A century and a half of legislation to give women equal rights and to abolish laws that confined women to a limited, home-bound role compared with men has not seriously challenged women's key roles as parents and homemakers.[2] The wider society often assumes that women will run the home and family, even when they work. It is this homemaking function that lies at the heart of parenting and gives special meaning to the word 'home' itself.

In describing family responsibilities, mothers rarely mention fathers.[3] Most mothers literally do most things for their children, even though some mothers in the present study made oblique reference to help from fathers. Women time and again made the decision to put their children and husband first and their own advancement second, as Annie in Chapter Two found in spite of her ambitions:

> "they depend on you. So I decided to give up university."

In maybe a quarter of the families in the present study, fathers play a clear role, although in only four of the 200 cases are fathers the dominant carers. When fathers play a strong parenting role, they too take on caring and nurturing tasks. Very occasionally there is agreement that the mother should work full time and the father take care of the children. Adam articulates his role clearly, looking after three children full time while his wife works. He explains how conspicuous he feels as a man when he takes his three children to community and school events. Louise in Chapter Seven explains how her partner decides to become the full-time carer while she goes back to work. Angela, later in this chapter, explains how her partner gave up work to look after her and to help with the children. Peter in Chapter Two played an important part too after he had an accident at work. Two-parent families can often create more shared roles.[4] However, even where there are two active parents, as in Annie's case, mothers generally dominate the home and take on more of the parenting voice.

All the lone parents we interviewed bar one are mothers, and most only occasionally refer to the father playing a role. Sometimes this role is negative, as in Flowella's or Joyce's cases; sometimes it is more positive, as in Phoebe's or Becky's cases. Sometimes lone mothers rely on relatives as Sola's daughter does, but sometimes they cope on their own. This puts great strain on limited financial and emotional resources, as Fatima's story showed; although some of our lone mothers were quite bullish about these responsibilities.

Parenting in a city requires more money than it does in less urban areas and low-income parents struggle to meet even basic costs for their children. Few parents complain directly about poverty, although many mention money as the element that would help them most. Often they explain how they could not take their children swimming or on buses or outings because of the cost. More income would broaden children's opportunities, as costs of organised activity act as a bar to participation. Low income becomes a bigger handicap as children get older, because their need to go out and meet friends becomes stronger.

The introduction of Working Family Tax Credits helped many parents into work; the expansion in basic training also helped mothers into service jobs in schools, childcare and so on. The number of mothers working rose from 26% to 66% between 1999 and 2003, partly due to children getting older. However, this still left most families with far below average incomes since such work was generally low paid and often part time.

Bringing up children is such a major responsibility that it is often simply not possible for mothers to work as well as care for their children, particularly for mothers on their own with young children. Lone mothers, like Phoebe and Flowella, decided that they simply could not work for these reasons. Eighty-five of the 200 families in the study are headed by lone mothers, most of whom stay at home with their children, work part time or have precarious jobs.[5] Then money pressures become intense and this seriously affects parenting. Zoe, Phoebe, Fatima and Flowella live with the constraints of low incomes rather than try to combine the lone-parent role with full-time work.

A powerful protective instinct dominates childrearing, so parenting in troubled areas creates high anxiety.[6] Flowella explained that her "community" was all right for her as an adult, but no good for her as a parent. She hated the conflict between guarding her child against harmful local influences and allowing her the chance to develop. A big worry parents share is other parents' difficulty in controlling their children. Peter, in Chapter Two, explained how people need to organise things for the children to "save them from their parents". The burden on parents in a disarrayed environment can be overwhelming. Working mothers often worry because they are not always there to maintain tight control.[7] Parents who do work know that their absence can undermine their children's confidence. Joyce explained in Chapter Four the guilt she felt at leaving her boys while she worked.

The neighbourhoods trouble parents, mainly because youth in the area seem beyond their parents' control and therefore a threat. A third of all our families reported direct experience of crime in the previous year. Some mothers experience frightening incidents that generate an expectation of trouble. The idea of unleashing their children onto the street is terrifying and children's stories often confirm these worries. Parents report their children's lack of confidence in the wider environment. Fear becomes a dominant influence over how parents exercise control.[8] Parents fear that negative influences in the street could undo their efforts, so mothers do not want their children to think bad behaviour is normal. They try to inculcate different values, but they see the street as the place where their teaching can be derailed. As a result, parents restrict their children, particularly when they are little, which in turn limits their social contact. Annie, a well-balanced mother, explains this:

> "I don't let the youngest out of my sight. I'm too frightened to let her play out. That's why I take her to an after-school club.... And on Thursday evenings we go to my mum's. On Friday I take her dancing … anything that's supervised properly. But just to let her outside the front door – it's just like I'm afraid – no way."

Without tight controls, multiple supports and resources, parenting difficulties can overwhelm parents and children can go off the rails, as Jane's story shows.

Jane's story – when parenting goes wrong

Jane was born and grew up in the Northern inner city where she still lives. She has eight children: five boys and three girls. At our first visit, she lived on her own with her two-and-a-half-year-old daughter in an almost empty block of 16 flats. Jane is white, her little girl is mixed race. The estate, near Phoebe's, was gradually being demolished around them. Only her brother and one other tenant lived in her block of flats. The surroundings were bleak and intimidating. There was a lot of broken glass from smashed windows, rubble outside the front doors and some graffiti around the block. Out of the adjoining block of 10 flats only one was occupied.

"You have to be referred by a social worker"

Most of Jane's family and friends lived around the area, including an adult son "who's just got out of a young offenders' institution and lives round the corner". Jane was a real local, yet she cut a lonely, isolated figure. The four younger children lived with their dad and her other children were in the area, in prison or elsewhere in Yorkshire. She did not have much contact with her parents or other relatives around the area.

Jane volunteered few details about her life and yet was unusually blunt about the awful things that happened in her family. She simply accepted what went on around her. At the same time, she hoped that her youngest children would "make it to college". Her ambitions were for them to "be healthy, go on to college, get a bit more money". She was doing courses herself and was keen on learning.

Jane's health was bad. She was very thin and said almost casually that she might be bulimic. She had asthma and arthritis and was constantly seeing the doctor. Some of what was happening was hard to explain: where were her missing children; what happened to the different fathers; why did her extended family not help more; how did she end up in such terrible conditions?

Jane was very hard up, managing on less than £90 a week, so everything was a struggle: "We go to the multicultural festival because it's free. Big bands used to be there but now it's £7 each and on Income Support you can't do it". She struggled to feed her boys when they visited. The main problem was that they did not arrive alone: "My son comes round with his mates. I don't mind them smoking weed. But when they get the munchies, they eat me out of house and home".

Jane wanted "more activities for children in the area", but she definitely thought that "Sure Start helps. They've set up quite a lot of things. Some parents are involved". She was disappointed that "you have to be referred by a social worker though and then they come round and give you babygrows and smoke alarms, which I could do with, but you have to be referred". She worried that there was so little for children near her, although she said she took her little girl to the park three times a week and sent her to the local nursery, run by a women's community group. Jane enjoyed "going to the park and swimming. I would love to see the paddling pools in use. The kids love it". She thought her children fared worse than her because "there was lots more for us to do when we were kids".

By our third visit, Jane's daughter "Anoushka's at nursery five days a week now, 9am to 4pm. I can't afford it but it's doing her good. Educationally it's so good for her. I had her down for another, but we couldn't make the open day and I haven't heard anything else from them". By the time of our fourth visit, Anoushka was going to school two days a week. However, Jane did not choose the school and did not want her to go there: "My daughter's brainy and they're holding her back. I'll move her if it gets no better. It's getting worse. Poor quality. They're not pushing her. It's always been bad at homework. There's lots of bullying still. She doesn't like school at all". Her other children did not like school either.

"I got caught"

Jane worked sporadically after she left school at 16, and had her large family along the way. She had to leave her original job because "the women were bitchy so it was either leave or get into trouble". She had been advised by the benefits office that because only one (later two) of her children was with her and the father (also on Income Support) had four children, she would have to contribute more if she was working: "I'd have to pay too much CSA for the other kids. I went to the lone-parent adviser and even she said it wouldn't be worth my while. I've done some work on the side and really enjoyed it, but I'd have to pay full rent as well if I worked officially. I love fiddle work and I can get it but you get caught". Once she had "signed on while working, for three months, out of desperation. I needed the cash, but I got caught". Jane borrowed and lent between friends and family. If she bought things, she did it in instalments. She tried to build a little security for her youngest child by "setting up a Post Office account for her, to save for her". By the second interview, her 15-year-old son had come back from his father's to live with her. She only commented: "My son's come to live with me, so I get a bit more money".

Jane had done a few courses through Sure Start and was keen to learn more: "I want to do computer and learn how to put up shelves. I've done massage and DIY courses. They sorted the computer course but I only did three weeks, family things came up. I want to do it now. I haven't got a clue". She also liked the health centre because it offered health-related courses alongside childcare: "They have different things like keep-fit and stopping smoking. They look after the kids". She also used to do keep fit at the nursery centre.

Jane liked the area and did not want to move away although the imminent demolition was causing terrible conditions: "Well, there's supposed to be a caretaker but I haven't seen him for a while. The surrounding area is not gravelled, it's all broken glass. There are steps which are used as toilets and there's vomit and everything". She thought that children's behaviour was deteriorating because of the lack of provision for older children, who saw the half-empty blocks as a good target: "It's getting worse, because of boredom with the kids. There's nothing for them to do so they destroy the empty properties. After school and in the holidays there's a play centre, but it's not for youngsters and the older kids are just caught in the middle".

She thought that the holidays were worse because there were "too many kids walking the streets with nothing to do".

"If you're frightened by things like shooting..."

Jane did not have much confidence in the police, mainly because of her own experiences: "The police are slow to respond to problems. There was a crack house where the empty flats had no shutters. The phone boxes are all smashed and the phones ripped out. There are cars set on fire. When I moved into the flats, I was upstairs but they broke in next door and nicked boilers and radiators and flooded my flat. They set fire to the chutes. The flat upstairs was always full of smoke. Most locals feel the same as me. Community police are no good either". But she saw them on foot every day following some serious drug crime in the area and she was glad about this.

When we asked Jane whether the police responded to incidents in good time, she replied: "It depends. If they think the person is armed, yes; if not, no". Some incidents Jane reported were frightening: "Two weeks ago one person got shot and one got stabbed outside. They both lived in the area. It's the drugs. They're thinking of building a big police station near here, but it'll just drive it somewhere else. People want to get out because of the shootings, but they're after the big boys, not just anybody. There are lots of tensions because of the problem with drugs. It's not just here".

Jane thought that the violence was getting more serious and more visible: "It's less safe than two years ago if you're frightened by things like shootings". Jane explained that the real trouble was in the early hours of the morning and she could cope with that: "It would be different if it was during the day". But a few weeks after this conversation, there was a shooting in the afternoon. The police then moved into the area. Jane felt "nothing round here would make it safer for my little girl. She loves the adventure playground but I have to take her. I just keep myself to myself and try to avoid trouble".

"Ending up like their brothers"

Jane greatly improved her conditions by moving: "They're going to demolish the block and I want a house for the baby, with a garden. But I don't want to move out of here. I like it, it's central for the town. Everyone's friendly and helpful". By our third visit, Jane had moved to a quiet street near the centre of the area. She was much happier with her house and was in the process of decorating. The new house was a brick-built terrace, with a small, bare front garden. The house and garden were generally quite tidy-looking, except for the windows, which were old with peeling paint. The street was a cul-de-sac of similar houses. It was very quiet and no graffiti or vandalism were visible, although there was a broken front door at the bottom of Jane's garden.

On this visit, Jane had two black eyes and looked dreadful, bruised and "done over", but did not explain how it happened. Still, she was generally positive about her new home: "It's getting better. There's a little girl next door and Anoushka's got friends round the corner. It helps you all get on if your kids are playing together, and it makes you feel part of it on the street. But there's still not enough for the kids to do". Jane would have liked to use her Right-to-Buy if she could, but she knew her finances would not allow this. She still worried about crime, but less than before: "Drugs are a problem, not so much since we moved here, but in the empty flats nearby you do get discarded needles".

During this visit, Jane explained how the broken door had come about. It was smashed in by police who had arrested one of her sons the night before while Jane was in town. Jane's address was his bail address, and they were searching for evidence. He was arrested for being in possession of cannabis, but he was sentenced for affray, not for drug possession or dealing. Jane told us that she went to see her daughter in a nearby village, and "to visit my other son in prison. He's in prison for three months at the moment". Her adult daughter and baby visited and sat in during the next visit.

Jane's worst news came at our fifth visit: "My son has just got eight years in prison and his brother is on the run. He'll stay on the run 'til he's caught because he is facing a long sentence". This meant that four of Jane's five sons ended up in serious trouble and Jane was afraid of her younger children "ending up like their brothers, into crime". Jane had almost lost hope for her older boys, although she still helped them, protected them and visited them in prison.

"You could be dead and no one would know"

Jane was attached to her community in spite of her troubles: "I know lots of people in the area, relatives and friends. Most live in the area". She thought there was community spirit, but added: "Mind you, you could be dead and no one would know". Although she said she could trust "everybody", she also said that the person she could most count on in a crisis was her "support worker". Her health visitor also helped a lot. Jane only saw her parents if she "bumps into them".

Jane thought that "community, it's like everywhere". But she had had problems with her neighbours in the old block of flats "when someone gets up your nose", and she was fed up when new neighbours moved into her new street and "started causing trouble. I'm pissed off because I'm having trouble with these new neighbours". She linked this to more minority ethnic families moving in, particularly Somalis. But she was happy that "my little girl has friends from other groups, African, Somali and mixed parentage. She knows them from school. Anoushka says she wants a little brother, but he has to be brown like her". By our fifth visit, Jane also thought that there were "less drug dealers around. It's getting better".

Jane liked community events, such as the local festival: "We go every year. It brings the community together". Jane also did what she could to help others: "I help regularly, all the time with other children. Whoever wants it, I do it, friends, family". She thought the only socially excluded group was "maybe the elderly". But when we asked who she felt really appreciated her as a person, she said no one, and there were only two people locally with whom she exchanged favours. Her big worry for the future was her younger children. She still felt that the area "lacks everything, there's nothing for kids".

At our fifth visit, Jane explained that she was hoping to get married to her new partner: "Then we'll live together. He's only just come to this country". Jane told us that he worked 12-hour shifts on a production line and earned £160 a week. Maybe he would help.

Parenting problems and social unravelling go hand in hand

Jane has overwhelming parenting problems. Her older children are acting out the consequences and Jane ends up in difficulty every way she turns – neighbours, the law, violent crime, environmental conditions, poor health, weak support, inadequate finances. Her parenting problems govern her life, while she controls so little. Her personal problems play directly into neighbourhood problems. Her children are her social environment – poverty, violence, prison, isolation. Yet Jane wants the best for them and hopes the younger ones may do better than the older ones – even go to college. Her parenting hopes are far from her parenting realities. Jane faces an extreme version of the conflict many parents we talked to face.

Social problems are more common in disadvantaged neighbourhoods: more poverty and ill-health, more violence and crime, more antisocial behaviour and disturbance than average.[9] Parents see the environment affecting their children; for example, witnessing violence disturbs some children. One of the parents' biggest fears is that their children if unleashed on the neighbourhood might become one of the youth that they so fear; some mothers are particularly fearful for their sons. The parents feel that their control is undermined by the environment, where children on the street often reject adult authority.

When parents see their children under threat – in the school playground, on the street, in the park, on school buses – they withdraw, undermining informal social controls and catalysing social unravelling within the neighbourhood. But parents do have ideas about solutions. Even Jane, who has reason not to trust the police, thinks visible formal controls prevent bad behaviour. Police officers "mainly in cars and vans" do not create the direct contact that is vital to confidence and to preventing trouble. Parents want more accessible, more visibly human security and more 'enclosure'. More defensible space makes parents feel more in control.[10] Being a social housing tenant gives parents almost no sense of control. Parents argue for a responsive, sensitive, visible management style with clear rules and strong enforcement through the physical presence of people who check up on things

– rather than disrepair, extreme need, poor environments and lack of authority. Some parents, like Annie, bought their council properties in order to have more control, but Annie still felt an acute lack of it.

The disorderly social environment puts parents and children on constant alert. They compare how they were brought up with their children's experience.[11] In more 'old-fashioned', more stable communities, parents imposed basic rules that evolved over generations. Most parents – and grandparents, who were often close by – had a similar view of what was and was not allowed and more people knew each other, at least vaguely. In this more controlled, safer environment, children were allowed a great deal more freedom by their parents. As a result, it was less menacing to play out on the streets, go to the shop or school unaccompanied, call for neighbours' children, or play in the park with friends.[12] Now parents find it harder to control their children in a general environment of change and unclear boundaries, with many strangers, beset by constant traffic creating noise and danger within communities.[13] Far from encouraging their children's confidence and sense of purpose in the outside world, parents in disadvantaged neighbourhoods hold children back out of fear. Yet parents know that they simply have to give their children some freedom.

Most families feel safe once behind closed doors and most mothers feel safe walking around their areas during the day, but they do not feel safe letting their children out of their sight – even when they are old enough to handle the street and local shops with some independence. Parents try to be philosophical about the dangers, and hope that their children learn to cope. Special provision for young people is a top parental priority.[14] Parents like Flowella, Phoebe and Becky argue that only by giving children and young people sufficient space in properly maintained and organised areas will things improve:

> "If the kids live in an area without facilities, it will affect them. If the money isn't there … the people who live there suffer." (Annie)

Angela, whose story is related next, is determined to keep control over her family life and parenting is a source of pride to her.

Angela's story – pride in parenting

Angela has five children, three teenagers and twin boys aged eight. Angela lives on a large, mainly white Northern council estate where "most of my family live". Tom, her partner, also has his family nearby. She had her first child when she was 15 with Tom, who helped a lot with the children. Angela believed in being strict and when talking about the children she said, "I think I've got everything sorted". She had health problems including depression, but Tom was very supportive: "He had to give up his job when I was ill last year. Now he can't work, so he can help and be there for me". She drew a lot of support from the community: "If I need someone to talk to there's someone round the corner, instead of being stuck in the house".

She relied a lot on them to help with the children. "Sometimes my mum does help. But my dad's real poorly so I don't like to ask. Tom's mum has them all the time." Angela was close to her own mother and spoke to her and saw her at least three times a week. Angela liked the area "because I know everybody here".

"What I got fetched up like, I don't want them to be"

Unlike most parents in the area, Angela did not think that it had changed much: "It's just the same really. I don't think it'll ever change. Nothing has in 25 years". She thought it was "OK to bring up children", but she, like other parents, worried about drugs and the environment. However, she hoped her children would have a different, better future: "What I got fetched up like, I don't want them to be. Not that I had a bad life, but I've never had a job and I want them to have one. I don't want them to be around here. I just want them all to have jobs when they grow up, not like me, just do well for themselves".

By our fifth visit, Angela and Tom's oldest son was working and Angela was clearly proud of him: "He passed his exam with distinction. He's been doing work-related training. They've kept him at Asda. He's done well. He knows what he wants and has it all planned". She explained how he had to work his way in: "Rob did a work placement. They kept him on after it. He wasn't paid for about a year and a half, which he accepted, rather than go back to school. But he did two out of five days at college". Angela would love to work herself but was scared: "It's really hard to get a job because it just depends how long I can last without coming down with it and I don't want to be ill". Her only paid job was for one week in a factory, until she became pregnant at 15.

At our first visit, Angela worried a lot for her young twins. She only let them go to the garden gate: "You don't know what's about". She never went to the park: "I won't let my kids down there. It's a bit rough down that end. They all go drinking in the park, all the kids. They just go in on a night and smash bottles all over". One of her top priorities was to make sure that parks had "no glass in them. They should tidy them up and check them out and make sure all the stuff's safe. They've taken the play area out. The twins used to use it. I don't know why they've taken it up".

"As long as you know people, you're safe"

Angela had ambiguous views about the area, although she liked her part: "I tell everyone to move into this area because you're safe. You won't get broken into, there's always someone round you. As long as you know people, you're safe. Where I live at the bottom is really quiet". Her relatives were also territorial about their part of the estate: "My niece wouldn't move down here. She says people gossip down here". The contact and gossip were exactly what Angela liked: "It's nice here at the community centre because there's lots of nice people who come for a chat and a cuppa. Everyone helps you, everybody's there for each other. We come here on a morning and don't leave until school home-time.... Then I go around home. I don't do much really" except spend time with friends. Angela was a regular at the community centre.

On our second visit, Angela was finding things difficult; she just wanted to get away from the estate and parents who did not control their kids: "If I could pick up my house and take it with me, I would. I just want to be off this estate now. I just want a change. It gets on your nerves. The only people you really see out and about are the gangsters up here. I don't think it's people not getting on. It's people causing trouble, all the kids. There are gangs but we have nothing to do with them". Angela sensed the instability of the estate: "There's quite a few people moving out. It's just the people who they move in. You don't know who they'll be. Yeah, there's loads of newcomers and you don't know where they've come from. Loads of strangers about".

By the next visit, she had become more positive again: "I love it where I am. I'm staying where I am". When we asked why she had changed her mind, she explained: "I've just got on better with everyone on the street. A lot happier. I'm just doing up my house and garden now where I am".

Angela and her neighbours were taking security measures: "Everyone's getting grilles. Half of them have bought their own. I've had it nearly a year. It makes me feel safer". She thinks "To bring up children, it's not too bad. The only thing is there's lots of drug dealers round our area. But I suppose you'd get that anywhere. Everyone says it's rough but the trouble has been dealt with". However, some of the council's more popular steps had a downside, for example "The council have taken away the bus stops so there's no vandalism. It's better. There's no smashed glass. But it's not better for the pensioners".

"I know I've got control"

Intimidation was a big problem: "I wouldn't tell the police about drug dealers because it's too much of a risk with your house. Quite a few people have said they tell the police and the police say they won't say anything but then their window goes through". She knew the area had a tough reputation: "Our neighbourhood's a lot, um, I can't call it rough, but everyone says it's rough round here.... But I like it here". Her main feeling is, "If you keep yourself to yourself, you're OK". But Angela is quietly glad that the police are being more proactive: "I like it more since the police station is just over the road".

All of Angela's children kept out of trouble. She made sure her oldest son was on a tight rein: "Rob is 16, but I know I've got control. I think they're quite safe now. I'm strict. He has to be in at 10.30. I just want them to be safe. I hope they'll not do drugs. I hope I've fetched them up properly". Jason, her second son, did start "bunking off" but his younger brother,

Matthew, offered to help: "He was truanting but he learnt he couldn't get away with it. His brother says, 'Don't worry mum, I'll keep an eye on him for you'". The school helped sort it out: "They managed to deal with it and he's not truanting now". Matthew was very different from his older brother: "Matt gets upset if he gets into trouble. He's as good as gold". She knew Jason needed more support: "I help because Jason finds it difficult at school. He's got a teacher who takes him out and spends time with him".

Angela complained about poor youth facilities in spite of the local youth work team: "They don't do youth groups any more. There's nowt for kids to do at all, except football and judo. They don't all go. They just hang about the streets. If I were in charge of it all, I'd change everything – houses, parks. I'd put more on for kids so they're not on the streets. Kids drove cars about as if they owned them, then police came in". Angela herself felt unsafe at night and always got Tom to pick her up: "Until 11pm it's OK, then I get really wary, looking behind the houses. I feel unsafe just because of what's happened. A girl got raped six weeks ago. Tom picks me up all the time". By our fifth visit, the council had introduced estate wardens who, Angela thought, really helped: "I think he does try and stop most of what kids are doing, because he's seen kids doing it a few times. The police come straight away if he rings. So I think it does make a difference if he's around and catches them". Other things were getting better too: "There used to be a lot of needles [for drugs] but I haven't seen any in the area".

"We never had 'owt like that before"

Angela was involved in community affairs. Not only was she a mainstay of the community centre, she was also part of the credit union: "I do the books two times a week. You get to know people and get on with them". She was pleased with Sure Start: "They come down here and do a toy library. We never had 'owt like that before. Quite a few at school are involved and some parents have been employed by them". She had also heard about a special health project in the burnt-out pub: "They're taking over the pub for mental health, to help people who feel they can't cope, as a drop-in". She noticed that some incomers to a very white area were "different" and she thought it was all right: "They've got a lot of Iranians who've started working at the supermarket. I have black friends as well. Rita is one of my mates, she comes here quite a lot and is a close friend. I think they do get on, I don't think it bothers anybody, not that I know anyway". Peter, whose story is related in Chapter Two had similar views but it did not match the general reputation of the estate as racially antagonistic.

"I always go to the school events"

Angela liked the schools her children attended, particularly the primary school: "The twins really like going to that school. I've never heard anyone say anything bad about it". She liked the community events that were attached to the school: "Community events do make a difference to the school and to the kids. They raise money for curtains and school gardens, to make it look better for the kids. They're always fundraising and I go to see the plays". She also thought that the secondary school was helping her older boys: "They really come out of their shells at high school. They speak out now. I always go to the school events. They do make a difference to the school".

Even though the secondary school was more difficult in some ways, Angela still liked it because of the teacher support she and her boys received: "They do get a lot of trouble because there's gypsies down there and we had trouble with bullying but they've sorted it out. It's got better since the new head started. He doesn't stand for any nonsense. They have to have full uniform". Angela had to sort out some problems one of her sons had and the school was very helpful: "Once Jason got his bus fare stolen on the way to school. I got in touch with the school and the lad got suspended. I always stress that they must tell me. He's not been getting enough help with his maths. They've sorted it out now. Last year I was up there every single day, well, because he was having problems with his teachers. He's changed, himself. I don't go to shows now but I go to parents' evenings.... I keep getting told there's lots of drugs but, touch wood, nothing's happened. It's fine and the children are so polite up there. I enjoy it".

Matthew received special support, which helped: "I think Matthew's teacher is good. She's not a special needs teacher but she goes in and sorts it out when he's loud. He likes her". Homework was another story: "He never fetches it home so he won't do it. Their dad says they go to school to work. They're not at home to work". Angela admitted later that the boys "don't like going to school as they're getting to that age. They both like going on school outings".

"The kids are into names now"

Angela did not have much money and occasionally worked cash-in-hand when she was very short. But she said she spent "loads" on the children for Christmas: "Honest to God, loads. They're all into label clothes. It's very rare that I get new clothes for myself. The kids are into names now". A lot of money also went on pets, which mattered a lot to them. They had "a dog, cat, parrot and a gerbil. The parrot cost £450 because it was rare. The dog was £250". Their only other extravagance was "once a week, going to MacDonald's, costs £15". Angela and Tom went to bingo on Sunday evening at the community centre while a relative minded the kids. They went on very few outings apart from this, but Tom did take the children on a big treat: "The last day trip was about two weeks ago, the family went to Blackpool and it cost about £250. I didn't go actually. Tom and the kids went. When I went on an outing last, it were September last year, to Scarborough, with lasses from centre". Angela could not remember when she last went on holiday, although she and Tom did occasionally get a weekend away, while a relative stayed with the children. Her big hope for the family was "to all go on holiday together. My mate's offered us her caravan for nothing".

Angela was glad things were getting sorted out on the estate: "I love my house. It's the best house I ever had. I tidy my bit up. You get to know people and get on with them. I'm in and everybody just talks to me". She also thought the children were doing OK: "They're quite safe now". In spite of health problems, low income and instability in the community, Angela felt confident as a parent.

Schools and other local supports

Supporting parents makes a big difference to family and community life. Parents in the present study, like Angela, say they are confident of their own efforts, in spite of surrounding problems. Extended family provides support and protection against trouble, particularly in the large, fairly settled Northern estate where Angela lives. Schools also make a big difference, particularly when parents are directly involved. Angela is constantly in touch with both primary and secondary schools in order to keep her children "sorted". Parents like continuous, positive feedback on any progress, and where there are problems, parents and school can work together.

For the vast majority of parents, the school provides a powerful anchor, helping them in many social as well as educational ways. For this reason, most parents prefer their children to go to local schools, in spite of neighbourhood problems. The known feels safer than the unknown. Mothers explain that the familiar local contact provided by other parents at the school and their children's need for local playmates contribute greatly to parenting support. Their children feel more secure if they know local children and are part of the local community. Becky, whose story is related in Chapter Three, explained how bothered she was by her children not attending the local school. Parents value the informal supports schools provide. In this way, the negative impacts of neighbourhood life – instability and threats of trouble – are countered by a positive sense of community, with known institutions, particularly schools, offering security and familiarity.

When parents in poor neighbourhoods aspire to the best, it is often the best within their local community because of their need to be close to where their children are. A few parents choose to send their children to schools outside their area because of particular local problems. Alan and Debra in East London explained that it was a straight choice between a 'violent' local school and a 'peaceful' school in a neighbouring, equally poor neighbourhood. In spite of general support for local schools, parents often feel insecure about their children's safety and progress.

Parents identify with the schools in their efforts to help their children to do well. Most support the idea of homework and reading at home, even if many have difficulty getting their children to do it, although some mothers feel pressured by it and worry about the pressure on their children. Meanwhile, parents whose children have special difficulties often speak highly of the efforts teachers make, of the recognition given to their child's needs and of the close liaison with parents over what is happening. However, some children do "slip through the net", as

Phoebe and Zoe explained; then parents' confidence shrinks. Some of the parents with the most severe problems simply feel that the school and other services have let them down. They are alarmed at the realisation that neither they nor the school can cope adequately, making the whole environment seem arrayed against them. Because of their difficulties, their contact with other parents is reduced, leaving them anxious and isolated. Sola felt: "I've had no help". Another mother worries about post-school support:

> "Serena's finishing school this year and she's special needs. I'm not sure what's the next step." (Judith)

Parents look to schools for help with social problems, as well as for social contact. They often look to teachers to help solve their parenting difficulties, but schools do not always cope with their children's particular needs. When parents take their worries into school, teachers sometimes find it too much; parents often need a lot more of schools than they are equipped to provide, as Ellie's story at the end of this chapter will show. Even so, schools are the most important and potentially valuable bridge between the home and the outside world.

Many parents find the transition to secondary school extremely difficult. School is usually further away, bigger and more inaccessible to parents than primary school. Like Flowella and Annie, many are terrified for their children. Parents who do not have confidence themselves fail to give it to their children. Almost half the parents say that their children have experienced bullying. But they realise that it is a widespread problem so they rationalise their fear. Some parents tend to accept the situation and feel it is best ignored. Older children try to stop their parents getting involved at school in case it rebounds on them. Yet in most cases, parents do manage to get heard, at least in schools, where these parents say 80% of bullying happens.[15] Bullying seems to be part of the general environment parents bring up their children in. It reflects both peer pressure on children and a weakening of control over behaviour. In this schools are both part of the problem and part of the solution.

Most parents believe that their children have better prospects than they had themselves, partly because they see that "the school's good". But most of the mothers had limited education in poor schools where they "weren't pushed". So parents like Annie, Phoebe, Peter and Becky accept lower academic standards as inevitable. A majority said "I just want them to be happy", but they also hope that their children will do better than them. Most worry for their children's future and many want their children to grow up somewhere better. Families such as Deliah's move around the country or the world to where they think their children will be safer and have better opportunities. Ironically, newcomers move into the very areas more established families are trying to leave, because they see them as centres of opportunity, as Chapter Six on 'incomers and locals' shows.

Parents are invariably positive about local support groups that bring parents together to share parenting problems. One mother with a severely autistic child found it a lot easier to cope when she joined a support group. Ellie, in the next story, warmly praises her foster carers' support group. Other parents are upset when support groups they belong to fold, or existing groups are too "cliquey". Several parents talk warmly about a parenting group, attached to the school or to Sure Start, which helps them with parenting skills without suggesting that they are inadequate. Parenting groups reinforce and underpin what parents need to do. At least one parenting group organised outings and other events for parents and children.

Parents have very little money to spend and choose highly local activities. Children like swimming, football and after-school activities, so parents try to fund these whenever they can. Parents enjoy playing games, going to the park and taking picnics. They can only rarely afford outings further afield and most do not have regular annual holidays; none of the 24 families we interviewed go away regularly but three families sometimes have use of a caravan. Time and dedicated activity, outdoors and indoors, with their children make them feel better parents. Most of the parents feel positive about being a parent and want to "stay on track"; even very young parents take their responsibilities seriously. Parents say they enjoy being together at home – just sitting and playing and talking. And they find the neighbourhoods far friendlier than average, which helps. When parents feel that they have contributed to their children's progress and success, however basic, they experience intense pride, and an immense sense of relief. Ellie's story illustrates how much parents themselves invest, how much they want to contribute and how more support could help them in their parenting role.

Ellie's story – a parent with broad shoulders

Ellie is a traditional East Ender. Both she and her husband are white. At our first visit, they had three adult children, several grandchildren, an adopted son of 17 and two foster children. Ellie had lived in and around the area all her life. All her family lived there too. She had no illusions about the area and basically accepted that it would not change: "You get used to an area. It's like the devil you know. I know what the problems are. At least I know what to expect in this area. If I was put in a different area I would be worried about what I didn't know. But I'm very dissatisfied, both with the area and bringing up children here".

Ellie is in her early fifties and reported just how much the area had changed: "It was safer before. The children could play out a lot more. The kids seemed to mix more. Now the kids are always rowing. If you tried to say something now you'd get a load of abuse. The kids are different now. The area seems to be overcrowded with more traffic".

Ellie and her husband moved to their neighbourhood "not through choice": they could not get a place to live where they were previously. "I'm here because I came years ago and my family are all here, but I would never advise anyone to move into it." Ellie did not have much hope that things would improve in the area: "They're going on about all the new stuff that's going to happen. But I haven't seen anything yet. They've put up a new gate on the market. I don't know what that's supposed to be about". They bought their council house a few years previously because they planned to move out of the area: "Eventually we'll move because as me and my husband get older, we'll want to feel safer. Hopefully we'll try and move somewhere quieter and safer … I wish I could take my whole family and live somewhere else".

"Putting something back"

Ellie enjoyed having her adult children nearby: "I like my house and I like having my family and children around". She also liked fostering, seeing it as extending her parenting role into the community: "It's involving myself in local things, because I'm helping local children. When I got laid off work I wanted to do something. At first I thought about childminding but I wanted something where I thought I'd be putting something back looking after local kids … I don't know how to express it, it's something more rewarding. Fostering takes up so much time, I'm not involved in much else. I don't have time to be on committees because of my fostering. There are things for over-fifties, like dancing in the Market Hall and a swimming group at the pool. But I foster small children so I'm not a typical 50-year-old. That's why I prefer the foster carers' group – it meets monthly for carers who work across the borough".

Ellie fostered children of British, African, Turkish and other nationalities. She was very protective of her foster children, thinking of them as hers while they were with her. "I couldn't let my foster children out there to play because I'd be worried all the time." But "you can be overprotective with young kids and can't take a risk. I won't let them out without me". Ellie wanted to see more space and activities for local children, including her grandchildren and foster children: "I would still like to see more parks for children. Really there's nothing for young children. With older children you couldn't let them play out, you'd be too frightened to".

Ellie got involved in school and play activities as a result of fostering: "I'm involved with education when I have school-age children. I go to parents' evenings and reading classes. I take the kids to the health centre. The current baby needs a TB vaccine and they're taking ages, six weeks. It gets very busy down there but they work as well as they can.... Hospital waiting times are diabolical".

"Kids with special needs don't get all they should"

Ellie was worried about gentrification: "I think they're trying to make it upper class. All down the market it's all food places. I'd prefer to see a supermarket. In the short term if the upper class came in, they'd have to make the area better because they'd be more forceful. But in the long term perhaps all the working-class people would have to move out because it would be unsuitable. They would be priced out of the area or something". She felt more positive about different ethnic groups in the area than she did about 'gentrifiers': "It's more interesting. You walk down the high street, you see all different cultures, all different food stores. I think it's more vibrant".

At the same time Ellie had real worries about the pressures immigration brought: "They've concentrated so many refugees. It's just too much. It's not being racist. I just don't think they should keep putting more in. They should share it more equal. The schools seem more overcrowded and the children don't achieve as well as they used to … I think they've put too many asylum seekers into the one area. It's affected the schools. They have to concentrate more on the kids who don't have English as a first language, whereas other kids with special needs don't get all they should".

All Ellie's sons had learning difficulties and did not receive sufficient help. She saw conflict between resources for the special needs of local children like hers and the language barriers of immigrant children: "One of my sons was dyslexic and played truant a lot. The head wasn't very understanding. He did get some special help but it was too late. My son's teacher said he felt singled out because he was the only white kid in the special needs class and the others passed him because their problem was not having English rather than a learning difficulty. But he's never had a problem getting a job. He can bluff. He's got the personality".

Ellie thought that children often needed individual help: "All schools should have full-time specialist teachers for one-to-one work with children who have reading and writing difficulties and they should be there continually. The children should have it all the time, not just for one term and then be told there are other children that are a lot worse. My other son also had problems but he didn't have the personality to help himself out and he has had a lot of unemployment.… He has to get us to fill out forms for him. He brings them round. My 17-year-old is also dyslexic. The school got tests done on him and got him some special help but it's too late once they're at secondary school because they feel embarrassed at being singled out".

Even Ellie's daughter had problems in school: "I took my daughter out of school when she was 15 because she was being bullied … that was getting a rough school. My daughter went on to work experience in a bank, then to work at a travel agent. She's worked in a lot of companies.… She's got the confidence and personality". Now Ellie's grandchildren were in school and the problems were repeating themselves: "My grandson's teacher can't believe how bad the children are. It's not their fault. They've had really bad teachers who've changed all the time". But Ellie still praised the school for helping as much as it did: "I like the school. They've always done their best for them. I like the head. They always had extra reading lessons, but they should have had extra help in the school". She knew teachers needed extra help: "Children still aren't getting enough. I know that from the foster kids; so many are dyslexic, can't read or write. Why so many?"

"Teenagers aren't very tolerant"

Ellie liked things that brought people of different backgrounds together and helped them get on. For her, fostering did this: "From what I see they all seem to mix quite well. I've got a black neighbour who I get on well with. Young kids at school, they don't seem to notice. It's only when they reach their teens they seem to start separating". When we asked, 'Do you have friends of other ethnic groups?' Ellie said "I've got a black friend ... she adopted one of the children I fostered. I did have other black friends who visited the house but they moved from the area. I have black social workers come to the house. They're associates, not friends, but they're very nice. I certainly think people have got to be tolerant and communicate with other people".

But at our fourth visit, Ellie thought that tensions were growing, especially among teenagers: "Race relations, that's always gone OK here, I think it's just the teenagers. It's the black teenagers more than the white ones". Ellie saw black teenagers facing big barriers to employment and security: "Maybe because they've got nothing to go to, no job. Whites accept going on the dole, but black kids don't accept so easily this lack of a future. There's a community club here that's mostly black kids and they fight among themselves. There were kids messing around with fireworks terrorising residents. More violence. The night after I spoke to you last time my grandson got mugged again. A 14-year-old nearby got beat up by a gang of blokes the other day. Crime is a serious problem. You always hear about people being broken into. I worry about violence for my grandchildren, and peer pressure. Teenagers aren't very tolerant. That's when they seem to change". The tensions bothered her: "You can only feel better if you protect your kids".

"Outsiders think it's rough and they're right"

Ellie had criticisms of the council, particularly over fostering: "I'm fairly satisfied with my foster job. It's fairly, rather than very, because of the state of social services – not enough staff". But she trusted her link worker and found her very supportive. She found the environment difficult: "Traffic noise is serious. You get a lot of traffic in this little turning. I don't know why they use it as a cut-through. If it was posh houses down here, they'd get it stopped". The streets were dirty but she didn't blame the council: "It's hard because we're on the market and rubbish blows along. So we get a lot more mess than others but it's not because they don't collect. It's not their fault". She thought that the borough was "too big an area to manage" and that they should split it back into smaller areas: "This place went downhill when they put the boroughs together. All the problems from up there came down here". Ellie had little confidence in the future of the area: "I would like the area to improve to make the way of life better, but that's not likely to happen. I've lived here long enough and it ain't. There's too much dishonesty in the council". It needed more control: "They should have more policemen on the beat. Outsiders think it's rough and they're right".

Ellie felt upset that there was so little for kids and teenagers to do locally, and keeping children occupied was one of her main goals: "I would like to see clubs for teenagers and children to keep them off the streets at night. More playgrounds and nurseries and a local play-park for the kids". She was particularly bothered by the charge for the swimming-pool: "My 17-year-old uses the pool. He knows the lifeguards so he gets in free, but other young people can't afford it. It's lovely to have the sports centre on our doorstep but it don't benefit normal people, kids whose parents are out of work". The same applied to play schemes: "the summer play scheme at the leisure centre, it's good but expensive". Ellie linked poverty to feelings of social exclusion, particularly among kids: "Kids are cut off because of the lack of money. I've never felt I've been cut off. I've always had family". Her biggest fear was that her children might move: "One day if they've saved up enough money they could leave".

"My friends are my kids"

Ellie liked the sense of community in her neighbourhood: "Community spirit brings better understanding of other cultures and beliefs. You see it in the way people react to each other, in the street, round the school, you see people getting on, like with my neighbour. When she was having problems, I looked after her baby. At school concerts you see all the mums getting on, black and white. But community, you don't really see it, in the schools there is; the mums of the school children all get on together. In the foster carers' group there is a sense of community as well. We all mix together, different races. But on a wider basis I don't know".

"It would be nice to be in a multiracial women's group." Ellie got on with anyone who "wants to get on. I get on with people. I relate to people no matter who they are, with parents who come round here. It's easy to relate if people want to get on, but not if they're abusive. The spirit's there – there are a lot of good people who live in here". Ellie, like Peter, Annie, Joyce and other parents, tries to understand why people might act badly in some situations: "Getting mugged does make people more aggressive".

Ellie was an active mum and saw her kids often: "I see my daughter daily, my sons one to three times a week. 'A son's a son 'til he takes a wife, a daughter's a daughter all her life.' My mother used to say this to me and it's true. My sons tend to see their mother-in-laws but my daughter comes to me". Even so, she saw her boys every few days! "My circle is my family. My friends are my kids, they visit me. We do things with the kids. We don't have any interests other than that."

Ellie was very proud of the combined wedding for her two sons. One daughter-in-law "is Turkish and there was an issue about her getting married in the church as her family is Muslim. In the end her father agreed to be there". The other daughter-in-law had fallen out with her parents so Ellie's husband walked her down the aisle. They had a great party afterwards in the local pub. This was parenting at its best.

Parents like Ellie bring up their children to cope with troubles. Ellie 'parents' many other people's children too. She would love to run away, yet she chooses to stay and create a 'global family' in her neighbourhood, with her husband, close to her own children and grandchildren. Parenting is her life and this stops her from escaping.

Cities can only function if parents play the role of helping children become good citizens. But to do this parents rely on surrounding supports, such as schools, the police, doctors, local spaces and facilities to help them. They also rely on family and friends. Parents struggle to maximise opportunities for their children and minimise risks they face in venturing from the family into the neighbourhood.[16] In the next chapter, we look at the pressures on parents from the perspective of newcomers whose lives are made more fragile by the weaker foothold they have in the community.

Notes

[1] Quinton, 2004.

[2] Finch and Groves, 1983; Goldschneider and Waite, 1991; Bruce et al, 1995; *The Economist*, 2005.

[3] LaRossa, 1988.

[4] Winkler, 2005.

[5] Mumford and Power, 2003.

[6] Ghate and Hazel, 2002.

[7] Utting et al, 1993; Utting, 1995.

[8] Farrington and Loeber, 1998.

[9] SEU, 1998.

[10] Newman, 1973.

[11] Mumford and Power, 2003.

[12] Young and Willmott, 1957; Newson and Newson, 1968.

[13] DETR, 1999; Power and Houghton, 2007.

[14] Davidson and Power, 2007.

[15] Evidence from 200 families (2006).

[16] Furstenberg et al, 1987.

SIX

Incomers and locals – a shrinking pot?

Cities are born of incomers, people who arrive seeking better or escaping worse conditions. Incomers often reflect high ambition, energy and youth, and cities flourish and prosper because of them. Over time, people become rooted in areas of settlement and think of themselves as belonging to a community. They become 'locals', people who have lived in an area long enough to feel that they belong. Urban enterprises depend as much on stable local communities as they do on incomers, which is one reason why families play a big role in creating and anchoring local communities.[1] But a rapid growth in incomers can upset the fragile social links that families build. In this chapter we explore parenting difficulties and neighbourhood problems, through the eyes of incomers.

Luiza's story – a divided sense of identity

Luiza and her family are definitely outsiders. She and her husband are of mixed race and from Venezuela. Their little boy was 18 months old when we met. They rented privately in East London and often ended up moving on, forced either by a landlord or poor conditions. At our first visit, they lived on a busy road above a shop. Luiza told us: "I want to move somewhere, if only not sharing with others like now. The accommodation is not good; problems with the bathroom, old carpet, leaks, bad, old condition of the apartment. They're renovating the accommodation, so we have to move anyway". At the second visit, they liked their new flat and were happy to pay £450 a month because they had a small garden. But they had to move again: "The landlord wants to refurbish". They moved three times over the course of our visits. By the fifth visit, Luiza had become wary about the number of strangers, in the area, people of different backgrounds and "clashes of values" between newcomers and more traditional residents. She felt vulnerable and sometimes scared.

Luiza was an asylum seeker with unclear legal status although she had been in the UK for eight years. "I asked for Income Support, but I didn't have the right to claim because I was waiting for my asylum case to be decided. We get no benefits because the asylum decision has not been made." Luiza did not really want to talk about her status; it seemed that she was refused asylum, an ongoing problem for her family: "The GP did not want to register us permanently. They said they were not certain we would be living here, despite my assurance that we were. We were only temporarily registered, so they didn't see my child when he was ill. One night my son was very ill and they said they couldn't register him. So they didn't treat him. We had to take him to the hospital. At least they saw us ... but the service was bad".

"They don't accept us"

The family's unclear status upset Luiza. At our third visit, she told us she was worried about her mother in Venezuela and wanted to take her son to see her as she "doesn't even know him. The Home Office hasn't given me a visa. I cannot go back home.... They're keeping my passport. I should have never [claimed asylum]. It's stupid. You cannot leave. You have to wait for them to decide". Luiza realised that being asylum seekers also made them a target and she faced occasional abuse: "Some people are angry, they don't accept us. The older people say things. When they see you're not English, they say, 'You're trouble, go back to your own country, you don't belong in this country'". She also could not vote.

When Luiza's son went to nursery, she started working unofficially as she could not get formal work: "I'm doing cash-in-hand now. My employer prefers this" – even when she was working for a West End company. Her husband worked in a cafe when he arrived. He now worked as a courier, using his own motorbike. "My husband was robbed and they vandalised the bike."

There was a much more serious attack on Luiza's husband just before our fifth visit. Luiza explained: "I didn't bring my son to nursery school today because we're tired after what happened last night". A group of youths had gathered outside their flat at night and started to vandalise her husband's bike so he leant out of the window telling them to stop. They would not do so and the argument became very heated. The boys then kicked in their front door. "The police came too late to do anything. We must have some rest now and fix the door." Luiza's husband wanted to become a taxi driver as he thought it would be safer.

Luiza also witnessed violence on the streets: "They fight a lot, especially the black ones with other black ones. I saw a fight in a shopping centre in East Ham. It was about someone's girlfriend I think. Two boys were inside a shop and one said something like 'Your mother's bad'. And the other one said 'Yeah, your mother too'.... And they started fighting ... I took Marcus [her son] out. The boss of the shop did nothing. You see lots of people smoking marijuana. The law says they're allowed to. I think it's not good. It makes people more violent because they want to enjoy it, they want to relax, and if someone comes up to them and says something, it's like they're disturbing them and they react badly". Luiza encountered other nasty incidents: "There was a teenage boy and a woman in her thirties having a loud shouting match. The woman was crying and the boy's body language was very aggressive".

"I try to teach my son to respect other people"

Luiza was ambiguous about her life in East London. When we asked her whether she felt that her child had better prospects than she herself had, she said "Better, because in Venezuela everything's very difficult. In my time we were five children and my auntie lived with us. Marcus is happy because he's the only one. He gets everything. We do everything with him". There were many material advantages to being in Britain despite their illegal status, insecure accommodation and low-paid work. But Luiza hankered after home: "I was brought up in Venezuela where things are very different. Shops, doctors, food is better, bigger houses and gardens, better medicine. We don't want to stay in Britain. We want our own house. We want to be a typical Venezuelan family and have more comfort". Ironically, her status as an asylum seeker was what prevented her from going home for fear of never being able to come back.

Inevitably Luiza did not feel she had much say in what happened: "One person shouts, many don't do anything. There are many powerful people who make the decisions". She wanted more open ways of doing things: "it's really important to know what others think". But she thought they would agree that "we need to keep the kids busy; and do it with fathers too, like Sure Start, trying to do things with the parents. We need after-school programmes for young people. We need to teach them to appreciate what their parents do too; and teach them to work with older people, to respect them". She would like to do more: "Sometimes I think about joining volunteer services, helping with disabled people, but I haven't contacted anyone yet. If you want to get your area better you have to take action".

"We live together very well"

Luiza kept positive about community relations: "There is community spirit in the area. My neighbours are very friendly. It's very mixed and everyone gets on well. There isn't much racial discrimination. People are used to one another". With each move Luiza managed to establish rapport with neighbours: "The neighbours help because they know us, so this helps things be safer. Community spirit helps everyone, people help one another". She saw this in the fact that she got on well with her neighbours and other mothers. She knew she had to make herself part of the community "because I live here. We try to make friends. We try to talk with other people, to be good, because we think that it makes a difference. My brother lives here – I can count on him in a crisis".

Luiza saw neighbourhood pressures growing: "The area's too full, it's got too many people and they don't understand each other. There's lots of Venezuelans around and Colombians, and Indians. People are just grumpy with each other. We've had different educations, depending on which class, which country we came from. I know there are difficulties everywhere, including Venezuela, financial and all". However, Luiza was glad of the mixture because it made people feel more accepted, and because generally people accept each other: "There are Angolans and Portuguese, Brazilians, Indians, English, Chinese, Africans. I think there are no problems living together. It's good for children to see people of other races. It's very positive. We live together very well. Racial harassment isn't a problem, it's a very mixed area".

"They try to show us someone's taking care"

Luiza was full of praise for efforts to help people: "The community centre is good for the youth of the area. Also the Sure Start programme is bringing people together". Luiza was particularly positive about Sure Start, although she was very late finding out about it, which saddened her: "The person who could tell me about things is my health visitor but she's too busy, so she's not much help. She told me about Sure Start after a long time. The toddlers' group is closed so I'll go there in September".

When she did join Sure Start, she could not praise it enough for what it did for children and parents: "My son has been taken by my babysitter to some of their events. They arrange activities and this makes it better for the children. For my son, it's great. Parents are involved. They take their children every Friday. They offer lunch as a way of supporting parents, meeting with other parents, learning how to take care of their children. Sure Start organised weekend fun-days in the parks. They bring stuff for the kids to play with and stuff for the teenagers like karaoke. There's music and food. And they give lessons about violence and crime. They explain what we can get for our children's support and things like that. They try to show us someone's taking care".

By our fourth visit, Marcus was at nursery school. In spite of problems over their status and the attacks, they wanted to stay in the area because of the school: "I take Marcus to nursery school for two-and-a-half hours; … it takes so long to get there, but he really likes it and wants to go.… It's his choice, he's happy". This made her feel "it's a good area for us. Marcus' school is nearby. His friends live here". Luiza was very grateful to public authorities: "I think the government tries very hard, but it depends on the parents too". Luiza usually thought positively about local services. "I think it's good. There's lots of places to go. The buses are fine. Sometimes there are problems, but it's not too bad". She says of the area manager: "They try. They want to take care". But she experienced some poor services: "The park is terrible. My friends get ill and want medicine and they don't provide a good service. The doctors still haven't registered my child". She worried about his asthma, particularly as she could not call on the doctor for help.

"The kids are so difficult, they don't have proper education"

Luiza's view of the area changed with each move, as each part of the neighbourhood had its own atmosphere. She felt the first flat was "very safe during the day. I go out with my child. There aren't many people here". Then in the second she felt that "the area is getting worse: rubbish on the street, loads of newspapers, cups, cans. Kids now have scooters and they ride them without helmets, really fast and the police don't do anything". The third place, despite the problems, was "better, because they're doing roads and pavements. It's not cut off because the station's nearby. There's lots of shopping, supermarkets".

Luiza also saw many problems that needed tackling: "It's a nice area generally. But it doesn't have everything, like a bank. BT have given up mending telephones.... Park benches are vandalised. People rob cars, mainly adolescents. The park isn't very good for kids. Dirty people in the area throw things in the road. Vandalism and hooliganism and crime are a serious problem. The kids are so difficult. They don't have proper education. They just sometimes start shouting in the street. They use bad language all the time. A few months ago they beat my husband's motorbike, just to try and break it, not to steal it. It's something you see every day here. And I think the area where we were before is even worse".

"It makes us feel better"

Luiza praised the police for trying to help: "Police are walking around all the time.... It's much better than before. Some people say they hate the police but I have confidence. Sometimes they take time but they always come". She was impressed with the community warden service, set up especially to increase people's confidence: "A community warden knocks on people's doors and tells them what's going on. To see people like this trying to do something makes us feel better".

There was one very frightening incident that could have destroyed Luiza's confidence. Instead she chose to see it positively: "Marcus once went missing for a few hours. I called the police and they didn't come to me. Two ladies found him and took him to the police station". But the police did not call Luiza to say that he had been found. So she went to the police station to find out what was happening, and discovered that he had been found safe. She was so relieved that she did not blame the police for not telling her sooner. It is possible they could not trace her.

"I stay home"

When we asked Luiza what barriers she encountered as a parent, she felt that it was "difficult to say because I just stay in or I just go to work, and only go out to do shopping ... I stay at home a lot. There was a time before when I was very depressed. I wanted to work and put him in the nursery but then I'm shy and I have a bit of trouble with the language". Luiza's shyness held her back from joining Sure Start, from sorting out her status, from getting more secure housing, but as Marcus got older and settled into nursery, she gradually overcame her fears.

When we asked her what helped her cope, she replied: "The church". She took her religion very seriously: "I read the Bible to Marcus". When we asked with whom she had most contact, in the absence of her family, she said: "Friends from church. I saw them last Sunday". When we asked what she most wanted for her family, Luiza said: "God, respect, a good education". But there were normal fun things she enjoyed doing with her child: "We go swimming, we go shopping, to the park, play at home".

Luiza was determined to build a better life, either in Britain or back in her own country. This drove her. She hoped "that Marcus would always be a good son and a good friend. We want to do everything good for him. We will try to lead him not to be blind, to see things clearly". Luiza thought that she was going about it the right way: "I'm very confident anyway, as a parent".

Integrating incomers takes time

The families in this chapter do not feel they belong. The scale and pace of turnover are more significant than the fact of movement, which city parents accept and are often part of. Families see limited local resources stretch to breaking point in schools and housing but also in understanding and tolerance.[2] Luiza's story shows just how wrong it is to attach blame directly to newcomers, where in reality bigger pressures are in play. Her story highlights not just the hurdles facing incomers, but also the ways they find to integrate, build supports and gradually gain a local foothold. Incomers experience both the hostility and acceptance of locals.

Incomers often arrive via some known link and they find space more easily in these areas than elsewhere because such places are generally unpopular. Incomers will accept living there precisely because they are less sought after and in lower demand.[3] Yet new pressures mount through the influx of newcomers, as has happened acutely in East London,[4] where people see the council replacing outmovers with 'problem families', and there is an assumption of deteriorating standards as a result of public action. Even to Luiza herself, too many incomers cause too much instability and feel threatening.

Most incomers to poor areas are either newcomers to the country or people with few resources, or both. Becky and Phoebe, whose stories are related in Chapter Three, are both white English 'newcomers' to particular areas. As families, newcomers usually come via social housing, like Becky and Phoebe, or rent privately from low-cost landlords, like Luiza. The constant flow of needy families into unpopular areas puts pressure on low-cost housing even though newcomers generally fill spaces other people are choosing to leave. Councils are obliged to help families with children without a home or at risk of becoming homeless.[5] By definition, recognised refugees fit this category and some of the most vulnerable families we have met have arrived via this route, such as Kali, whose story is related later in this chapter. The local issue is who gets priority, since people already established in an area are not usually classed as in extreme need compared to more recent arrivals. Often the housing needs of incomers are so acute that they have no choice but to accept the worst areas.

Unknown outsiders in precarious and transient communities greatly increase community anxiety. This can make an area or parts of an area almost unmanageable, as many of our 'local' families like Annie, who is black, and Ellie, who is white, have explained. In the three neighbourhoods in the study where there are big minority ethnic populations and major influxes of newcomers, there are also big regeneration schemes that disrupt things further, displacing established residents like Joyce, Flowella and Phoebe, rendering them powerless. There is a circular process of area decay, exodus of established families, inflow of newcomers, deteriorating standards and accelerating turnover, leading to eventual community breakdown, major intervention and sometimes the decision to demolish.[6]

Areas housing many vulnerable newcomers are difficult to manage because local families who hit trouble of one kind or another – for example, a marriage break-up, domestic violence, lone parenthood or extreme low income – are forced to compete for the same housing priority as newcomers, making these areas the gathering points for local families in great difficulty, like Jane in Chapter Five, and families of incomers, like Delilah in Chapter Four. The most immediate shared need of families is housing. Accessible and affordable housing is invariably in short supply, made more acute by demolition of the most low-quality homes.[7]

Inevitably, services in these areas are overstretched, and people providing services – teachers, doctors, health visitors, the police, housing managers – face many more demands and a much less settled and less predictable community than more stable areas. Incoming families, who desperately need a little security and stability, are immediately prey to these local tensions that undermine community identity. Incomers are fearful of attack because they know they are readily identified as outsiders and they also know they have weak leverage on services. They are often unsure how to connect with the local community to build a greater sense of belonging.

It is quite common for 'outsiders' simply to be overlooked because of the difficulty in connecting to local provision. Like Luiza, they may have trouble accessing a doctor if their status is illegal; and most worrying of all, the police may be slow to respond or simply bypass their calls for help, as happens with Yonca in the next story. Incomers sometimes fail to get their children into pre-school and they do not hear about what is available because they are not plugged in to local networks. Poonam complains about this later in the chapter. In this vacuum, relatives can be an absolute lifeline as there may be literally no one in the wider community they can call on. For Luiza, the arrival in her area of her brother is a huge relief.

It is much harder to settle in an area that is precarious and unstable, because there is a less clear social structure and existing resources are overstretched. It takes time to move from 'outsider' to 'insider' status, which will open up contacts and opportunities. Yet newcomers offer potential resources, as Luiza's desire to do voluntary work with disabled people shows, even though this is hard to convert into a useable service.

Even for people who grew up in Britain, there are many barriers to belonging, some recognised, some hidden, as Becky in Chapter Three explained. As an incomer to her neighbourhood she felt like an outsider. A common reaction is to follow the reserved English habit of 'keeping yourself to yourself', as Peter's wife explained in Chapter Two, hoping that ways would arise for you to cross over onto the 'inside'. Even when there are events or meetings or invitations, many incoming mothers feel too shy to respond unless someone directly asks them to join in. It may take an incoming family the whole of their children's childhood to adjust to local conditions and develop a sense of belonging.

Schools and doctors are important common ground for incomers and locals.[8] But health services are often overstretched in poor areas, and if people have questionable status they are not be eligible for some kinds of help; exclusion of certain incomers may be growing.[9] Local schools on the other hand seem to help all comers, with few questions asked, as long as they have places available. Schools in particular harmonise local relations and anchor families. Children help create strong bonds at school and Luiza's son provides an important anchor for her in the community through his school friends, once he is old enough. Usually, however cut off the parents are, their children make friends, and this enhances the parents' sense of belonging, even if they still feel like outsiders. But for local people, giving equal priority to 'outsiders' and newcomers makes them feel that their own children may suffer, as Ellie explained in Chapter Five. Her sons with learning difficulties received limited help because of competing needs, for example from children who spoke English as a second language. A Northern mother explained how schools, in attempting to be inclusive, can make locals feel excluded in their own community:

> "The school's alright, but they need to cater for everyone. The children were taken to the Mosque in school, instead of the Mosque and the Church. They're only catering for other children. My son thought everyone believed in Allah. It's a bit one-sided." (Megan)

Religious schools are generally popular and therefore restrict their intake to 'practising families'. This can cause overt ethnic friction, as Poonam's story will show later in the chapter. Schools find it hard to balance such diverse needs.[10]

The outspoken fears of 'locals' underline the threat that foreigners pose to their confidence in the area. Many white 'born and bred' families no longer feel comfortable in an area where extremely rapid change has displaced their traditional community. White 'locals' with few choices begin to feel marginalised in the place where they thought they belonged and resent it. Chapter Seven explores this issue.

Even incomers see further waves of incomers as a threat to their fragile attempts to gain a foothold. Thus Yonca, whose story comes next, condemns Nigerians as "dirty" and "noisy" and "coming in too large numbers". Luiza sees the new waves of incomers hanging around on the streets as a cause of disturbance and disorder. Population change makes the position of 'outsiders' more vulnerable as more incomers destabilise the area further and make all 'outsiders' a growing target of local resentment. The street violence that Luiza and Yonca report is caused by gangs of black and minority ethnic youths. Kali, a refugee whose story comes later in this chapter, sees "too many Pakistani youth and too few whites" as the cause of bad behaviour.

Immigrants tend to be young. It is the lack of an older generation that can create an atmosphere of instability and disorder, as Yonca shrewdly comments. The riots of the early 1980s raised this issue of the loss of older, more stable residents, just as Yonca does:[11]

> "More young people are moving in. If they were older people, they wouldn't be making all this mess."

Virtually all the mothers in the study highlight the barriers created by ethnic difference, whatever their origin. Until people can find a way to integrate themselves, by speaking the language, joining groups where they share common ground, making friends across the ethnic divide and making themselves useful, they are really stuck as 'outsiders'. Yet the very lack of these bridges cuts them off. Yonca's story shows just how isolated a foreign family can become in a hostile environment.

Yonca's story – an outsider who cannot join in

Yonca and her husband had moved to London from Turkey 15 years earlier. At the time of our first visit, their daughter was two. They lived on the sixth floor of a very run-down high-rise block in the East End of London. They had lived in the flat for nine years and in other parts of the East End previously. "We were offered the flat by the council, and not offered any other place. We had friends living in the area and my husband was working in this area." So they accepted the flat even though the block was in a bad state, with conditions being far worse than elsewhere in the area. Its entrance reeked of urine. The lift was dark and smelt badly. Yonca told us: "You often see dog's mess, urine and garbage bags in the lift".

"I trust no one in the area"

Neither Yonca nor her husband understood English and they seemed isolated, depressed and homesick when we met them, and, four years later, conditions, if anything, were worse. They seemed cocooned in a little world of their own because they spent most of their time at home. Yonca said that their little girl misbehaved because "she is constantly cooped up inside", but Yonca and her husband would not let her go out as "it's not safe". Their isolation made their child suffer: "Even my daughter is depressed, as she doesn't go anywhere and sometimes she wants to fight with me. It's not good". A sense of helplessness surrounded everything they did. "It's time to think about nursery, but we don't have much information." They contemplated sending their daughter home to Turkey: "[My husband] doesn't want his daughter to grow up here. He is thinking of sending her home to have her educated".

At the beginning, Yonca said that she could "trust no one in the area. There is no park nearby and I can't take the child downstairs because of the language problem. The child doesn't speak English… We don't use the parks. They're very far, in the next area". Yet Yonca craved space: "A garden is more important than the house for us, because we don't go out. It would be an outlet".

Neither Yonca nor her husband were working throughout our visits: "We both left school at 12. We worked in clothing factories. My husband's workshop closed.... The most important thing is to get a job. When my husband was working, he was working full time, but they made it look like part time. The company pretended we were receiving less, to avoid tax". Yonca was desperate for her husband to work and sometimes seemed annoyed with him just sitting at home. Because of the language barrier, they had little idea how to secure employment. Yet the family's finances were unclear. They received Housing Benefit and Child Benefit, but apparently no other form of support. Yonca explained: "We can't get residency because we haven't been here long enough so we lost financial support"; this sounded like a failed asylum claim. "If we were lying to the state, as some people do, then we would get all the benefits. But we never wanted it that way. That's why we can't receive benefit." We referred the family to the local Turkish centre for help over this.

"We don't speak English"

Yonca said what would most help her family was "a job and to live in a place without fear. We went to an employment agency to find work. It wasn't helpful because they said since we don't speak English they couldn't help us. My husband can't find a job because of that". By our fifth visit, it had become impossible for him to work because he had hurt his back and neck; Yonca was trying to find a job. As they knew, their biggest handicap was their inability to speak English: "Since I don't speak English, I don't have communication with people from different ethnic groups. As long as we have a language problem we would experience this everywhere".

They could not see how to begin to move from the flat or area: "We haven't tried. The lady upstairs has so many points, she's scared of heights and is on the seventh floor and has been waiting five years. Another woman has a heart complaint and the noise is too much but they still haven't moved her. So what chance do we have? If we had financial means, we would move out and buy a flat. Maybe they sent us something but we didn't understand because of the language". Even moving around London was difficult for them after 18 years: "how can we go anywhere near the centre? We don't have a car and we can't speak the language, so we can't even ask people the way".

Yonca and her husband felt very alienated from the local community: "There is no community spirit. I don't belong to any community groups". Most of their contact was with Turkish family friends and they knew no one nearby to babysit: "If we go out, we go with the child". Yonca said that she could "only count on my sister. But I'm married so I have to take care of the house and I don't have much time. It's always my sister who's the closest. I trust no one, just my mum and sister. And there's been no need up until now. Three other Turkish families are living in the block, so we have some contact with them but not with the rest". Actually, Yonca travelled as far as Haringey to visit relatives; and nearby to tend to her disabled mother and to shop. They were still very closely linked with their family in Turkey: "Last year we went to Turkey. We borrowed money as my husband's father was ill. We're still paying the debt for that". It was unclear how they paid this debt.

"It's a problem, me wearing a headscarf"

Yonca felt that neighbourhood cohesion could be improved. She thought that people were very selfish, an attitude she and her husband realised they had adopted: "The motto is you look after yourself. That's what we believe". But she thought that if people respected each other, social exclusion would not exist and many problems would vanish: "There's not respect among people. Everyone is individualistic". She felt that she was different from most local people and stood out: "There are divisions for sure. Everyone belongs to different ethnic groups. I see the English as different and I'm sure they see me that way". She realised that her background created barriers: "Certainly it's a problem me wearing a headscarf, people are more reluctant to communicate with me as a result".

"I was robbed"

Yonca and her family had two experiences that destroyed their confidence in the police and the area. In the second visit she told us: "I was robbed four-and-a-half months ago; I lost a lot of money and jewellery. My bag was taken but I didn't realise at first.... The police said they didn't want to search the people in the shop where it happened. I haven't received any information from the police since". She felt very bitter about this inaction, but she had not reported it straight away because she did not realise until later, so it was too late for the police to search the people who had been in the shop.

The second incident was worse: "My brother was attacked in the corridor – he's 25 and he collapsed. He's alright now, but he was in hospital. We don't know how it happened. They were a gang of five or six people.... They also beat my brother-in-law up terribly. There was a guy passing in a car and he helped. We informed the police about the attackers but they didn't respond". Yonca no longer trusted the police: "We have distress from the police". She felt she could count on nobody in the area, making her insecure and negative: "It's very important to us, not feeling trust. We don't trust the authorities in the area. We were preparing to travel and had thousands of pounds on us when the robbery happened. We went to the police and they did a report but never contacted us again. I was very ill from this and went to the doctors, but they didn't take it seriously and didn't do anything. So how can I trust anyone after this?"

Yonca constantly harked back to the same incidents, but it was not clear how it all fitted together. They said they had no income apart from Child Benefit, yet Yonca said she lost thousands of pounds. She also said that the police ignored the robbery, although she said she reported it. At the same time, when our interpreter explained, in sympathy with their problems, that her own Turkish husband could not get an entry visa into Britain, Yonca's husband offered to put him in touch with someone who could "fix it".

"How can I trust anyone after this?"

Yonca thought that these crimes were not isolated incidents: "It's very unsafe, there are gangs round here. It happens all the time, people being beaten up; there are other incidents. Thank God we're not involved with the police and don't know much. We're not happy with them. We haven't seen them walking a lot but I've seen them passing in the car".

The police actually increased her fears: "We get warning letters from the police saying that unless you're expecting someone, don't answer the door". But Yonca partly blamed the council for making their block of flats so troubled: "All the burglars are placed in this building. This area has never been good. Even if you ask English people, they will say the same. And yet we are obliged to live here".

Yonca, like other families, interpreted environmental signals along with happenings. She saw the area deteriorating as a result of more foreigners, "We're not happy, we don't like the changes: the dirt, the noise, changing it to more filth. They have even broken the security door at the entrance, it's a group of African kids".

Yonca worried about the bad example this was all giving to children: "When children grow up, it's difficult to control them. They may get into drugs". But she believed that stronger management would improve things: "The very first thing I'd do would be to clean up this building and to hand over the management to other people. It's very good we have council housing, the flat is fine if you look after it, but it's a shame the block is not maintained by the council. There's no security, that's the main problem. There's a caretaker who comes here five times a week. But it seems to make no difference. Within no time it's back to its messy state."

"Meetings with parents bring us together"

Yonca did not like living such an isolated life, even though she took few steps to change this. She explained what she would do if she was in charge of the neighbourhood: "I would build some kind of community centre, for people like us to chat and socialise so that we can get out of the house". Yonca liked things that brought people together – "a community group to socialise". She added: "I would build a supermarket nearby as lots of people don't have cars and have to carry the shopping from far".

Before our third visit their daughter started school and they noticed a big difference: "She likes to play with her friends. She loves her teachers". Yonca enjoyed this new contact; it changed her view of the area and its people: "At school, meetings with parents bring us together". This contact meant she no longer rejected people who were different, but wanted to get to know them. For example, at our fifth visit, Yonca was happy she could help her neighbour who was ill: "when she needs to go to hospital, she trusts me and leaves her child with me". Yonca was also impressed with being invited to give her views on what should happen in the block of flats. Being told that everyone could voice a view gave her some confidence that they might be heard: "Everybody in the block is being consulted about the improvements but we don't speak English so we don't go. We think we would be taken notice of if we went". She added a word of caution about newer incomers, "even if they change things in the block, they need to do something about the people who live in the block".

"More opportunities"

At our fifth visit, Yonca explained that she could not have any more children, but had positive hopes for her daughter, in sharp contrast to her depressed view of her and her husband's situation. She seemed to want to stay in Britain because she thought it might help realise her ambitions for her child: "My childhood dream was to be a doctor, but my father didn't let us go to school, so I would like her to follow my dream to help others. She has much better prospects, more opportunities. Here and now, there are more opportunities for children to do something with their lives". This dream of a better future for their child helped explain why they were willing to eke out such a bare existence in a society where they had so little sense of belonging.

Incomers look for local links

People who spent their entire childhoods and formative adolescent years in a totally different environment and culture miss the familiar sense of belonging that this bestows and feel acutely conscious of their outsider status in a new country. This in turn inhibits joining in and developing a new sense of 'local' identity.[12] People may have uprooted voluntarily but they may miss and regret the loss of roots, particularly when they become parents.

We do not know why Yonca and her family came to Britain. We know they return to their home country freely and without fear. We also know that Luiza has no fear of going back to South America, only of not being allowed to stay in Britain or return here. So these families have questionable status here but not in their home countries. When they are subject to attack for their identity they feel particularly vulnerable.

Incomers fear rejection. So both Yonca and Luiza stay indoors most of the time and get depressed. They cannot see a ready way of crossing the threshold of belonging. Yet as families they want this, particularly for the sake of their children, who have to cope with school and need to survive among other local or 'outsider' children from different backgrounds. Somehow most parents manage to find links, often through their children.

Mothers often talk about the need for community space, meeting places where it is safe, friendly and open. Even Yonca, our most isolated 'outsider', wants this. Having a place to go where you can meet others is also what Kali, in the next story, craves. In theory there are already many such places, but they often fail to make incoming families feel accepted, make human contact or break down their sense of isolation. Even in the more settled, large Northern, mainly white, estate, Becky, in Chapter Three, who is a 'local outsider', explains the problem of cliques within communities and how excluded they can make people feel. In Chapter Three, Phoebe cannot settle in her new area because she feels so 'different' and sees the 'locals' as "too stuck up".

Few of the barriers mothers face apply to their children in the same way, as children instinctively make friends in school. This indirectly helps to integrate them, as even shy parents like Luiza and Yonca explain. As a result, incoming parents see a brighter future for their children and many opportunities that they did not have in their own childhoods in faraway places. 'Locals' also recognise the opportunities:

> "There's loads, spoilt for choice, city farms, local swimming pools, sports." (Debra and Alan)

It is not unusual for incomers to face outright hostility, and we came across several nasty cases of racial violence – much worse than the frightening attacks Luiza or Yonca experienced. The worst of the incidents was recorded by our interviewer:

> "Desirée and her family originally came from Nigeria, and had been harassed throughout their time in the East End. She knew that her attackers were neighbours, all supporters of the local British National Party. But other local children often joined in the abuse. Eggs were thrown at her house. Vomit and faeces were left on her doormat and cigarette butts were put through her letterbox. She and the children were targeted with racial abuse when they went out. Desirée one day found her front door and her doormat doused with kerosene. This suspected arson attack finally provoked the council into moving them to another area of East London. Throughout all this, their elderly

> neighbour, a white pensioner, proved to be their strongest and most loyal supporter. All minority families have now been moved away from the area."

The strategy of moving victims of racial attack simply reinforces the power of racial abuse and violence in a hostile, formerly white community. This part of the East End is notorious for its history of overt racial hostility, and yet it has always been an area of immigration because it is near the docks. The wider area has the highest growth in minority ethnic incomers in the country.[13] The instability, too fast to adjust to, creates inevitable conflict over what is happening.

Community change can be deeply upsetting, leaving some people unable to adjust to the rapid transition under way. One of our fathers sees the population shifts in East London as a real threat because of the sheer speed of change, in spite of wanting to be positive about incomers. The receiving community comes under pressure as competition for subsidised housing and school places comes to the fore, even as the area renews itself through incomers. Many parents believe that time spent waiting in poor conditions should advance their position in the queue for housing. Joyce in Chapter Four detected unfairness and corruption in the selective system of "needs-based" allocation of homes.[14] We return to this contentious issue in Chapter Seven.

The more strangers there are in a community, the more all mothers, locals or incomers are affected by a sense of unfamiliarity. Newcomers feel this lack of community acutely because they have left the wider supports of their own family, although Luiza and Yonca are joined by relatives. Newcomers do not like to complain or push for themselves, but they share the worries and fears of more 'local' families. They fear crime and drugs particularly, but they are also worried about inadequate policing and the visible presence of youths on the street in gangs. Close as their views are to locals, their fears are heightened by their inherent insecurity as outsiders. They read closely the visible signs of disorder on the streets, seeing noise and disturbance as signs of trouble. They worry most of all about groups of youths, mainly young men, especially if they belong to a different ethnic group; 'gangs' spell trouble. Sometimes 'locals' are the problem so incomers like Yonca find it safer to be exclusive.

The need for activity that brings families together makes Luiza see Sure Start as a true landmark in community relations, recognising as it does the need for mothers who are strangers to each other simply to get together – a simple, direct and deliverable idea.

Daniel, an African father, explains the need to close the gaps:

> "There are no activities that bring us all together. It's easier for people to be together in their own groups, Caribbeans with Caribbeans, Asians with Asians. We're not divided but things don't bring us together. At home in Ghana, it's the things we do that bring us together."

Yonca for her part sees 'new management' as the key to sorting out the violent troubles of her block, and wants strong control of negative, sometimes criminal behaviour. This tackles city conditions at the bottom of the urban hierarchy, where poor people are pulled together by the magnet of underused spaces. These require more, not less, supervision as a result, because the arrival of incomers, while not the cause of urban decay, feeds into it.[15] Many mothers think likewise, underlining the fact that incomers need not just community links, offering ways of gradually becoming part of the community they want to join, but also a level of urban management that makes it easier and safer for them to use neighbourhood spaces.[16] Cities may thrive on change but if conditions are undermanaged, more established communities erode, as we show in Chapter Seven.

Our next story underlines the barriers to integration, even where a family is coping and the children are making progress. Kali lives in the same area as Marissa who, in Chapter Two, explained that people lived together adequately, but did not really mix. It worried Marissa that foreign families were not well integrated and it worries Kali too, from the other side.

Kali's story – a quietly determined refugee

Kali is from Sudan and had been in the Northern inner-city area for 10 years, nine in her present house, when we first visited. She saw herself as different from her neighbours and clearly an 'outsider'. Although her English was limited she managed to communicate and expand on her main feelings. Kali expected quite a lot of the council and was frustrated by her lack of control over conditions and her own life. When she arrived in Britain with her husband and five children, she was put in a homeless hostel. She felt that they were not treated very well: "When I came I had temporary accommodation … I was on the waiting list for somewhere else but they sent me here. They said only here. We have not choice but we're not animals. They said we were overcrowded, but they only sent us here". She definitely thought that they were overcrowded now, as their terraced home had three bedrooms and Kali now had eight children aged three to 18, six boys and two girls.

"I feel alone"

Kali was separated from her husband and was entirely dependent on benefits. "It's hard. I cash it and it's gone. You've got nothing straight away." She seemed quite upset about her financial problems: "I have to pay £25 a week bus fares for the children". She tried to move to a bigger, easier place, driven by her sense of isolation: "Two years ago, I was wanting to move to another area because I feel alone. I can manage all the children, but it's difficult, all the hills".

In spite of the problems, Kali was ambitious for her children: "I hope for a good future for them, so I hope they'll get good grades, good education and get to university. They're all different. One wants to be a doctor". At our fourth visit, she told us: "Yasmeen [aged 18] has finished [school] now, and is thinking of university and is looking for a job for a year. Abdul is in the second year of sixth form". Kali thought her children would do well: "They have better prospects because they don't waste their time, they do well at school". She thought that it was much better for them to be in Britain than in Sudan: "Of course, of course! They are safe and have benefits here. If you work you get benefits and education. When they finish school they want to work". But she was sceptical about the quality of the secondary school, although it had a brand new building: "I won't say it's getting worse because it looks really beautiful. I can say it's OK, not higher. It could be better.... People say it's getting better but I don't see that, I don't like it very much".

Kali thought that more segregated schooling undermined teenage behaviour: "When you look, a lot of them aren't white. Most are Asians: Pakistanis. I'm not saying they don't behave well, but it should be more mixed. White people have more respect and are better behaved. There aren't many whites; you can see one or two or three whites. If there were more whites, maybe they'd behave better. It's 90% Asians at the school, it's not good, and behaviour is very low there because of it". The primary school was different: "It's fine, it's always been fine. Teaching is very good, they teach well".

"We don't know the neighbours"

Kali believed in keeping tight control of her children, as she was very worried by the behaviour she saw and wanted her children to do better than the local average: "My children come straight home from school and they can't go out without me. Even my daughter isn't like Sudanese people. They say she's posh. She hasn't got many local friends, even Sudanese. She has a good education and she wants to go to university. They haven't got friends on the street. When they were young, they didn't go out playing because it's not safe. We don't know the neighbours because when I look at the behaviour, they have bad language in school and on the bus. I have control over them. In Sudan swearing is bad and you have to behave good".

Kali found teenagers a particular challenge. She felt that there were a lot more pressures on them now than in the past and parents had less idea what they were up to: "When your child is a teenager, it's very different. My son is nearly 16. There are a lot of teenagers around and he told me he wanted to play with them and I said no. I'm not sure what they're doing or what they wanted. But they're in a group and I don't like to see that. My son says he's just having a play but I'm not sure. You do see teenagers with drugs. Maybe my son would catch it, so I say no ... it's no good for teenagers, they only go out with me". Kali saw the influence of other boys as something her son might 'catch', and her only answer, like Angela in Chapter Five, was to give her older son a tight curfew. This issue did not seem to arise with her eldest daughter: "I don't have any problems, even though I saw so many different problems".

"I want to learn more"

Kali tried to educate herself so that she could help her children more, particularly with their homework: "I didn't go to college. I tried for a home tutor but I couldn't find one. I teach myself to speak English. I do what I can with the children's homework ... I am good for reading some words but some I just don't know. With maths it's very difficult because you can't teach yourself but it's very important. I want to learn more but I'm very busy with the children, cooking, shopping, washing, going to and from school with the younger ones. I do try but I can't help much. Sometimes I feel bad because I've not got enough knowledge to help ... I don't know if it's good or bad what I say".

Kali was ambitious: "I'd like to work in the future and do some learning". Her most immediate ambition was simple but elusive: "What I really want is home tutoring, one or two hours, but I can't find it". Even though Kali understood English fairly well, she felt shy, like Luiza, and needed more contact to build up her confidence: "I haven't got white friends to talk English to". We gave Kali possible contacts but by our fifth visit she still had not found a tutor. However, she was holding on to her ambition for herself and her children: "I go to English classes on Tuesday and Wednesday mornings, but it's very difficult to organise with washing and cleaning ... I'd like to be a student and go to university but that's very expensive".

"I'm a busy mum"

Kali felt isolated from local families, particularly white families. She felt that "it's not safe walking round the area. I only walk round in the day", although "I did enjoy seeing things when I'm out with the children". She would like to be more involved but she was "too busy. I'm a busy mum". In describing how she spent her day, the demands of coping alone with eight children were clear, although the older ones helped, so she thought of them as her friends: "I get up at 5am and do all the breakfasts, walk the younger children to school, and then I do chores or go out somewhere, do coursework, collect them from school, cook for everyone and then I'm tired. I just look after them". She often said: "I feel tired, very tired". As a result she did not join in with local activities: "I've got enough of my own children. I've never been to meetings, I've no idea what they're like". She sometimes agreed to go but then failed to attend: "When I say yes to meetings, I'm so busy I forget. This year I've missed two appointments with the children".

When we asked Kali if there was anyone she could count on in a crisis, she replied "not at the moment", then added "the children". She said she "would like someone to help". Kali did not really have friends, "just the neighbours". She said she had no contact with her husband or other family and therefore no help, although on one visit her daughter went to find her at a relative's shop. She trusted her doctor and seemed to draw support from discussing problems with her, particularly about the children: "It's a woman, anytime I can go and tell her about me and she respects me".

However, Kali felt that the community would rally around in time of need: "Of course people help each other. When teenagers get into trouble, where can you go except to ask the community's help? I worry about that, they're growing up and you don't know what will happen". Kali did not mind her street in spite of her fears: "We have no trouble with neighbours in the road. In some areas kids are out, but mine can't go out without reason". She liked the fact that "it's always been mixed. All of my children have Asian, black and white friends".

The family lived peacefully but Kali maintained a minimum of social contact. Kali explained that indoors it felt "very safe to sleep". The eight children kept each other company and they seemed to have an easy relationship with their mother, albeit within the tight bounds of her authority. They were often in and out during our visits, playing together, laughing and joking with their mother.

"Not being able to meet others"

Kali's isolation, like Yonca's and Luiza's, was fostered by a lack of places to go with her children and meet other mothers and children: "There's nothing like a park. When you're a mother it's very difficult to do everything. I don't have any problems in the area. I'm not sure what's good. I'm always with the children ... I just go to school with them. But sometimes it's sad not being able to meet others". Like Yonca, she thought that to bring people together you needed "a centre to go to". She could not get out of the area much, and going to a nearby park was a big outing for her family. She was disappointed that this did not bring her into contact with other mothers.

In spite of difficulties in meeting people and her family responsibilities, Kali noticed small, incremental improvements around her. She admired the effort to upgrade the neighbourhood, and felt a sense of pride in the changes: "The main street is beautiful now". She felt she could not really judge the area because she was not well enough connected to know. But she disagreed with those who felt there was no progress: "I've no idea how the area's going, I just heard it was getting worse. I've been here 14 years and had no problems, me and my family, so for me it's better, not one big thing at all, no, just gradually getting better".

Bridging the gaps within communities

Arriving as a newcomer is like jumping on the bottom of the up escalator. As long as it keeps moving, there is always space at the bottom, but pressure at the bottom dislodges people further up too.[17] Incomers need to survive so their very presence and reliance on public and community services makes them, in local eyes, 'predators on the community', the 'cause' of the shrinking pot. It is then easy to blame them for all the ills of the community. The 'incomer' families we talked to are desperately trying to be 'good citizens' and would like to join in.

They want to contribute, but they also want to better themselves, which means in effect having their share of the available resources. The locals meanwhile see the turnover in population, the influx of newcomers and the pressures on conditions as a form of "ousting".[18]

Many of our 'local' families are at pains to say that they get on fine with incomers and have 'nothing against them' but simply feel that they have lost their 'community'. White families tend to feel this most acutely as they are usually the longest-standing residents and are used to being in the majority, but black and mixed-race families with roots in the areas experience this same pressure alongside white families. Mothers revisit this theme in the chapters in this book. Nadia, coming from Ireland, married to a North African, explained in Chapter Three her desire to escape an uncertain and rapidly changing community.

There is an inherent tension between insiders and outsiders as change creates gaps in understanding, communication and contact, but families particularly dislike the self-isolation, which Yonca and Kali describe. Incomers reverting to their roots, natural as it is, reinforces separation, as well as giving people an alternative sense of security that they cannot quickly find in their new community.[19] Kali regards children in Sudan as better behaved than in the North of England and she keeps tight control over her children to stop them being influenced by bad behaviour. Yonca explains how she half-wishes her child could be educated in Turkey. Luiza harks back to Venezuela as a happier place with more going on. This identification with their community of origin distinguishes incomers from minority ethnic groups already embedded within neighbourhoods, who feel they belong, albeit with a distinct identity. Fatima in Chapter Two explained how her family had several identities as devout Muslims and "the modern ones".

The lack of safe common spaces reinforces distance and tensions. Shared collective space helps anchor families together and builds social contact.[20] Parents of all races need and want to link up, but contact in transient areas needs organising. Local activists are critical, but the effort required to make things work deters all but the most energetic. The sheer volume of people, the diversity of ages and needs, the constant turnover of community, require careful management, as Yonca said. Disorder, disrepair, decay, neglect and ultimately violence are a consequence of urban evolution without urban management.

Poonam's story, which is related next, helps explain why it is so hard to break down barriers. In many ways she is very much a part of the large Northern estate where she lives because she is married to a 'true local', and yet her distinct ethnic background makes her feel separate in many ways. She, like other 'outsider' mothers, feels the need for bringing people together.

Poonam's story – fitting in is a slow process

Poonam is British Indian and was born and grew up in another part of the Northern city in which she now lives so she is much more local than the other families in this chapter.

However, she is not considered a true 'local' in this nearly all-white council estate, where many extended families live. When the interviewer was first visiting she asked a neighbour if she had seen Poonam. The reply was: "Oh you mean the Paki? Mind you, she's OK". This was her way of placing Poonam as an 'outsider insider'. When we met Poonam, we thought she lived alone with her three-year-old, half-Indian half-white son, Jonathan. She was shy and seemed isolated. She was seven months pregnant with her second baby.

Poonam got her O-levels and went to college to do geography. But she also did hairdressing and other courses and ended up as a supplies supervisor. She was keen to go back to work and study more, but had to delay this because of her second baby: "I'd like to go back to college to brush up on accounts. I was going to go back when he started school, I can't because I'm expecting".

At the second visit, a year later, we learnt that she was married to a 'real local'. At our third visit, her second boy was 18 months old. We learnt that her husband worked long hours and weekends too. At first he was self-employed, then he worked for a company. Poonam explained how little she saw him, because "he works seven days a week and gets home really late". This partly explained her lonely life. Poonam was reluctant to discuss their income, and seemed a very private person. But in many ways Poonam belonged: "Mum and dad-in-law live round the corner" and she saw them often. When her son started school, she took her sister-in-law's children to school too.

Poonam explained how she came to live there: "I used to work up here and it was close to me. This bit, I'd say, is quiet and there's easy access to the shops". She saw her mother at least once a week, but none of her own family lived in the estate. She rang her mother every day but could not leave the children with her because she was "really old. I spend holidays and weekends at home. I have most contact with my sister and nieces at the weekends". She relies on family members for help: "I'm very funny about babysitting. If I did go out, it would have to be family".

"We watch out for each other"

Poonam liked her part of the estate: "Where I am, the neighbours are nice. We watch out for each other, my neighbours on both sides and one on the corner. We do watch out here. I speak to them every day if I see them. But further afield, I don't know". Poonam did not have really close friends on the estate and knew "hardly anyone". She did not experience much trouble: "You get the odd mischievous kid but it's OK generally. Some little kids used to get into garages at the back and peeped in the shed. That's all. There's no crime really". She really liked her house and wanted to stay: "I'm happy with it. I want to buy it. It's quiet. We've put a lot into the house. We're settled. It'd be a shame not to buy it". Her house and garden and immediate surroundings were neat and tidy. She liked the new shopping centre nearby: "We'll have to see what that brings because it might attract kids. But there'll be shops surrounding it. It'll be ideal for me. The people I know are OK with the area; no one's passed any comments".

"Mine aren't allowed out"

The only real trouble Poonam had was on the bank outside her house, a magnet for children: "The kids do play on the grass round here. The large tyre in the front garden, they rolled it down the bank and broke my fence. I reported it to the police and they said 'it's supposed to be a no games area, and the council should make sure it's enforced'. It's happened twice now. They told me to tell the council, so I told the rent officer but nothing's been done. The council at one stage put a sign saying 'no ball games', although this didn't seem to work. Summer's here now and we've got kids mucking about on the grass. The lads on mopeds are inconsiderate. They've no care whatsoever. They come close to being knocked down themselves".

Poonam accepted that some disturbance was inevitable but there was a bizarre incident in her garden the following year: "Someone got into the garden and took the screws out of the hinges on the shed. That was it. I didn't report it. That was all this year. So far so good. We've not had many break-ins. Not had anything except rolling stuff down there". Even so, Poonam did not feel it was safe to let her children out: "Mine aren't allowed out of the garden. Sometimes I daren't even leave him in the garden. It's a shame I have to be outside with him. I shouldn't have to be doing that really. The oldest is sensible but it worries me if the youngest gets out. He's more of a lad.... That's the only thing that worries me. And the older one could be hurt by them rolling things down the hill. He plays in this garden, or goes to his nana's and plays in the garden there". Poonam thought that other parts of the area were much more problematic: "It's quieter here. Where my sister-in-law lives it's noisier and a bit rougher, with boarded-up houses. Each area's different; it would influence the way you live".

At our third visit, Poonam expressed a lack of faith in the council as improvements to her home had been massively delayed, even though some improvements like overcladding, or 'bricking' as they called it, were going ahead: "I have noticed the houses being bricked up and they're doing painting and new windows. I'm still waiting. Someone came a month ago but I've heard nothing. They said they're going to do it and a year on, nothing happens".

"There's nowhere to meet people"

Poonam thought that a sense of community was very important but felt it was undermined by conditions: "I do think it's important because it's one way of knowing who you can trust and who's there for you. But in this day and age it's difficult to trust people". There were few local activities that Poonam heard about: "No events for the community, just school ones, school fairs. I go to them. They make a difference. It gives the young 'uns something to do and you get to know people in the community". She was not sure whether community spirit was getting better as she still felt an outsider: "I haven't been here long enough. I hope it's getting better but I can't really say. It'll be interesting to see how it changes. It's a shame they haven't built something or allowed someone to provide a unit where kids can go". She thought a lot of problems stemmed from lack of facilities: "It's boredom for kids. I don't know what it is with the generations, but we used to make up games. We used to find things to do. They don't seem to do that any more and end up on the streets".

Poonam, like Luiza, wanted to know what other people thought before deciding what would help improve the neighbourhood: "I'd do a survey and find out what people wanted and I'd probably find most wanted something for kids to do". Poonam herself wanted more places where families could go and more things to bring people together: "It would be nice to have somewhere for the kids to play. There's no social area for the kids. They end up outside the job centre. It's a shame there's nowhere for them to go – a park or play area. I don't know what they had in the past. There's nothing local for kids at all. Usually I go to the main city park. I take them all over the place because there's nothing near here." She, like Olivia, wanted the council to "mend the potholes".

Poonam greatly enjoyed "playing, reading, going out" with her children. She felt their chances were better than her own, although she was a little sad that they needed to be so 'wised up' about life. She did worry, like all mothers, for their safety: "Just the security of the kids, you don't know what's happening. Since they've built the houses over the road, some of the kids from over there have made me feel unsafe. Prior to that, I was fine. I think if I feel safe, my kids do. They pick up on how you're feeling. I don't think there is much in this day and age that would make my children safer".

"I'm not cut off because there's nothing to be cut off from"

Poonam seemed quite disconnected from what was going on, in spite of close in-laws and good neighbours: "It would help to know what there is round here that would help your lifestyle, information so that if there's something you need, you can get help. There's nowhere to meet people". Even Sure Start, which she did hear about and wanted to take the baby to "for him to play with other children", seemed inaccessible to Poonam. She put it down to physical distance, but there was probably a psychological barrier too: "It's a trek to get there. I would like to go but I haven't managed to get there yet".

Poonam explained how "cut off" she felt. She thought "neighbourhoods can isolate you" if there was not enough going on. "There's not a great deal happening here so I feel cut off anyway. There's nowhere to go, only the shops at the top and the Circle. I'm not cut off because there's nothing to be cut off from. I don't know what goes on round here." She explained that, in spite of good neighbours, she "never had a chance" to get involved; she did not exchange small favours with people who lived nearby and when we asked how many people she felt she could trust, she replied, "very few, obviously family and neighbours". She did not feel totally secure either: "In winter it's a bit iffy after dark". In spite of all this, unlike most mothers, she voted in the last election. She thought she should take her chance to have a say.

"Get the best out of school"

At our second visit, a big worry for Poonam was schooling. Being so cut off made her unconfident about what was best so she sent her boy to the school her sister-in-law's children went to: "To be honest it was the one I was told about. I would like to know more about the others, the results. I only know about this one because his cousin goes there. If I can find out more about the schools and there's one I think he'll benefit more from, then I'm sending him there. I've heard that the church school is better but it's just hearsay, so I want to find out properly. From the assessment he had at the school, I was quite pleased. They seem very organised and they will assess him on a one-to-one basis. So I'm quite pleased".

Poonam was worried at "learning pressures on five-year-olds. He's five and he gets homework to do. I think he's a bit young. He gets books and spellings to learn. He loves his books but it's a lot. They've started doing spelling tests. He does get frustrated, and to put that pressure on is too much, he does have to do it ... I don't think it's right. There's something not happening at school if he has to do it at home. I don't remember getting anything 'til I was in middle school, maybe 10 or 11. But I'm 100% confident reading with him".

Poonam was ambitious for her children as well as for herself: "I want him to get the best out of school. I'd like him to go on to further education and go as far as he can, but I also want him to be happy. That's why it's important to know about the schools in the area. My mum and dad, they did their best for me and I don't think they were wrong. I think it's important". Generally, she was happy with her son's progress: "When he gets things right or has achieved something, he does feel good about it".

At our third visit, Poonam asked us to help her find out more about schools because she had become quite keen to move her son from his school. This school was not her first choice and problems started to mount up after a while. She described her attempt to transfer Jonathan after a nasty incident of bullying: "At one stage he was getting racist comments. I reported it but I wasn't too pleased with the head. Jonathan did tell the dinner ladies but it got ignored and he didn't want to go to school. He pointed out the lad to me from a distance and I had a word with the form teacher and she did deal with it. I did have a word with the head but she was more concerned about taking an assembly than seeing me, so I was mad ... Jonathan seems quite happy again now, but he does get pushed sometimes. It's bad. Now the school's got worse; one-to-one reading is reduced. The head wasn't interested in what I had to say. It's out of order". There were racial overtones, and one of the things that upset Poonam most was that Jonathan's "innocence and lack of awareness of being different from other children" was destroyed.

"His attitude stank"

Poonam and her husband tried to get their son into the local church school but she implied they encountered an undertone of prejudice: "My husband thinks it's a better school, he went there. I would have liked him to go to there but I got the information pretty late so I was a bit rushed. I got told they had places and when I rang up, they said no problem. But when I went up to apply, the head didn't even want to give me the form. They were very reluctant to take him on. Then later I found that some parents from our area had got their children in. I might try to get him in for next year". Poonam had a similarly upsetting experience with her doctor: "As Jonathan was growing, he was a bad eater and I didn't get much support. He was feeling ill one day and couldn't walk, feeling faint and sick. I asked the doctor to come out to visit and he was very reluctant. When he did, his attitude stank".

Poonam was outspoken about the times she felt that wrong had been done. There was an undertone of deep resentment at being treated unfairly and unequally, particularly when she felt that her child was suffering. Poonam detected prejudice or injustice in the school over racist bullying, in the doctor's attitude to her son and in failing to gain admission to the church school. Poonam's strong sense of indignation at her 'exclusion' and 'separateness' made her pursue the right, particularly for her children, to be included. Poonam clearly felt excluded from the religious school and sidelined both by the head of their current school and the doctor. On the other hand, she really liked her health visitor: "she's a nice lady, she pops in now and then".

Poonam got on with life, with few complaints: "I get up, feed the kids, collect my sister-in-law's kids and take them all to school, come home, do the washing, shopping, feed the little 'un, take him to the park, collect the other kids, get them their tea, get them ready for bed, nod off on the sofa, then cook his tea, when he gets in at eight or nine, then bed".

By our fifth visit, Poonam thought that the school was a main reason for not moving because they were happy, in spite of her earlier worries. She was also happy with her house and part of the estate. Many people around Poonam were nice. But Poonam struggled to feel part of the community in spite of her strong local ties. Although Indian by background, she was in many ways accepted within the community. Her husband's family was white and local to the estate, helped with the children, supported her and accepted her. Her neighbours "look out" for her and she for them. They thought she was nice, even though she was conspicuously different. In general, Poonam saw few divisions in the community in spite of the troubles she described to us.

Poonam's story illustrates the barriers that 'outsider insiders' face, and the struggle of precarious 'insiders' to belong. Psychologically we all instinctively seek known landmarks, familiar faces and trusted social contacts – a pattern of uses in our lives that removes the need for constant decisions in the face of uncertainty. In this chapter, four families explained how it feels to be 'outsiders' in unstable urban communities. It is a harsh and uneasy meeting place for families, where people feel squeezed and pressured. Yet the mothers have to find ways to survive, and crave for easier, more secure meeting points to break down the barriers they sense around them. They may be asking the impossible. For modern urban neighbourhoods are edgy places, with change and uncertainty pressing in on them. In these conditions it is hard to build firm, stable bridges or create safe spaces. Life is restricted in poor neighbourhoods and 'community spirit' helps you survive and cope. It is how you fit into the jigsaw of cities. Without fitting in, the isolation becomes hard to bear. So how families survive in such precarious conditions is the focus of Chapter Seven.

Notes

[1] Power, 1997.

[2] Home Office, 2001.

[3] Rogers and Power, 2000.

[4] Dench et al, 2006.

[5] ODPM, 2000.

[6] New Kensington NDC, Liverpool, visit, July 2005.

[7] Power and Houghton, 2007.

[8] Mumford and Power, 2003.

[9] Médecins du Monde, 2005; *The Tablet*, 2006.

[10] Lupton, 2003b.

[11] Scarman, 1981.

[12] Ratcliffe, 2001.

[13] Lupton and Power, 2004.

[14] Hodge, 2007; King, 2007.

[15] Power, 2004a.

[16] Paskell and Power, 2005.

[17] Latchford, 2007.

[18] Dench, Gavron and Young, 2006.

[19] Runnymede Trust, 2000.

[20] Worpole and Knox, 2007.

SEVEN

City survival within precarious communities – who pays the price of change?

Modern cities experiencing rapid community change develop a kind of "urban malaise".[1] Only locally tuned interventions and multiple community supports can counter this by working directly within such areas. The task of anchoring fragile modern neighbourhoods within the wider city requires a civic response, comparable to the earliest efforts of civic leaders.[2] Families in disadvantaged neighbourhoods need a similar response.

Lesley's story – a disappearing community

Lesley is an articulate, "born and bred" East Ender, with three children, married to another 'local'. Her husband is a builder. At our first visit, she was deeply upset by what she saw as the destruction of her community as a result of "all the newcomers. I've lived here all my life but it's not the same as when we were growing up. I don't like the changes. It feels like the heart's been ripped out of the East End". The main problem for Lesley was too much change: "They've just piled loads of people in here and pushed us out".

The rapid pace of change was hardest: "I don't want to sound racialist. When my little boy started school, there were six or seven ethnic minorities, all nice people. When my little girl started three years later, she's a minority in the class. I know people who've lived here all their lives who can't go to that school because they don't go to church". Lesley thought her children might not get in for the same reason. She went there herself and was really pleased when they did. But she constantly returned to the fast-shifting ethnic make-up of the school. At our fifth visit, Lesley said: "It's getting worse and worse for 'coloured' children in the nursery. There are 24 'coloured' for three or four white. As much as I don't mind them mixing, I do want my two-year-old to have her own mates. It's very sad that my children aren't learning about their own culture. I don't think it's fair".

"Community spirit matters because it's just nice to be friendly"

At our first visit, Lesley liked her street: "There is community spirit down this street. My nan lived here since my mum was a little girl. There's neighbours who'll get bread or sit with my little girl if she's asleep. It's nice, how it was when I was a kid, proper community spirit. I don't feel cut off because I have lots of neighbours and friends". But she reminisced: "I used to walk from here to my nan's and we'd go to the market, you'd talk to people all the way along. You'd know everybody but now we hardly know anybody. Community spirit matters because it's just nice to be friendly and pass the time of day with people.... Down this street we're quite friendly. The man next door will get bread for me ... I know there are people I can ring if I need something".

Family mattered a lot to Lesley. Her in-laws lived around the corner and the children often went there to play as the road was safer: "My 12-year-old boy stays in 'cos I don't want him hanging around on the street. He can go round the block, but only the immediate area. My little girl, age nine, doesn't play here, only round my mother-in-law's". Lesley's own relatives had dispersed, but her husband's family was still nearby.

In Lesley's eyes, community change was the problem: "The area has gone down the pan. It's absolutely full of 'coloured' people. All my mates are moving out for the same reason. They're being outnumbered. When they put their houses up for sale, the only people who come to view are 'coloureds'". Lesley felt under pressure to move out.

Over the four years of our visits, Lesley did not leave despite having bought her house under the Right-to-Buy: "If you've got your own house, you've got the freedom to sell and go where you want". But at our second visit, she explained that she was not sure where to go: "Let's put it this way, if I could move to an area tomorrow where there wasn't so many, I would go". Her mother had moved to Essex and she really liked it there: "If I go over my mum's, I feel quite nice being there. You can walk across the road to a duck pond, a nice little pub with a garden. It does make a big difference". She also had friends who'd moved to Canvey Island. But she was still uncertain.

"Too late to keep our own here"

Lesley clearly thought that council housing played a big part in community erosion: "I just think to myself, 'How come when you've grown up in the area, lived there all your life, you can't even have a house or flat when you get married and want to move out of home". By our fifth visit, she felt defeated: "It's too late to change it to keep our own here because they've all gone", explaining how isolated she felt. "An older lady who's lived in these houses since they were just built, now she's gone, because it's got to the stage where she never felt safe to walk to the local shops to get herself a loaf of bread. In the end you just have to move on. If I went to Tesco's and someone had just put me there and I didn't know where I was, I'd think I was in a foreign country. When we had our old neighbours, it was a lot different then. It had a little family feel to it then, but that's all changed."

Lesley pinpointed the competition for resources: "It sounds horrible but people that have been here all their life are more entitled. I just feel like people are just coming in from everywhere, walking in and getting their houses, getting school places and getting all the help. And we are all just getting on with it ourselves". The school exemplified the problem for Lesley: "It's a church school. The only people who go there now are the Africans because they go to church and people who've lived here all their lives don't get in any more". She quickly added that despite this, "I've seen an improvement between the children in how they get on".

"That'll be their world"

Lesley tried not to pass on negative attitudes to her children: "I've never put it in them to be racialist. I have coloured children over here to play with my little girl. All three children have mainly African friends. That's all they've got to make friends with. Actually I do think they mix quite well. They're all friendly, and get on with each other. And that'll help them when they get older because that'll be their world".

Lesley saw deeper problems: "It's a harder world now than when we was young. It's tougher wherever you live. There's nothing for children now. If it was still as it was, then you wouldn't want to move. Now it's a strange place. You walk along the main road and all there is is down-and-outs drinking extra strong lager". So, lack of facilities, a bad atmosphere on the street and a transient population made things worse.

Lesley believed in helping and getting involved: "I go to whatever is going, six or seven times a term. I used to help with reading and organising stalls 'til I had the baby". She had a lot of contact because the school went out of its way to link with parents: "Every day I see teachers because they come to the playground at the start and end of school. So you have a quick conversation with them then. The kids're well behaved and I feel good about that and I tell them not to bully other children. Their reports are so lovely, it makes my job easier. There's also a parents' evening once a term. The school brings people together. I'd meet up with other mums at coffee mornings, that brings us together". So the school, for all its bias towards churchgoers and its changing ethnic composition, inspired confidence in Lesley, linking her in to a community where she had lost her bearings.

"You want to feel safe"

Lesley felt that the basic environment was less cared-for than before: "The place seems dirtier and rougher from when I was a kid. You must think I shouldn't be living here if I feel like this. Well, I wouldn't if I could get out. It's getting worse because now it looks all dirty and scruffy". This made people worry about what might happen: "I don't feel it's safe enough to let children walk around". Even parks felt threatening to her: "Now and again I take them to the park. The other parks are a bit big. I wouldn't go to a big park with just me and her. The big park is lovely but it's quite secluded. I've been over there a couple of times but I've never felt 100%. I'd feel better with another adult with me".

The basic problem was lack of supervision: "It could do with some improvements. When we was children, it always had a park keeper, so you did always have someone keeping an eye on it. There's a big bit of greenery but the dogs can just run all over the park". The devaluing of parks was exemplified by the major road-widening across the area: "They took a bit of the main park away to widen the road. There's a lot of gangs of Africans up there, and drunks. I would be wary, stepping from the car to the shops. You want to feel safe, so that if you want to put a baby in a pushchair, you can". Luiza made the same point about the same row of shops.

Lesley lost her handbag in a smash-and-grab raid on her car outside her house. She reported it to the police but said "they done nothing. They just simply wasn't interested. They gave me a crime number and sent me a form and that was it". She did not want to be too hard on the police though: "They're doing the best job they can. There used to be a small police shop round the corner but it's shut now as the building it was in was demolished".

The cuts in local police, park keepers and youth clubs hit Lesley hard. She wanted more facilities, particularly for children and young people in the area, "like there used to be. I don't feel there's enough youth clubs. When we were children, in winter three or four nights a week, we did have a youth club to go to. There used to be the youth centre and another youth club every night of the week. But there's nothing like that now. Nothing is put on for the children, so you make your own amusements with them". Her children were lucky because they had a family caravan they could go to at weekends.

"They say things'll get better but I don't think they will"

Lesley knew that schooling was the key to children's future: "I would just like my kids to have a good education, to get them a good enough job not to have to struggle through life". She had no complaints about the primary school: "The new headmistress has done a lot to brighten the education up. It's quite a friendly little school when you go over there. The head and teachers are quite friendly. I'm pleased. They do after-school every night: homework, football, other sports, computer club. They've got a bit of everything. Basically they've got everything covered". Lesley's support for the school overrode her worries about race.

At our second visit, Lesley was much more worried about her older son's secondary school, which would be further afield: "I did consider moving my son in with my mum so he could go to secondary school there, but it's not family life, doing that to him. He's starting secondary school in September and I'd like to have left by then. It'll probably be an impossibility. Another thing worrying me about secondary schools is you hear there are people selling drugs to children and nicking things, like mobile phones to get money for their own things. It's only what you hear, I'm not convinced it's as bad as all that".

At our third visit, her son was very pleased with himself for making the transition to secondary so easily. But Lesley felt: "I wanted him to stay in primary school where I knew where he was, there, across the road". By the fifth visit, when her older boy was 14, he was hanging around the house instead of attending school. "I don't know what he dislikes, I think it's just school."

"I ain't got no one left here now"

Part of Lesley did not want to move: "They say things will get better but I don't think they will. You can only hope, 'cos it'll be better for us". She noticed transport improvements, which definitely helped: "I did go on a train last year, two school trips with the kids on the new tube. To get to places, that's pretty good". She thought that newer residents who did not have the painful memories of a disappearing community might be more optimistic: "People who've come here more recently probably think it's getting better: the new tube and new university".

Lesley felt nobody listened: "I can't influence decisions. We campaigned against buses down this road, also against the airport, but they always have to have their way". For Lesley the only thing that could really help was "to move out and mix more with our own, if that doesn't sound too horrible". In the last visit she explained sadly: "I ain't got no one left here now. I feel on my own".

Community relations require careful brokering

Lesley, a long-standing white resident living in the East End, explained how undermining it felt to be a mother without community supports because 'her community' had been displaced by newcomers. Newcomers to such unstable places can only imagine how precarious a neighbourhood feels to families like Lesley's; they do know how unwelcome they feel. Lesley's story starkly reflects gaps that open up under pressure of change – the gap between stability and uncertainty; incomers and locals; community breakdown and community tolerance. Lesley articulates views that many mothers share without expressing them so openly, including Annie, Flowella and Delilah from earlier stories, all from minority ethnic backgrounds. They all talk about the sense of unease they feel among too many strangers.

Some families adjust more readily than Lesley to the constant turnover, but her area is undergoing extreme change and she feels a deep sense of loss. The demolition plans for the area compound her uncertainties; Annie in Chapter Two showed how unsettling these plans were. They pushed Joyce, in Chapter Four, into moving out altogether, and made Flowella, in Chapter Five, feel that it was pointless making an effort in the community or in her flat. City improvement plans can damage family and community life in spite of their promise.

Lesley has done quite well out of public services so far. She owns her own ex-council property and got her children into the local church school, which is very popular, in spite of not being a churchgoer. Yet Lesley saw mainly negative consequences of community change, whereas 'outsider' mothers, like Kali and Luiza in Chapter Six, saw opportunities, in spite of suffering deeply from a sense of exclusion. The rapid ethnic change in this East London borough during the 1990s inevitably created tensions over resources. The lack of control that families feel over their 'community' and immediate environment shrinks their capacity to cope with instability, so many families typecast newcomers as a threat.

None of the parents we talked to in Lesley's neighbourhood is sure that they will benefit locally from regeneration plans because they know that the aim is to attract a more 'mixed', more prosperous community. So they feel squeezed from both sides – by better-off people the council wants to attract and needy minority ethnic groups whom the council is required to house as a priority. Some families, like Flowella in Chapter Five, positively welcome the gentrifying incomers. If families like Lesley's, Annie's or Joyce's understood the regeneration plans, and their own entitlement, they could possibly adapt more easily and work with the grain of change. In practice, even government is unclear about the direction of change and does not appear able to control it.[3]

There is tension over subsidised regeneration and gentrification to attract people who are well off already, compared with the acute basic needs of local families, but the strongest tensions arise from programmes that prioritise minority ethnic groups to equalise access. This can upset even the most open-minded and tolerant community representatives, who question ethnically directed government funds.[4] Many think that incoming minority ethnic groups get too much help, and some minority ethnic parents worry about the reputation of newcomers for cheating the system.

Cities thrive on movement and change, on fresh blood and new ways, but population turnover disrupts extended family links, which are particularly important to mothers and children. It is hard for different parts of the family to stay together as the pressures of mobility intensify. Lesley's relatives have all moved out of the area. Josephine, an African mother in Lesley's area, understands 'white flight':

> "There's more African people in the area and more whites moving away. Maybe they've seen a lot of immigrants coming and they don't like it, so they move away – because some of them are scared of our attitude." (Josephine)

The networks of support that help families cope in fast-changing city neighbourhoods are strengthened by more rooted families. So displacement carries a high social cost. By housing incomers and eventually helping them to integrate, low-income communities indirectly support urban development and wealth creation. Total regeneration of the area through demolition and new building places very little value on community stability.

Residents of low-income areas constantly renew cities from the bottom because cities need cheap fluid labour markets, and incomers are clearly service providers and wealth generators. As long as a city is functioning, it will suck in and expel people, goods, resources and waste at the lowest possible cost. Housing competition from incoming families is the other side of the need for low-paid and active workers. In this way, cheap housing in poorer neighbourhoods close to service centres may be a major driver of the wider economy, as Nadia's North African husband, a restaurant worker in central London, showed in Chapter Three. But for the families who live there, the absorption capacity is limited by finite resources, including community resources, the fragile but crucial social networks that enable families to survive and that recur as a basic need in every family story.

Neighbourhoods act as sponges, not just for people, but for wider resources needed to keep them functioning.[5] Yet parents often find it hard to get action on problems that only the wider services of the city can solve. Individual families and local communities do not have the power to control communal behaviour, nor the authority to tackle communal breakdown, nor the resources to reinvest in run-down buildings and services. Actions of a public nature require a wider authority, otherwise the vacuum in authority leads to inaction, sometimes with serious consequences.[6] But that reinvestment has to work with the community, rather than ignore it as so many mothers claim. Cynthia, whose story we relate next, highlights the deficits and promise of local interventions.

Cynthia's story – a true survivor

Cynthia came from Sierra Leone to London 18 years before we met. She broke up with her first husband and stayed with her auntie while expecting her first child. The council agreed to rehouse her and she had been in her present flat for 11 years when we visited in 1998; her eldest daughter was about to go to secondary school. She remarried and had a baby, but in the interim she struggled and "took a private loan from a loan shark, so now I'm in a vicious circle". Cynthia could not move because of her rent arrears. She was trying to pay off both the loan and the arrears. Cynthia has struggled to bring up her two children as she wants. She sets very high standards for herself and for them, despite immense difficulties.

"I'm capable of doing more"

Cynthia worked hard at a London hospital: "I like the job. It's just a cleaning job, but I've got a lovely day ward; it's so clean and everybody's nice, but personally I think I'm capable of doing more and I feel a bit frustrated. They can tell that, because I keep applying for jobs". Cynthia explained that she had previously tried to study: "I got a place, but didn't have the fees of £600, way outside my budget. Now I have a partner, I maybe could afford to go. But I've got two children and I'm older". Cynthia wanted to train as a nurse and be paid while training. She'd been offered an opening in West London: "I'll really grasp this opportunity at Chelsea

Hospital, even though it's far. I'll get paid, plus I'll get training. I'm not taking the local one. They know me as a cleaner. I'll have a hard time fitting in as a student. But over there, they don't know me. I'm going to start afresh and I'll feel more comfortable. I've done the test and passed. I did well, so I'm going for that one. What I need is something I'll get paid for and get trained. I've got to do something or we'll run short of money again".

At our third visit, Cynthia had managed to get the job with training, offering her an NVQ in general nursing, but she had to do extra shifts and evening work to clear her debts: "Because I do shifts, I can't do the training. With the NVQ and the job, I have no time to study. I have a mentor for the course but even this doesn't help much because of the kids. I do extra work to make up the money. I go to college at 1.30pm and come home about 9pm. Sometimes I do agency nursing as well. I'm worried about Susie's homework. I have to leave her at the childminder's house, sometimes overnight, because of shift work. Susie's having to study a lot now and I've got two jobs because of the debts. I should be coming home at 5pm to help with homework. I want to give up my evening job to involve myself more with my children's work. I'm now thinking about setting up a business. I heard about a scheme that helps ethnic minorities set up their own businesses in the area".

By our fifth visit, Cynthia had become a full-time student nurse, a major upgrading from her previous position as healthcare assistant and before that as a cleaner: "I've done quite well for myself, for my career". She was still in a financial trap but said, "I will just have to go on paying my rent arrears". Her husband was now a self-employed joiner. "He used to work on the buses." He was a great support, she said. Cynthia really hoped things would work in their relationship.

"I don't want her to get involved"

Childcare was been a constant worry for Cynthia. She agreed with her sister to work and give her £45 a week to stay at home and help Susie as well as her own children. "My sister's very good with kids, she brought Susie up. She makes sure the children do their work.… When my daughter comes home from school, she can come back here because my husband is here. But I don't want her to be at home by herself, so I let her stay with my family because then she is with a woman and she keeps an eye until I come home … I don't want her just to come in here and start sleeping and then she might end up opening the door and start chatting to these girls. I'm not saying they're bad or anything, but I see some of the things they do and I don't want her to get involved".

With the new baby, full-time childcare became a big worry: "They only have a few places in nursery, and you have to have the money. It's about £90 for the week or something like that. If you're on Income Support it's free, and I think, 'There we go again. What's the point of working when you can't have nothing free?' I'm not saying it should be free, but if you're on Income Support, it's free". Her sister could not take the baby full time so Cynthia was looking everywhere: "I got a list of registered childminders from the council. I couldn't see anyone I knew. It doesn't have to be someone from my country, because for a while my Susie was going to Liz, she's an English lady and ever so nice. I've known Liz for years and I know what she's like at home". Cynthia did not want to leave her baby with a stranger, so her extended family came to her rescue: "I found this young cousin of mine who's just moved into the area. She took over from my auntie looking after baby. I want someone I can trust for babysitting, I had such a gap between them".

Cynthia sometimes regretted her decision to work as it not only deprived her children of her time and care, but also prevented her getting help: "Now they say mothers should go to work, but I should have stayed as I was. If you're not working, you get things. But if you are working, you don't get anything. When I was at home I was better off just with two cleaning jobs. No childcare costs". The cleaning jobs were 'off the books'. Cynthia worked "all the hours God sends".

"I want Susie to do better than me"

Cynthia sent her daughter to a Catholic secondary school: "There's lots of discipline and you're not allowed to go out of school in the lunch hour. I went to a Catholic school in Sierra Leone. My daughter didn't get into the Church of England school. She had a good behaviour report. The main reason was we didn't go regularly to the church. You get a form of attendance, then this goes to the school. I have lots of worries about secondary school. I didn't think she'd be able to get on a bus on her own". Cynthia also thought of applying for drama school: "Susie does very well with acting. I've got the forms to apply for the famous Italia Conte School". In the end Cynthia was happy with the Catholic secondary school.

Cynthia was even more ambitious for her children than for herself: "I never miss a parents' evening or school play or funfair. I want Susie to be better than me. The new head makes it clear that she's good at some subjects but not others. Whereas before she was bunched with everyone including those brighter at maths, now she's in a special group, which I prefer; that's helped. Back home you can repeat a year but not here. The new head's really done a lot. The school's gone up the league table. They set targets at parents' evening and say it's up to you as a parent. Susie's now stopped going to extra maths classes. Instead, I pay a teacher £10 an hour every Tuesday. The teacher leaves Susie lots of homework, so now she's coming up".

The school supported parents a lot: "The school has some fairs, jumble sales and parties. There are after-school things. It will give the kids somewhere to go … I find if you push yourself and get involved, they help your child too; otherwise they don't help as much. I would like her to go to university; she shouldn't be in a rush to go to work. I'm closely involved, but only in the school community", not the wider neighbourhood.

"I want to get out of this area"

Cynthia worried a lot for Susie because "she's been through thick and thin", she really wanted to protect her. At our second visit, she explained, "Some conversations of the girls on the buses are frightening. Their parents aren't aware of their behaviour. I like Susie to mix with her cousins. I'm not prejudiced but I don't like what I see". Cynthia was unsure of keeping control over her daughter's activities, in such a little flat: "I've got my daughter coming up 12 now and I get worried. My daughter's growing up and she can help me more, but soon we won't have enough space. There's no garden for her to play out. I can't see me letting her go out there ever and I know it's going to bring problems. Susie doesn't go out, but she's bored".

In practice, Susie did sometimes 'play out' if she went with someone Cynthia knew and trusted: "She's allowed to go to the park with a friend. I wouldn't let her go alone. I don't let them because I've seen how the kids grow up round here. I see more police around the shops, that's where all the trouble is. The off-licence was robbed at gunpoint recently. But there's more police presence now. There's little parental control in this area. My daughter doesn't play around here at all. That's why I want to get out of this area. I'm worried about Susie because I come home late and get scared". But Cynthia was immobilised by her debts: "I'll have to move out of here before she gets to that age; that's my plan. Trouble is, I've still got rent arrears from before I met my husband. I will have to go private or something".

Cynthia felt the loss of more-established white tenants was weakening community control: "When I moved here it was mostly old people in this block. When I was going to work, I used to see them, you know, the old ladies who stand together in groups and chat for hours. One opens her door and one opens her window and they talk. I talk to all the old ladies. They look out for everyone. Everybody knew everybody then. We could chat in the lifts, or by the lifts. This place has turned out to be noisy now. It used to be a lovely quiet area. There's too much noise and too many kids round here. Now everyone is trying to keep their business away from each other".

"Before I come to that lift, my heart is thumping"

Cynthia felt particularly threatened by groups of boys who hung around her block: "I mentioned before that we have these boys sitting on the wall. Well, there's a whole load of them now coming in this direction where the lifts are and they're there, every time I come from work. Before I come to that lift, my heart is thumping, and I'm thinking 'God, am I going to get mugged before I can even press for the lift?' Sometimes I see the things they do. They're breaking the lights downstairs. The boys come in and smash them. We had a letter from the council to say they were aware.... They fitted new ones. Every time one of them comes in there, they just finish it off, break it. Half the time we don't have lights in the entrance and stairwell.... What can you do? I just watch and I feel terrible. I know they've done something wrong and they're running away. I think, 'My daughter's growing up. Some of them are girls and I'm getting worried. They're smoking and doing all sorts, everyday, every evening. I think they need some activity".

By our third visit, the gangs had got worse: "The area is getting better. But then again we've got this pack. What I notice is, it isn't the same boys that used to sit round the other end. They've grown up now, so we've got a new pack. I used to know them when they were little and they've grown big now, about 14 and 15, hanging about there and I'm terrified of them. I think the kids need something to keep them going, like a boy's club or something. They're improving the area, yes they've worked on the renovation, fine! But what about recreation for the children?" Cynthia, like so many mothers, felt powerless: "I can't see my voice influencing ... I wish I could get my voice heard".

Cynthia hated what she saw: "The same group of boys ... they were bullying another boy. He was asked to go and do something he didn't want to do. He was running away, and this big one just grabbed him by the shirt and said 'You're not going nowhere, you just stop with us. You grass on us and I'll beat the hell out of you'. And I thought, 'If that was my son, or even if I knew the parents of that boy I'd tell them to do something'. He didn't want to be with them or to do something bad. But he couldn't leave because he might've got beaten up or something. I've seen those things and I think it's horrible. Another day, there was this man outside my door. I opened the door and saw a quilt and everything and he said, 'What's the time? What's the day? What's the month?' I was so terrified. I thought, 'Oh Lord'. Then he left and there were needles on the stairs. The druggies don't really live in these flats. They're not from this area. They live elsewhere and come and gather here. It's like the kids".

"This block is now full of outsiders"

The worst incident happened late one night: "The baby was ill, it was about 10pm. We called the ambulance and went downstairs to wait. Then a man came rushing towards us, gushing blood from a stab wound. He had come to deliver a take-away and the woman he was delivering to said she hadn't ordered anything. Two boys came up and stabbed him so the ambulance that had been called for my baby took everyone to the hospital at the same time. I could see the bone in his arm. This happened next to the lifts on the ground floor. Boys are always standing by the lift. I'm not saying they did the stabbing".

At our third visit, Cynthia felt that her block had become very unsettled: "I've lived here 12 years and I only talk to the ones that have been here a while. Funnily enough this block is now full of outsiders. You can hardly count an English person in the block, apart from the two old ladies on the third and fourth floor. I met them here when I moved in. They are the ones that really made me feel welcome".

"Of course when I moved here I was a single parent and they used to see me struggling going to work and coming in. This one old lady used to come by and say 'I could hear the baby crying, are you alright? If you need any help, drop her by and go'. Now the rest of the people, I don't know half of them. I've seen new families, Asian, Turkish, a lot of Turkish people. The two old ladies are very involved, they're white, long-term residents, very friendly. When the lift is broken, they always know when it is going to be fixed. When I left my keys in my door, they saw them and kept them for me 'til I came home".

Cynthia tried to explain her attitude to white people: "I get on better with an English person than someone from Sierra Leone because I've lived here longer. I feel more comfortable and relaxed talking to somebody like you, rather than my own. I wouldn't let them know my business". Yet Cynthia relied a lot on relatives and neighbours: "I'm lucky with my neighbour who speaks the same language as me. One good thing is neighbours nearby".

"We decided not to move"

By our fifth visit, things were looking up in Cynthia's block: "Better, definitely. We've had central heating put in. The environment looks cleaner. They've got more after-school clubs for children. The improvements are not on our side of the estate yet, but it's coming towards us. Now we have things down here, that's good. They've improved the local environment a lot. They have wardens now. With graffiti and vandalism, it's got much better. The area looks cleaner, the rubbish has got better". However, big social problems remained: "The social life hasn't got better. Crime has got worse. I've seen a lot round here. A young boy hung himself in the next building. The police found a body in a bin a few months ago". At least the police were targeting the area, following all the violence: "I see more police around the shops, that's where all the trouble is".

Cynthia felt more optimistic, now the efforts to improve the neighbourhood had started to work. Previously she had thought "those renovations wouldn't work in this block because it's more open. You couldn't have an intercom system like the other block. It would all end up with graffiti. Even the doormats get stolen". But at our last visit, Cynthia said: "They've done the new front door and a new intercom at the entrance that stops the kids coming in. The lifts are cleaner".

Cynthia's outlook changed completely as a result of changes in management: "We're getting our money's worth. When we need repairs, they come right away. They gave us an incentive to move, some money to move us on, but we decided not to. The rubbish is now picked up every day. Before you just couldn't enter the lifts because they were in such a poor state. So I used to struggle up the stairs. The lifts are a bit cleaner now, although people still wee in them once in a while. But they're doing a lot to the buildings".

"They're listening to everyone"

Cynthia was also more hopeful about community involvement: "Community spirit, I think that's the way you get your voice heard, as a group rather than an individual. I'm talking to you and I don't know how far that will get all these problems. As an individual I don't think you can get far". Involvement helped: "Generally they're involving tenants more, and now everybody goes along: families, refugees, they're listening to everyone. It's made a difference. We're all in on the community meetings. It used to be only senior citizens, only white".

Social exclusion for Cynthia was not about her family or her difficulties as a parent, but about the place where she had to raise her children, and its reputation: "I didn't realise this area is so cut off. You don't get anywhere if you come from here". But she decided not to move, because of the positive changes under way.

Community involvement can help shape provision

Cynthia advocates both public intervention to improve conditions and a stronger community voice to shape interventions because she sees things improve when the wider city responds to local need. She recognises the efforts of teachers and housing managers, but she knows that the contribution of parents is critical. She worries how little time she herself has, even to give to her own children, let alone helping the "packs" of young people that threaten community safety. Cynthia has direct experience of these "packs". Her older daughter is entering her teenage years and she fears for her safety. But she tries to see the problem in terms of what young people need, rather than how much harm they do – even though in her eyes they do many bad things. She believes in sorting out problems rather than letting them overwhelm you.

Provision for young people in the neighbourhoods is a top parental priority but responsibility for meeting their needs lies between parents, community, voluntary initiative and public services. Young people need help to cross safely between home, the spaces in their neighbourhoods and the independent activities that will lead to adulthood. But matching disoriented youth in difficult areas to the wider opportunities requires intensive handholding that is simply not on offer to most young people in these areas.[7] Certainly government 'frameworks' and 'strategies' for youth are little more than fine words, unless something changes on the ground.

Local parental involvement and direct engagement with young people are key, but youth initiatives rely on secure funding, as experimental youth projects often win headlines, but do not make up the shortfall of regular after-school provision, for which funding has steeply declined. Mothers reported on youth club closures or restricted activities and hours, borne out by evidence from Sport England.[8] At the same time, organised youth activities tend to attract more purposeful young people and have difficulty catering for more alienated youth.[9] The distance between failing young people and the rest of the community is wide. Only rarely does a youth activity galvanise the children who 'hang out' on the street.

Limited resources are a major constraint on provision. More affluent areas support sports clubs, dancing classes, music lessons, discos, outings, expeditions, summer camps and bus and train fares to events, because parents can pay for them. In the areas where our families live, community facilities are far more expensive relative to incomes. It costs about as much to swim, with far less available cash, in the East End as in Kensington. And you are less likely to find an ice rink, cinema, adventure playground, paddling pool or supervised park. As a result, young people have more time on their hands and fewer places they can go.[10] Their 'idling around' the area helps to create an atmosphere of disorder and mothers blame this on the lack of structured activity as well as on parents. Youth provision could fill the gap between the capacity of families to control what happens to their young and their need for space and adventure. Supervision needs to be combined with alluring but safe activity.

Trouble is almost inevitable when children experience poor schooling, a harsh environment, negative peer pressure and shortage of positive role models. Lack of skills, lack of money for the 'extras' that link young people in, lack of fares to go elsewhere, lack of youth-oriented spaces, push them 'under their hoods' – symbolically at the very edge of society.[11] Annie, an involved parent, concludes in Chapter Two: "There's no future for the children here". Yet the wider world, where youth are bound, can seem a frustratingly unreachable destination.

The lack of resources for young people applies equally to more general services that the average person takes for granted – a range of shops, banks, cafes, cleaners as well as social facilities and other services. Delilah, in Chapter Four, compared her area with West London, asking "Why can't we have half of what they have?"

The lack of local spending power keeps neighbourhoods poor and therefore deters other people with more resources from moving in. This vicious circle depresses families. It is why some families, like Flowella's or Annie's, support the building of unaffordable housing in their areas – just to create a better climate for investment in local services. Creating more mixed communities within existing areas without displacing existing communities would help these problems.[12]

One powerful response is local self-help. Many of the most powerful movements to tackle disadvantage begin with community self-help, reflecting a form of collective altruism, which in turn evokes public concern.[13] Local community effort galvanises the support of the wider society as it demonstrates self-reliance and reciprocal relations as well as reinforcing the urgency of problems. Phoebe, in Chapter Three, sees a direct connection between local-scale community action and wider change, and many mothers see community involvement as a key to progress. Yet too often clumsy government interventions crush the fragile efforts of local residents.

Involved parents are frustrated by the difficulty of welding together structures of intervention and local needs. This happened in two New Deal for Communities areas in spite of major efforts to involve local people. A community representative and father summed up the difficulty, saying "communities are chaotic systems" (Adam). In spite of this difficulty in harmonising local needs and wider interventions, the cooperative instinct at least in part explains why people in low-income areas with little spare capacity find ways of accommodating and helping each other.

Overriding visible ethnic tensions and resource conflicts, this mutual aid often crosses ethnic lines, as Cynthia's story showed. The old ladies of Cynthia's block took on a community role and watched for problems with entrances and lifts. Frequent breakdown menaced Cynthia's security and undermined her precarious confidence, but white older neighbours proved her strongest allies.

The threat of urban breakdown is countered by local services that both older residents and families need, regardless of origin. Lift breakdowns need not only local vigilance but external intervention to fix technical problems. So external services need to tap community knowledge and communities need both outside help and local organisation. The local community cannot fix everything on its own. Kamal, in our next story, thinks a lot about how communities hold together, what young people need, how public bodies respond, what makes areas decline and improve, how his own community can become more open, better serviced, more mixed and integrated.

Kamal's story – communities have untapped assets

Kamal, his wife and their two young children live in a three-bedroomed, inner-city terraced house in a pleasant street in the North, but they're uncomfortably near a busy main road, which bothers Kamal.

Kamal played a big role in childcare, as he was unemployed throughout our visits. His baby son cried when he went out. He remembered as a child in Pakistan, roaming freely while his father went off to the fields. Here he "can't let the children out of my sight". His wife never went to school, except the Mosque school. She did not speak much English and did not join in the interviews, although she was often around.

Kamal had many worries about the area although he was clearly attached to the community and very involved: "It's a trouble spot. The shop over the road, the teenagers hang around it, which isn't a problem in itself. It's when the drug dealers come. It's a safe spot for them because it's a cul-de-sac. I say to the shop owner that people need to feel more confident going to the shops, especially families and children". Drug dealing was a big problem and Kamal had personal experience: "A year ago I was attacked outside the shop by drug dealers. I called the police and they came out. There's just lots happening in the area, crime, but they got caught and got 10 years. After that it dispersed".

"It avoids being a ghetto"

At our first visit, Kamal worried about his house losing value: "The homes have gone down in price in this area. I'm looking at half the price I would get [nearby]. This house was £47-53,000 in 1988, £45,000 in 1990, and in 1999 it's valued at £38,000". However, three visits later, Kamal saw real progress: "The area has changed, I think. It's going to turn full circle. In the 19th century, professionals owned these houses and I think those types of people will come back.... The conditions were worse before. I was thinking of moving from this house but staying in the area, now we might stick it out and apply for an improvement grant. We need double glazing because of the noise of trucks outside the shop".

By our fourth visit, Kamal's "little patch" was really starting to improve: "We're going to get a facelift on our road next.... If they improve the houses on the outside and confidence builds up and other things get done, prices will go up". Kamal saw housing as key to making the area work: "Communities change if housing is improved. The housing image is a big problem". He liked the idea of the area becoming more socially mixed. "Image-wise, the facelift scheme has changed the area: new home owners, a mixture of young families and professionals and social workers and council employees. There's more white people coming round here to use the shop. It feels more comfortable. It's good. It shows that the image has changed and is breaking down. The media portray the area badly. But it avoids being a ghetto".

Kamal was pessimistic about crime, in spite of physical regeneration: "They'll never fully resolve the problems of drugs, but you can tackle them. The police don't help by telling people not to buy here. Hearing that made me want to stay in the area but it made a lot of other people move out". Marissa too had been told by estate agents not to move there. Kamal suspected: "It suits the police and those in power because it then concentrates the drugs and crime in this area and then it's not in their backyard. I didn't want to move out because of the image. What I wanted to do was stand my ground and stick with it so people might see me and say it's worth living in the area."

"They're not the heartbeat of the community"

By the fifth visit, police had cracked down on crime, but with perverse consequences for Kamal's family: "The police are in cars so they aren't doing a lot. It would be better on foot. Community policing is not visible. I used to work with them, so I was shocked when they raided my house. I did have confidence in them. They apologised but not officially. So now I'm suing them via a solicitor". Kamal was very upset by this incident. It felt like a personal affront after all his efforts to contain drug dealing in his street. He never recovered his confidence in the police or in public authorities.

Kamal had been a youth worker and was actively engaged in many local projects. He had lost his job during cutbacks in youth work: "When I was made redundant, it was very unfair, like deliberate dismissal. You've got to start all over again. I've seen all the youth work being disbanded and now we youth workers feel we're wasting our time as a profession. It's been deprofessionalised and anyone can do it. I'm glad I'm out of it now". The club he had worked in attracted lots of young Asians, who were now causing trouble hanging around on the streets.

Kamal felt that professionals who made most decisions were not in close touch with the neighbourhood: "These people in middle-class occupations sit there and say, 'Isn't it terrible that lower-class people have to live with this'. They need to analyse it properly. They don't have an understanding of the area. They need more training. The problem is that the people giving directions do not do the work. They're not the heartbeat of the community. We, the ordinary residents, never get recognised. It's people who shout loudest". Kamal assumed that white professionals relied too much on self-appointed religious spokespeople, especially within Islamic minorities, "White people listen to them".

Kamal saw the community as weak: "I think campaign days are over. It's meetings for meetings' sake. You've got to be more strategic. You've got to understand politically what you're doing. If you don't tailor what you do to the government, they won't fund you. There are different groups in the area. Some people are saying we don't get services because we live here. We should be treated the same".

"If the council don't demolish, it'll be more attractive"

Kamal wanted to promote local integration: "I think there's harmony. It's multicultural. The only way to fight racism is on the ground. If you live somewhere else you don't know. It's getting better but a bit slow". Simple things could be done: "Some bits are very bad but there are lots of things they could do without massive investment. It's maintenance that's the problem. A car was dumped over the road. I had to put pressure on the council to trim the trees outside. I have to ring them up and complain". Kamal saw opportunities gradually opening up: "We need businesses. Up the hill lots of shops were boarded up but now they've opened. There's no bank or petrol station in the area but it's quite near to the city and the transport is good. We need to get more investment in the area. Recently a shop selling clothes opened down the road. It's multiracial, cosmopolitan. Years ago people wanted to move to other areas. Now professionals are starting to move in. If the council keeps Cliff Street and Anne Street up and don't demolish, it'll be more attractive".

Kamal had many ideas about how to improve the area: "If you go to the main park they've got a cafe and a football pitch and tea and coffee and a little hut. They have other activities too like fairs. We could do with that down at our park and save on petrol and be appreciating the area and attracting people from outside". Kamal recognised the neighbourhood's assets: "The area's therapeutic with all the greenery. You don't want to be somewhere depressing and oppressive. I think it's become more environmentally friendly as well and I don't always use the car. And it's got history. It goes back to the Romans".

On the other hand there were serious environmental problems: "There's a lot of pollution. It's the landfill site that causes pollution and illnesses. But it hasn't been proved". The city incinerator was well known for its emissions and Kamal had a constant bad throat and often coughs. He worried about cars too, particularly "safety-wise with the traffic, we can't let the children out of sight because of maniac drivers and because of abductions. We need road bumps".

"They're draconian"

Throughout our visits, Kamal was very sensitive about the council since he lost his job: "The social put me on training but it was a waste of time, so I started doing my own. I've taken a job with a community development centre because in the council it just depends if your face fits. The ethos in the council has changed since the elections and they want too much control over you. In the voluntary sector that's not quite so much the case. The job I'm doing will involve mediation". This job failed to materialise, but Kamal was involved in many groups: "I'm a school governor at the primary school and I'm involved in the City Forum. I was in the Asian Youth Movement". He was also a devout Muslim.

Kamal criticised heavy-handed, insensitive council interventions: "When a tragedy occurs, action happens. We're scared of the council taking action because they're draconian". He preferred to work outside the council after his youth work experience because its bureaucracy required narrow conformity. He was even critical of Sure Start, unlike most parents: "Sure Start, they're just repeating local authority speak". But Kamal had high praise for the city's action against racial intolerance: "Here it's OK compared to Burnley where three BNP [British National Party] were elected. There's been a lot of anti-racist work and local people have taken it on. We're lucky we have skinheads who are anti-racists".

Kamal wanted his children to identify with their own culture: "People shouldn't forgo their own identify. I think generally the refugee issue is topical and it's horrendous what papers like the *Sun* say about it. It's what white people here in this area say about asylum seekers". He wanted different communities to be on an equal footing: "When my daughter was talking, I got the impression the teachers were patronising to ethnic minorities. It's important for teachers to be positive about the culture she comes from. Originally parents had problems with teachers not teaching about Muslim cultural events. Now people are feeling positive about the school and the new head is good".

Kamal thought that schools were trying to respond: "There was a problem in the school two years ago. The headline in the paper was 'Racism'. I was there. It wasn't racism, it was lack of awareness of cultural differences. The new head is better".

"We need to shout from the rooftops"

Kamal felt that social exclusion particularly affected local older, mostly white, people: "The elderly are cut off because they can't get about. Some won't even open their doors because they're so scared. It's caused by drugs, crime and antisocial behaviour because the elderly on the estate and other people are scared of drug dealers. When they move the kids on, you see women and elderly come out to the shop". Kamal tried to help: "I went to the shopkeeper and said, 'Make sure the drug dealers don't hang around the shop or I'll try to get you closed down'". He hoped that "the yuppies'll move in and they'll have an impact. I don't want the youngsters outside as role models for my children. I tackle them outside the house".

Kamal wanted to involve everyone: "I think there are those who are excluded and want to be heard, but I think some people don't want to be included. Business people have their own lifestyle. They don't want to be included, 'til the council won't give them planning permission". Parents' voices were often not heard because of childcare problems: "A lot of people come to meetings with no families so kids' issues are not dealt with. We need to shout from the rooftops but all the time morale is low. I couldn't go to the parents' evening last time but I would bring things up if they weren't doing their job properly. I'd be the first in there speaking out".

Kamal worried about the future: "My children will meet all the obstacles, similar to myself. I just hope they'll challenge them and be more confident than I was". He wanted to help young people build confidence: "Confidence can come from sport. You have to prove yourself in football and cricket. I've done work in the sports ground, combating racism in football. You can help understanding". He was proud of his children: "The way I see my kids studying to make positive things happen, not negative things, they're picking up that way of doing things".

"You can't measure it"

Kamal was a community man; he tried to be open: "In society people keep themselves to themselves, but if you open up, people are very friendly. We treat the neighbours with respect". However, his neighbours were difficult: "Our neighbour's in dispute with my wife over the washing line. It's bad. To be honest we don't know the people next door and they work all the time. We don't mix". On our second visit, Kamal explained their occasional desire to leave: "We can't cope with too many people around. We want somewhere quieter". This contradicted his deep commitment to the local community.

By our fifth visit, Kamal wanted to do more: "I'm restricted because of the family. Otherwise I'd be very heavily involved. I have to be selective. But some of my ideas are coming to fruition. People like me have the involvement from living in the area. I don't have motivations to get a job through it. I don't want to work in the area". Kamal received a grant to set up a local radio station. "In 2000, Radio Islam asked me to get involved in a radio station for the area. It's an interest and expertise of mine, something the area needs." He was proud of this breakthrough. At our last visit he announced: "We've got the money for the community radio station". He was also involved in the local newspaper. But he was depressed that he was still not working. Various possibilities fell through. "I don't think New Deal will help me but I hope young people will benefit."

Kamal believed that community spirit was the wellspring for the future of the area: "If community spirit is low and demoralised there's no confidence and people won't move in". But he believed: "There's a sense of community and inclusiveness. It's good for our well-being to feel you're part of something. It pulls people together and benefits the area. You can't measure it, but you can feel it".

Making resources work harder for communities

Parents have an innate desire to be involved because the only way they can shape their children's future is by shaping their environment. Being involved also reflects the human drive to solve problems and in these areas it is hard to ignore problems. Parents can achieve more if they live in harmony with other families; they only survive if they can find community links. The exchange of favours and services is rooted deep in universal cultural patterns, because it ensures that in times of need the bonds of sharing are stronger than the drive for autonomy.[14] Because we all at different times are aware of this need to be part of something bigger than our individual selves, most people feel some impulse to help out. We cannot be sure when we will need help, so mutual aid survives in an individualised world.

Some individuals, like Kamal, go to extraordinary lengths to help others in the community. Kamal was a youth worker in the neighbourhood until the service was cut back, and is determined to remain active. Kamal's involvement at so many different levels is unusual. As a father and neighbour, he cares about everyone – children, young people, neighbours, older people, even gentrifiers. This takes him into contact with the local shopkeeper, who might encourage drugs by providing a local gathering point; the local youth, who might intimidate older white residents because they gather in groups and offer a bad example to his children; the older people themselves, who may become isolated and for whom he feels a sense of responsibility; his children's school, where he is a governor and where he sees many cultural and social tensions played out; the youth service, including local sports provision, which he sees as vital but inadequate; the regeneration organisations, like New Deal for Communities, which renew the area and attract a wider mix of residents; and the local media, which can help or harm community relations.

City government is not close enough to particular problems to recognise the often invisible linkages, the informal checks and balances within communities. At the same time, our stories make it clear that without wider support many families simply would not manage and without exception families rely on external services and interventions. But they want to shape what happens more closely to their priorities. They want less heavy-handed, lower-scale, often less costly but more continuous actions and more care, more sensitivity to community needs and more community-level supports. Kamal recognises the central role of the council, but he realises that officials can be too heavy-handed. They are there to help, but they should operate through local channels on a scale that is tuned to local needs. Other parents articulate similar views; council-provided leisure centres illustrate the right action at the wrong scale:

> "It's no good having a smart sports centre if it's too expensive to use." (Ellie)

The neighbourhood scale is very different from the city scale.[15] Interventions in poor urban areas often ignore local priorities because decision makers and funders live far from local conditions. Often they do not even live within the city whose problems they are employed to tackle, as Kamal points out. Their distance makes them poorly tuned to the immediate environments facing low-income families, even if they themselves might have experienced those problems at some earlier stage. Jane Jacobs highlighted this disconnection.[16] So the structures of the wider city are generally governed and controlled by people who have a weak identification with its poorest neighbourhoods, responding to superficial and statistically measurable conditions, passing over the fine grain of local problems. This means that programmes to help poor areas are more attuned to wider programme requirements than to community priorities.

Regeneration should connect parents into the wider community by making conditions closer to the average, since investment gives a powerful signal that the area is of value and that family lives and children matter. Yet in two of our areas in East London and in the Northern inner city, poorer, less "valued" families feel threatened by it. In contrast, New Deal for Communities and Sure Start have a generally positive reputation among parents because they make parents feel more valued, supported and confident about the future. Some parents are involved in these special programmes targeted at their areas; some secure work and training through them; and most feel the interventions bring some real benefits. It would be relatively easy to secure the much bigger benefit of anchoring, stabilising and supporting local communities.

As society becomes more affluent and more consumption-oriented, poorer neighbourhoods are inevitably left behind unless extra investment equalises poor conditions. Area improvements, in contrast to area demolition, help to anchor communities, reducing turnover, maintaining some stability in local schools and nurseries and tackling visible problems, as Cynthia's story showed. While many families want to move because of immediate housing and area problems, fewer want to move away from the areas altogether. As areas improve due to public interventions, families like Kamal's hope they might round a corner. Kamal, Flowella and Marissa want better-off people to find ways of living alongside poorer people without displacing them, injecting new resources into the areas. But many parents just see continuing inequality, displacement and localised divisions.

The distance between 'urban managers' and citizens can be narrowed through local delivery in schools, health centres and voluntary organisations. Sometimes new local vehicles such as neighbourhood management organisations need to be created.[17] Schools work directly with parents to try and create a sense of community within the orbit of the classroom. Sure Start is an unusual move in the direction of community involvement, with a highly local, parent-friendly approach to child provision. Its application to children's centres may weaken its community purpose.

Driven by the Treasury, Sure Start adopted a novel approach, working directly on a small scale with vulnerable young mothers.[18] It is a real breakthrough in approach, as Luiza and several other mothers explained; we learned about many unquantifiable benefits through our families' experiences. Louise, in the next story, puts it simply:

> "We feel better as parents."

The local approach could be extended much further – to regeneration, policing and neighbourhood environments. [19] Parents would value such immediate efforts.

As our society ages and households get smaller, we become less family- and child-centred. Thus, remote decisions by those in charge about parks and play areas, supervision and spending priorities, often puzzle mothers. The local park in Lesley's area used to have a park keeper and a swimming pool. Now the pool's closed and the park is unsupervised; so it has become underused and frightening. This leads policy makers to sell it off and build on the land, in the mistaken view that 'no one uses it so no one wants it'.[20] It makes the area less popular to families. Neglected open spaces are being lost throughout our areas and all over cities. Zoe, Lesley and Olivia highlighted the loss of open spaces through clumsy decision making and a misunderstanding of community needs.

Community involvement alone cannot close the gap. More inputs are needed. The education and skill level of the local population is lower than the national and city averages and therefore demands placed on teachers, colleges and employers are higher. It is harder to teach in a school with many languages or where many children have special needs.[21] Policing is more difficult where there are many crises to respond to and many displaced young people on the streets. Social services are more stretched because more children, young people, mothers and older people need special support and care. So there is a double handicap facing residents and providers in these areas: a lower level of basic provision because of the lower resources of the area relative to its needs; and higher demand because of the greater needs and lower resources of residents.[22] Local neighbourhood managers, teachers and wardens are familiar with local problems and therefore can manage local resources more precisely. If this became a common pattern, space for children and young people, safety, supervision and repair would become higher priorities.

Our last story in this chapter underlines the vital role of public provision and community support when a family faces acute need. Louise has an outgoing attitude, and cares deeply about her immediate and extended family, her community, and other families with special problems. She is a major bridge-builder but she also believes in community control and enforcement. She could not do all she does without the help of her partner and her relatives; but her family also rely on public support because of their special needs – the health service, schools and above all Sure Start. Louise needs many lifelines, showing how families with special needs survive, how communities function and how the wider city can soften its harsh edges through local and small measures that bind people together.

Louise's story – helping hands in times of need

Louise is a young, active mother on a large Northern estate. She had had three children by the time she was 23, and had her first when she was 17. Her mother lived nearby. Her father lived on the estate and helped a lot financially and with the children, as did her sister. Her auntie also lived nearby; they were the same age and very close. By our third visit, Louise's boyfriend, the children's father, had moved in with her. His mother, to whom she referred to as 'mum-in-law', also helped with the children. In addition, Louise called on her uncle and granddad, who lived fairly nearby.

Louise's mother lived in her street at our first visit. "My mum had me at 15 and nana looked after me." Her mother now had two small children of her own: "There's my mum but she's got a three-year-old and a little baby so I don't like to bother her". Louise originally wanted to move into the street because of her mother, although they did not seem to be getting on well at our first visit. She spoke to her "as little as I can". She explained: "When I fell pregnant, I felt so alone". Both she and her mother suffered badly from postnatal depression: "When my mother had my little sister, she had depression so I watched her and there wasn't anything for her to go to 'til she was two. I didn't know of anything either". Later Louise explained: "Now there are courses here to help with English and maths. She used to get bored just claiming and now she's doing something for herself. She's getting more money for herself too". Louise was very glad about this.

Louise was very attached to her community and particularly her extended family. She said on our first visit: "My auntie's four years older. She's like a sister. I see her every week and we take it in turns to cook. My auntie helps with childcare. My granddad comes too and he cared for the kids when I miscarried". Louise relied on her relatives but wanted to be self-sufficient: "I don't want to palm them off on someone else so that I can look after someone else's kids", echoing Phoebe's views.

"I had to push myself"

Louise was very much part of where she lived. Her street was "like its own little community". Louise liked it: "Before I lived here, I lived nearby and got burgled. I wanted this street because my mum lived here and it's safe. You can leave the kids and know they'll be looked after. If any strangers come to your door while you're out, the rest of the street know and tell you when you get back. My mum just moved off the street and she hates it where she is now". Louise's feelings about the area went up and down depending on who moved there. "They're a lot younger and don't seem to care. They're drinking and playing music 'til all hours. It's the youth more than anything. The older kids bring the trouble. You walk past and get abuse. They seem to think the world owes them a favour." Louise herself was only 20!

By our second visit, Louise felt better as families with younger children had moved to the area: "New families, there are quite a lot in the street. These have younger kids, so it's nice. The children have got more kids to play with on the street so I'm happy. The kids like to play out with friends". Even when they had a troublesome neighbour, Louise said: "I didn't really want to move for the sake of the street. There was a noisy young girl and all the yobs went in and out and so the street got together and got her moved. They've said they won't move anyone under 24 into the street", which is older than Louise.

Louise was worried about the impact of working on her family: "I was going to join the childcare team but finding someone to watch these while I watch someone else's, it's not worth it. When you're a single parent, it's finding someone to care for them. You don't know who's going to look after them. To me they go to nursery sooner than they should anyway. I suppose every mother feels the same but ... it's just going too quick".

Louise tried to put her kids first: "I could go to a group and talk to anyone but it's the children. I feel their need for me is greater than my need to do courses at the moment. They'll be in school before I know it and there'll be plenty of time then". As they got older, Louise joined in more with local activities, knowing that the children were happy and well looked after.

By our second visit, Louise had taken a job in order to be more financially independent: "It's just money. Their dad helps me out a lot but I'd like to be able to provide for them rather than other people looking out for me. I've been offered a job at the school. I'm just waiting for the police check. Maybe just afternoons and Bethany can be in the nursery. I was going to get a job on nights in an old people's home. Their dad said he'd help but this is better". She now saw working as "a way of building your own life. I had to push myself to get opportunities".

"The ideas have come from parents"

Sure Start was one of the programmes that made the biggest difference to Louise and her family and by our third visit she was involved as a helper in the programme: "I was a Sure Start parent before I started to work with them. Sure Start are doing well. It's helping families but it's only for the younger ones. We have lots of groups that people can escape to. I go to groups when I'm not working, to get me out. You can take the kids. Sure Start is mostly parent-based. The ideas have come from parents and Sure Start are there to encourage and support. Parents are a lot more involved once the groups have started. They have a bigger role".

Once she was involved, Louise started helping other parents: "I work for Sure Start now, but I also access it as a parent at the parents' centre ... and through complementary health. It's enjoyable and the kids like it. It makes a difference to be in the group. It's not just mums and toddlers, it's fathers too, and swimming. I take the baby to complementary health. It's free to parents. He's had five sessions of massage and he sleeps right through now. It's nice to be able to offer things we couldn't afford otherwise. Sure Start do training for parents and care workers in caring for children, which is a good idea". Louise knew that her area needed extra help: "By living here, we're more aware of people living in poverty and with lots of debt". She sometimes helped with funding applications for special projects.

By our third visit Louise's youngest had arrived. He was severely disabled, and her second child had developed a heart problem. "She gets tired easily." Their father moved in to help and Louise kept her job at Sure Start. "We have a support worker and that helps. Their dad lives here now and he looks after the baby and gets a carer's allowance. It's hard, specially three children with two years between them. Last year he gave up work to be full-time carer and it took 'til Christmas to sort his money out. He trained as a builder for two years and then moved to a suppliers'. He was a supervisor there for 14 years."

"I just need support in general"

Louise was full of praise for the health services: "He was born early and was in intensive care and forgot to breathe. He has a rare illness. They've really been good with Nicholas, and picked up his diagnosis quickly. The physio is good too". Louise knew how lucky she was to have relatives to help, as well as her partner and health workers. "I've got Bethany poorly and the baby's got a breathing monitor. I just need support in general." Her health visitor was a lifeline: "The health visitor's there for you no matter what. I like everything she does".

Louise's experiences became a training ground: "I'm doing courses at the minute. I'm delivering a parents' course for Sure Start voluntarily and in September I start a sports course so I can be a fitness instructor. I want to work with kids in a sports role and definitely do paid work like this in future. I'm also learning disabled children's skills. I trained with Sure Start and now I help with a group which helps disabled kids to achieve the milestones of other kids". Louise's partner was getting much more involved too: "He's just joined the parent group at the primary where our girls are. He volunteers sports-wise for Sure Start and does courses on Monday and gets involved in our kids' lives more and has an input into their education and hopefully that makes a difference".

"I like to be involved"

Louise knew it was important to be part of the community: "Community spirit matters, especially when you're bringing up kids, so they have a sense of where they are. I was brought up by my nana and I knew everybody and it was safe. Mine can go next door or in the street. One way has no kids but the other way has two girls and we swap nights for them to come round or mine to go there to have tea, so we speak more than once a day. We sit and have a natter or we go shopping together. People like to get involved in things. I like to be involved. We had an anniversary party for an elderly resident. It was in the street and the whole street came and it made her day".

Louise was not sure whether she would be able to stay in her home long term: "Maybe when the kids are older, I might want to buy a place. Other than that, I wouldn't move anywhere else. It's ideal for me here. I can reach everything and things for the kids. I'm happy and they're happy so there's no reason to move". But she needed to adapt the house for her children's needs: "I'm happy with the house itself. I've got central heating and all new windows. I'm just waiting for the council to decide if we can adapt the house for the one-year-old or whether we have to move to another house. It goes to a panel. If they won't adapt the house we'll have to move". This was a big worry because "he doesn't like change ... I want to stay and would only move if I had to".

"I don't think we're listened to"

Louise could not influence basic things, yet communities only worked if local people could solve problems: "It's important because if we're living here and bringing up children here, we should have a say. I don't think we're listened to. We've been trying to get a park. The nearest park is at Meadowfield so I'm trying to get it. One is going in here and they say all the residents were informed and supported it, but I knew nothing about it. Apparently it's been approved and I was annoyed because I wasn't notified or asked to give my opinion. Half the people don't know what's going on. They even put Sure Start down as providing workers for the park and Jimmy who runs it didn't know".

Louise worried about divisions on the estate: "The council don't move them in because they get harassed. If a new family moves in, they do tend to get trouble". She wanted her children to mix with children from other backgrounds: "People get on pretty well generally. I don't want them growing up not knowing why there are different people, and different groups. There's a lot in the nursery. My little girl was a bit confused. Bethany has a friend whose dad is black and she thinks he's marvellous. I explained everybody's not the same. It's quite mixed".

"Boys and girls standing around at night"

During our second visit, Louise felt particularly down: "I don't find it safe. I don't want to bring them up here. Community spirit is not as good as it used to be. They don't seem to come out on the street and talk. Everybody seems to stick to their gardens". Louise was worried about trouble at night: "You don't get a lot of trouble on the day. It's the night-time that gets you worrying, the noise and the group of boys and girls standing around at night. Just people hanging round on the corners and the rape that happened recently".

At our third visit, we asked Louise about crime prevention: "The street itself actually does it without being a Neighbourhood Watch. We watch each others' homes". But she knew that was not enough: "You do need more police for juveniles though. There's no police back-up. The portacabin I work in was broken into and two days later they came – I gave the police two out of 10!"

By the fifth visit, Louise felt the area had improved: "I'd say there's more police because you see them and when [you] first visited you saw none". But she saw strong local resistance to 'grassing': "To have a relationship with the police, you're best not living on an estate". Olivia shared Louise's view. Louise was pleased that neighbourhood wardens were beginning to help, but was fed up that they went "before trouble starts. They finish at 5.30pm, which is when the kids start up, but they do chase up problems like repairs".

"It's good if they modernise them rather than knock them down"

There were major local environmental problems in the area: "Rubbish in the area is atrocious. They don't always take it. I'm sick of cleaning up the mess. It's serious. Vandalism is on the increase. There's been an increase in dumped cars. Windows are smashed and so are bus shelters". Bus shelters were a favourite target in all the areas.

Louise worried about supervision: "Parks are not safe to use. The bigger kids do use them. They should be cleaner. There's glass and it's quite a trek. We thought there was going to be one on the grass area but nothing's happened. It would be a good idea because there's lots of young ones in this area. We don't use the parks at all. We go further. During school holidays it's noisy. Just a lot of mischievous kids. They do a play scheme but I don't think a lot of kids like it. We're lucky because the 'mums and tots' still run. My auntie runs it but apart from that, there's not a lot on".

Louise did not like demolition and her sister was badly affected by it: "I've heard they're knocking a few down and doing the ones left empty up a bit. My sister got given one of the modernised flats opposite the shop and now they're knocking them down. They'd just decorated and now they're going to have to start again when they would've liked to stay here. It's good if they modernise them rather than knock them down".

By the fifth visit, Louise was seeing definite progress in the neighbourhood and her doubts had faded. In her own part of the estate, she saw more intensive management: "Council supervision is better than it was. Police pressure is still not good enough, but it probably was at its worst when I wanted to move. It's improving a lot more.... There was a car done over in the street but that was to pay back a grievance. They're moving better families into the empty houses and doing them up rather than leaving them empty. There's a children's centre for working mums. They provide it up to 6pm and give them their tea. I don't use it but I might in the future". Louise noticed how the new estate management company was tightening things up and a lot of problems were being tackled: "The council are kicking them into touch, the bad ones. They're sorting out gardens and not leaving houses boarded up. And there's a special team that deals with juveniles, then there's Sure Start and the council itself".

"It's a good, nice street, a safe environment"

Louise coped with severe health problems, and helped others thanks to multiple supports: "The groups make a big difference. The group has helped me to understand my son's illness because initially it was a hard illness to deal with. It's helpful to talk to others experiencing it and support each other. Now I coordinate the complementary health clinic at Sure Start and do outreach work – visiting families with disabled kids, offering them support – and when I come home, my partner's cooked tea and put the clean wash away. Then I spend an hour with the kids, then put them to bed and sometimes I go for a cuppa with one or two friends to chill out and go to bed. It's a good, nice street, a safe environment".

Louise's story shows why public intervention needs to work alongside community networks and self-help. Wider problems, such as the racial separation that Louise observes, or the demolition plans that disrupted her sister's life, or the lack of a useable park and potentially the inability to adapt her council house for a disabled child, undermine her confidence, in spite of a supportive family and community.

Poorer areas are hard to manage and are cut off from the mainstream by the intensity of their problems, as Louise, Kamal, Cynthia and Lesley have all explained in different ways in this chapter. Staff shortages and high turnover reflect the management problems of difficult areas. Louise's experiences of Sure Start, the police and the area renovation, demonstrate that more local action generates more local confidence, albeit the resources need to come from the wider city. Locally focused, local-scale ongoing action more closely matches the needs of families than large-scale systems or one-off interventions alone can achieve.

Cities are living organisms, made up of constantly changing communities, requiring continuous reinvestment and reintegration. The bottom layer matters as much to the functioning of the wider city as better-off communities. For poor communities drive the services of the wealthy, which in turn generate the economy of modern cities.[23] Fine-tuning responses to family priorities within the communities where they live is the price of city survival.

Notes

[1] Hall, 1999; Hunt, 2007.

[2] Reader, 2005.

[3] Power, 2004b.

[4] Home Office, 2001.

[5] Lupton, 2003a; Paskell and Power, 2005.

[6] Gladwell, 2000.

[7] Holman, 2001; Sport England, 1999, 2003; DfES, 2005.

[8] Sport England, 2003.

[9] SEU, 2000.

[10] Farrington and Loeber, 1998; Sport England, 1999, 2003; Paskell, 2004.

[11] *The Guardian*, 2005; *The Observer*, 2005.

[12] ODPM, 2003b, p 14; Strategy Unit, 2005.

[13] Garrow, 1986; Thompson, 1990; Richardson, E. (forthcoming).

[14] Briggs, 1976.

[15] Healy, 2007.

[16] Jacobs, 1970; Power and Houghton, 2007.

[17] Birmingham City Council, 2003; DCLG, 2006.

[18] HM Treasury, 2000.

[19] ODPM, 2002.

[20] Groundwork, 2005.

[21] Lupton, 2003a.

[22] Power, 1992.

[23] Jacobs, 1970.

EIGHT

Conclusion – cities need families

Families are at the centre of the way cities work, an essential tier in all societies. If cities cannot support families then cities will eventually fail. Family life helps the social evolution of cities by strengthening social networks, or what families call 'community spirit'. How the poorest areas and their families fare within the wider city tells us a lot about the social health and overall progress of the city because these communities expose the most pressing social changes that affect everyone – the structure and function of families, the impact of rapid immigration in cities, the changing base of work. This concluding chapter draws together evidence from the families in the study:

- that disadvantaged neighbourhoods make family life difficult;
- that in order to survive families build local community links;
- that families make cities more humane; and
- that cities work better when they support family life.

In other words, families generate much of the social capital on which society as a whole flourishes.[1]

Cities comprise many different kinds of neighbourhood, which interlock with each other. Within neighbourhoods the most basic unit, the family, forms the smallest but most vital building block of the most complex of human social organisms, the city itself. Families tell us why cities can seem ungovernable, why community remains so important, what would make cities more integrated, fairer and therefore more humane.

It is helpful to think of the city as a living organism for two reasons. First, it is made up of people, anchored together by a 'sense of place', but changing, learning and shaping their environment. Second, people do not live as islands in cities that are strongly collective structures; therefore cities evolve as social organisms.[2] So if cities are living organisms in their social dynamics, families with children constantly recreate that social vitality from the bottom up, while incomers also do this from the outside in. All human society, including urban society, needs and therefore creates families, so families are crucial to the continuation of the city. Cities therefore thrive if families thrive within them. The family stories in this book reveal the scale of difficulty facing families in difficult areas.

The need for low-cost neighbourhoods

Modern economies have come to depend more and more on cities, but cities create an intense hierarchy of needs and neighbourhoods, based on wealth, skill and scarcity. All kinds of neighbourhoods are necessary to the survival of cities, and poorer areas also provide homes for low-paid workers. Only with low-cost neighbourhoods can low-income families survive in the city. Their need to survive at a bare minimum drives the conditions of low-income areas that attract the most marginal, least connected people into them, often the casualties of urban change and competition.

Without low-paid workers and a fluid labour supply, city economies do not work, grow and create profit.[3] Residents of poor neighbourhoods contribute disproportionately to the basic services of the city, while receiving far below average in return. Low wages reflect the ability of society to attract disadvantaged people from many different places to service jobs in the city. Health, education, transport, retail and entertainment would grind to a halt without such neighbourhoods and their families make up a large part of the workforce.[4]

As the local supply of cheap labour runs short and becomes expensive through the more general rise in standards, so new, cheaper labour is imported, hence the increase in minority ethnic communities and the replenishment of poorer neighbourhoods from underneath and outside by migrants, who, in turn, create families within the areas where they settle. It is this dynamic that our book looks at through the eyes mainly of mothers – a relatively unrecorded perspective on cities, neighbourhoods and communities. We have argued that without families, cities simply would not work, since cities are a human construct and human society hinges on well-functioning families. This implies protection for children, opportunities for their development and support for their families so that families can survive and build community relations among diverse people, many of whom are initially strangers. If cities protect and support families, then the economic backbone of cities, the service workforce, can help create harmonious conditions. If not, disorder will result. This is costly to cities.[5]

Cities and neighbourhoods

Because poorer neighbourhoods provide the essential underpinning for the economy of cities through their low-cost labour, city governments have long accepted responsibility for their management. If the city as a whole fails to respond to family needs that arise from their vital economic and social role, and if community relations disintegrate because of limited resources, then the spillover effects on the city as a whole can be very damaging.[6]

Cities often seem harsh, particularly to families. There is more crime, violence, disorder, dirt and human distress than in society as a whole – hence the popularity and continuing sprawl of suburbs.[7] Cities of themselves generate intense problems but they also concentrate problems in the poorest neighbourhoods, where conditions can become almost unmanageable.[8] The bare statistics show a huge gap between national, city and poor area conditions.[9]

We knew from the outset that our families were coping with far worse problems than average.[10] But witnessing the resilience of families within the 'underlayers' of neighbourhood life opens up a new world. For neighbourhoods per se are only the starting point. Neighbourhoods need to become communities, as parents socialise their children within these neighbourhoods, and long-standing residents have to share common spaces with newcomers. Interventions and supports often do not match the social imperatives of fragile communities – familiarity, security and opportunity.

The neighbourhoods where our 'city survivors' live are not typical; they are extreme in their condition and their concentration of problems, but they are typical of poorer areas within cities across Europe.[11] Families we talked to generally express caring, responsible, coping and sensitive attitudes towards others; they are hard working, active and deeply committed to their children. They have fewer resources and cope with far worse pressures than average, but they do, on the whole, cope because they are driven by the survival instinct. So they rely on non-monetary resources of family, community and city infrastructure in order to survive. Parents are shaped by cities in their search for progress. Generally they come before they form families, or are simply 'born and bred' in the city, so a dynamic relationship exists between families and cities; each needs the other and as social organisms at opposite ends of the scale, both cities and families prove adaptable and socially resilient, in spite of immense pressures.

Cities change

Cities worldwide are in constant transition, shaped by the wide forces we have observed through the lens of parents, possibly their closest observers. Urban neighbourhoods make up 80% of all built-up areas, yet neighbourhoods such as we describe in this book comprise only 5%; however, in major cities they comprise a third of all neighbourhoods.[12] Neighbourhood decline is a dominant urban problem. Some have argued that if it was not for the inflow of migrants into urban areas, cities themselves would have continued their rapid decline.[13] Even so, the repopulation of urban neighbourhoods with incomers adds to management demands, generates conflict over resources and weakens traditional social controls, adding to the pressure on unstable communities. The management of the collective environment of cities and their services is the precondition of family survival.[14]

Urban neighbourhoods have forever been in constant flux, forever been replenished by incomers, as existing inhabitants gain enough security and status to move somewhere better – usually outwards. So the poorest neighbourhoods comprise too many incomers and too many who want to move out. The demands created by the sifting and churning of people cannot be managed or orchestrated solely by the local community, in spite of its impact on local lives and its central role in the urban economy, because city neighbourhoods are not self-standing but part of a much bigger organism or structure, driven by wider needs. In the case of the East End of London, the reach of the city is global and so are the pressures on it.

The public structures created in the 19th century in Britain provide a frame within which local change can occur, while maintaining the basic order on which community survival depends.[15] Thus, cities can be both permanently rooted and constantly changing. Policing, cleansing, paving, lighting, health and education emerged as powerful unifying services for the inhabitants of urban neighbourhoods based on the cooperative, collective commitment of 'city fathers'.[16] These basic services are still emerging in the exploding cities of the developing world, but they have become more important than ever in the decayed areas of older, long-established former industrial cities where city survivors live.[17]

In developed countries, and specifically England, core cities have been worn, battered and depleted by decades of hard use – to produce, to trade, to cast off and to start again, forever attracting new people, new supplies and new knowledge while rejecting failures and neglecting weak survivors.[18] At the tail end of a long process of decline are the troubled places where our families live. Here lower-income people are attracted by the opportunities and innovation that pull the young and the hopeful to cities, starting on the bottom rung of the ladder.

Helping families in cities

In exploring the dynamics of urban neighbourhoods from the perspective of parents, we posed the following questions:

- What impact do neighbourhood conditions have on family life? Can unpopular areas be made to work for families with children?
- Do families with children help make neighbourhoods and cities work by strengthening community ties? Can they do this in rapidly changing communities?
- What form should interventions take to counter the uncontrollable pressure on families of extremely rapid change?

In the first half of the book we explored neighbourhood life through family lenses, with a narrow focus on family survival in what seems a hostile environment. Local social links provide a main support for parents and their children. The second half of the book examines why families rely on the wider environment, adapting to new pressures and seizing new opportunities as they emerge. Families focus inwards on their children's needs, but constantly operate within the wider neighbourhood arena where wider action can help families to survive.

Our main findings fall into six main themes. These low-income ***neighbourhoods*** are deeply problematic for childrearing. Parents live with a general fear of the surrounding environment and pick up many negative signals from what they see. This makes a majority feel torn between local ties and a desire for a better environment for their children. Parents can see possible solutions to many basic problems, such as maintenance and supervision, but they are often too worried for their children and too unconfident of their own position to want to hold out for better times. In any case, they feel unable to influence outcomes because they are marginal to where power lies and decisions are made. Neighbourhoods are more unstable in London than in the North and therefore more families want to leave. This is partly the result of faster change and greater instability, which in turn generate more social problems. These neighbourhoods do not work well as they are, although from our stories it is clear that some things are improving. There remains a big question mark in the minds of parents as to whether neighbourhood improvements will help families at the bottom, like themselves.

Community is the inner layer of neighbourhoods, more local, and more family-based, once removed from the wider and more threatening city. Community is the level at which mothers see their world and their children's – a peopled world with familiar faces that smile instinctively in recognition. But the notion of community is threatened by over-rapid change and too many bad experiences. London communities encounter more difficulty than Northern areas because London is more anonymous, faster moving, experiencing bigger changes, and traditional communities are disappearing faster.[19] All parents recognise the value of micro-links at a very local scale. Friendly contact counts for almost more than anything else.

In spite of competition over housing and schooling in particular, most parents display an openness to ethnic differences and a desire to make community relations work. They argue for meeting points and activities that will bring people together and make their children feel they belong. Certain activities encourage community spirit, such as fun events, but these require organisation and on the whole parents rely on 'community organisers' to bring the people together because rapid change has undermined this wider form of self-help – urban communities are not self-contained and therefore only partially self-organising.[20] To families, community is not an outdated idea, but the real value of community lies in familiarity, which evaporates under the turmoil of changing cities. Community matters more to families in difficult areas, who see it as under threat but need it for survival more than the population as a whole. Social and urban policy too often ignores the value families place on a sense of community.

Family life itself dominates community survival because families are the lifeblood of community life. Low incomes, weak entitlement, the status of newcomers, problems of debt, breakdown or a troubled past all shape family life and therefore neighbourhood and community life. So family and neighbourhood are inextricably intertwined. The families we talked to care most about their children's happiness.

Higher education and more money, two keys to a better future, often seem out of reach, although most aspire to better conditions, a better future for their children and an ambition to better themselves. Most families lead severely constrained lives and very few go on regular holidays or more than occasional outings.

Parents often do not allow their children to do normal activities, for example playing outside. But they do value fun things they can do together, such as having picnics or just playing together at home. There is a clear need for more low-cost activities for families. The schools help but the neighbourhood itself often does not. Parents are particularly worried about youths on the streets and gang formation. Yet families, even in the face of extreme pressures, want to make things work, exerting positive influences over the immediate neighbourhood, for the sake of their children. Families articulate a clear need for more support, for more accessible facilities and activities that will help them survive.

Parents expend much of their energy on developing their children's ability to cope with the fast-changing and difficult world around them. They see their active ***parenting role*** constantly threatened from outside the homes, including the poor parenting of other families, particularly if they are from a different background. The 'rough' activities of children and young people on the street are a source of conflict between parents as they try to exert control. Some parents have difficulty handling their children, although most seem to manage most of the time. So parents are constantly restraining their children, finding it hard to relax their controls and encourage outward-looking, free-ranging activities such as street play or the use of parks.[21] Their biggest fear is that their children may not follow their home example but be enticed to join the 'street culture'. Several families spoke of intimidation by peers to achieve this. In the uncertain atmosphere of rapidly changing communities, parents rely on relatives where they can, on schools where teachers are willing, and on more general supervision by neighbours, wardens and the police. Supervision is no substitute for informal community controls, but in fast-changing neighbourhoods where parents are afraid, it becomes a prerequisite for it. Many parents feel beset with insecurities, internal troubles and external fears.

Parents value community spirit but it is elusive, ephemeral and vulnerable to turbulence. Even though it is so important to families and particularly mothers, it is undervalued by society as a whole. Yet it can be made to work with effort. People need to find common ground and shared activities, safe meeting points and cheap outlets. This is particularly true for growing children. Parents are particularly preoccupied by youth. As they grow away from their home surroundings, young people realise their low status and weak foothold in society, so sometimes they rebel.[22] They have the power to destabilise communities and mothers know this. Our families think that young people's needs are the most urgent, serious and pressing but they want the wider community to help in ways that include, rather than exclude, troubled youngsters.

Incomers seem to pose a serious threat to communities. Rented housing areas generate a lower commitment to a future in the area than predominantly owner-occupied areas. This applies to our families, four-fifths of whom are tenants. Rented housing accommodates newcomers who are strangers to the neighbourhood. This is a critical function in cities.[23] Newcomers with families have the same needs as local families and they feel isolated and rejected when they cannot join in. Their experience of neighbourhood conditions is very similar to locals'. Schools are a big unifier because children of all backgrounds come together there and incomers rely heavily on schools to improve the prospects for their children. But schools are contested places too and the language and cultural needs of foreign children in the eyes of some parents supplant their own children's needs, even while they recognise the needs of others too. Schools show worrying signs of increasing segregation because of this.[24]

Racial antagonisms influence how incomers fit in, and how children fare. Some families are bitter but most try hard to understand, show tolerance and accept the new reality of ethnic change. A big unresolved issue is entitlement from the perspective of struggling local families. The competition for a 'fair share' of a small pot creates harsh and unresolved tensions within resource-scarce neighbourhoods, as we found in all areas. Parents offer a lesson in community adaptability; but they need more channels of communication, more social links and more common activities. They also need clearer information and informal rules, particularly for children, so that there will be less strife and more social harmony between racial groups of very different origins.

We found many examples of community tolerance and acceptance, and picked up parents' real pleasure when intercommunal relations worked well. This makes the investment in bridge building all the more attractive since the societal payback will be high if communities undergoing rapid ethnic transition can work. It is not an automatic process, as urban studies from other parts of the world show.[25] But special interventions in areas with high minority ethnic concentrations run the risk of provoking a backlash from local communities who see the government responding to the needs of 'outsiders' rather than people who 'belong' – a common cause of community conflict.[26]

Urban communities need ***wider support*** within an overarching framework of authority to cope with the intense pressures of the city's most extreme problems. While poorer areas act as an invaluable labour and housing resource for the city, they also act as a receptacle for wider city problems. They therefore need at least equal services to compensate for additional burdens. Equalising conditions and opportunities has to be a goal underpinning the social structure of cities.[27]

Making neighbourhoods work

Much can be done to make these places work better: modest improvements to common areas, particularly parks with park keepers, traffic-tamed streets and play areas with wardens, cheap access to swimming pools and local cafes.[28] The loss of provision for young people and the failure to maintain and oversee mixed-use open spaces have had a devastating impact on families. These provisions could be reinstated at relatively low cost. A safer environment requires communal maintenance on a continual basis in addition to more activities for youth, more childcare and more general care for the local environment.

More thorough and continuous basic services in all built-up neighbourhoods as a day-to-day routine of neighbourhood management would overcome many problems, but only dedicated funding would allow this because there are simply too many competing demands on limited city resources.[29] The critical balance between managing urban conditions with a light enough hand to foster community engagement as the families advocate and a strong enough hand to deter transgressions of community security, such as damage to the surroundings and common spaces, requires local structures and only an accessible, local, known presence can perform such a continuous balancing act.[30] This is not only a question of resources, but also of style, familiarity and communication. Parents have many ideas, tailored to their limited purses, their local perspective and their pro-youth concerns. Their closer involvement would pay dividends. Figure 8.1 draws together suggestions for wider action gleaned from the families during our visits, showing the need for both overarching, wider support and local 'hands-on' methods.

Families and cities

Interventions often appear mediocre, slow and insensitive because the decision makers are not directly facing the problems they are trying to address, and the families, who are natural problem solvers, rarely have a voice in big decisions. As a result, their lives are bombarded by problems not of their own making, such as constant traffic, which creates dangerous streets; parks without park keepers, and neglected and therefore unuseable play areas; inadequate policing and weak enforcement against crime. As a result the assets of these areas are undervalued.

Yet families cling to their local area because it is what they know, where things are familiar – "the devil you know", as one mother put it. At least bare survival is cheaper and over time local links develop. So from a family perspective, these areas are valuable, even though many mothers feel isolated, and all recognise the stigma the city as a whole attaches to their homes. To renew these areas without displacing people in them, as is happening currently in all the four areas in the present study, requires recognition of the value of community; more active programmes of integration using schools and housing as vehicles; and more opportunities

Figure 8.1: Family views as to how to tackle local problems through city interventions

Neighbourhoods	• Organising neighbourhood and housing management to tackle local problems • Developing local action plans • Maintaining streets • Introducing wardens and local policing
Community	• Local involvement – community development • Fun events – multiracial focus • Social spaces – play areas • Extra help for school outreach to families • Continuing support for Sure Start • Brokering local conditions with communities
Family	• Helping families stay near each other • Tackling housing access on a transparent basis • Offering family support through health centres • Reinstating health visitors and giving them more training • Making neighbourhoods safer and more family friendly • Supervising play areas and green spaces
Parenting	• Offering clearer parenting advice • Supporting parenting groups along the lines of Sure Start • Giving local schools a wider remit to support parents • Making local facilities low cost for local children • Providing open space within five minutes' walk of every home • Ensuring strong adult supervision, for example on estates, in stairwells • Providing for young people and involving parents where possible
Incomers and locals	• Using health visitors to make contact • Encouraging school leadership on integration • Supporting white as well as minority ethnic families • Prioritising shared meeting places • Giving positive signals to parents • Organising social provision that breaks down barriers
Support	• Delivering services locally • Brokering needs locally • Encouraging community roles and representation • Bringing frontline staff to ground level • Reinstating and expanding the role of local caretakers, park keepers and street wardens • Listening to local families

Source: Interviews with 200 parents, 1998-2006

for young people, reducing the hostility they feel to the wider society. These neighbourhoods do not need to be so distinct from the wider city.[31]

There is much that the wider city can do to help, building on a basic sense of justice and need for these areas. Local schools offer a tried and tested model of neighbourhood-based approaches. Schools have universal support since they plainly exist for the societal good and they help most families, by developing skills, helping most young people become productive and keeping them busy. At the same time, by secondary level, schools often lose their connection with local communities. The basic educational gap in poorer areas becomes wider as a result.[32]

Health likewise has universal backing because of the wider costs of ignoring health risks. Local doctors' surgeries and health centres are among the few local bases within which different residents of all ages and backgrounds come together, although the illegal status of a few families in the present study meant that they could not register their children for local healthcare. The power of doctors, nurses and health visitors to contribute to local well-being at a personal and social level could be far more widely used.[33]

Other social provision – libraries, sports centres, repairs, security, public transport and open spaces – are being modernised to become more private, more expensive, more inaccessible to low-income families.[34] Services that are not well used because they are not well run or not affordable then disappear from poor communities. Our families clamour for accessible supervised parks, cheap swimming pools and daily youth facilities but need and access are not synonymous. As society becomes richer, standards rise and the cost of provision mounts, so people at the bottom, particularly families, enjoy a new form of exclusion – from the public realm that most people take for granted.

Regeneration or bridge building

Any attempt at wholesale regeneration needs to measure the damage to families. The lucrative development gains offered by cleared sites near the centre of cities undermine the positive need to hold on to families and build on the links that already exist between people. Displacing low-income families into other poorer areas in the name of 'regeneration' destroys urban stability; it is damaging to families caught up in it. Nor does it help schools and health services. For in the clumsy process of demolition and rebuilding, many key services are lost.[35] Nor is such radical change necessary for the renewal of run-down areas. In Britian, we thoroughly tested the 'clean sweep' approach when we first built council estates that are now so troublesome and under threat of demolition. We must not make the same mistakes again.[36]

We can instead add to and reuse the many infill spaces and buildings within existing communities in order to create more attractive, more mixed and more integrated communities. We can upgrade, extend and remodel existing properties to create more choice, more value, more mix and more space within communities, rather than drive people out.[37] Restoration and reintegration far more than clearing away affordable but low-value homes, will make families want to stay and extend the range of homes within existing communities. It is an affordable, flexible approach that revalues existing assets, upgrades existing environments and supports existing communities by adding rather than taking away.[38]

The life stories of 24 families that this book tells suggest small, unpowerful people – mainly women and children, foreigners and 'failures' – coming up against big forces of economic and social change in an inhospitable environment. Community provides a low-cost form of local support that helps them survive. But interventions are often insensitive to the needs of local families who struggle to secure their children's future. Most services, if delivered at a community scale, would provide direct bridges between local service deliverers and service users, preventing deeper social cleavages.

The 24 families suggest intensifying neighbourhood pressures on family life, driving parents to educate their children to anticipate bad experiences, bad behaviour and bad people. 'Foreigners' and 'strangers' are often blamed, and yet almost all families are happy to mix with families of different backgrounds. The inability to broker local relationships in a threatening and unprotected environment is a most pressing problem. The families' high dependence on schools as a source of support, contact and community reinforcement, over and above education, reminds us of the interdependence of welfare structures and communities, of social support and individual progress, of local institutions and families.

Our first 12 stories about neighbourhoods, communities and families expose neighbourhood problems that most people cannot imagine. Three of the families actually did move away from their area during our time of visiting them, although one was forced to by prospective demolition; another four tried to move but could not find a way; a further three were torn, feeling that for their children's sake and particularly for their safety, they should move, but family and community ties held them back; only two out of 12 families were sure that they wanted to stay in their area, one because she believed that community links in a racially mixed and disadvantaged area gave her children the experience they needed for a humane and shared future; the other, a father carer on a large and homogeneous Northern council estate, was definite that they would stay because he simply felt it was where he belonged and where he wanted to be.

Of the 12 families in the second part of *City survivors*, four wanted to leave their area, two of whom were 'outsiders' and one was driven by demolition plans. These four, all mothers, really did not like where they lived. Five were ambiguous and frequently changed their views on their areas but because of community ties and some improvements were likely to stay. The three who definitely wanted to stay had local family and community ties, felt a sense of belonging and had some confidence in the supports and improvements they saw. They were worried by local conditions and opted for 'the devil you know' in the belief that familiarity and belonging mattered more than other measures of happiness.[39] London families were more anxious to leave the area than Northern families. Overall, 11 wanted to move or had to move because of demolition; eight were ambiguous but on balance would probably stay put; only five were sure they wanted to bring their children up in the neighbourhood they lived in.

Families regenerate cities

Families play a central role in urban neighbourhoods, because they are essential to a dynamic, healthy social structure. Like cells in a body, they are the smallest social organisms, vital to the whole, and their children help sustain a sense of social purpose and commitment to the future. Families are strongly community oriented so they are natural bridge builders because of their social needs and their children's constant outward thrust towards the wider world. Children are great unifiers because of this social drive. Literally all of the children in our families have friendships across racial divides. Children are a main magnet of sociability and the strongest drivers for collective intervention and collective responsibility, although as they get older they can be great dividers too, through the tensions they cause.

Young people can be reached and their behaviour held within bounds only by winning their commitment to and enthusiasm for the future. They need a sense of purpose, so work, money, achievement, college and sport all open up possibilities. These needs should force society to recognise both the potential of young people and the risk of neglecting their demands for attention.[40] Parents suggest a Sure Start approach for school-age children. Young people in the families we talked to usually make their way out of trouble through the routes that society opens up, but some do not. Parents cry out for more help for young people but they also want to help. This is a largely untapped resource.

Families are a positive force in neighbourhoods because they need each other, use social spaces frequently and go out of their way to create local contact. Families foster goodwill towards neighbours because they need to know who their neighbours are for their family's security. Thus, they contribute in small ways to helping others as well as themselves.

The experience of the families in the present study leads us to four main conclusions.

- ***Cities naturally create hierarchies through encouraging wealth creation.*** The more prosperous buy their way out of poor conditions into more private, more spacious, more high-quality areas. Services in these better neighbourhoods match incomes because residents have a stronger voice, more power to control and more resources to supplement local provision. As wealth grows, so demand for services grows and richer urban residents in better areas need cheap neighbourhoods housing people without voice or power to provide the low wage services on which cities depend.[41] Security, food, maintenance, home and childcare, street cleaning, retail and transport provide the underpinning for city survival at the top.

- ***Neighbourhoods change with economic change.*** Low-skilled, low-paid workers with manual or service experience compete with each other for low-paid jobs since the loss of industry made many manual workers redundant, and globalisation encouraged the flow of migrant workers to cities.[42] They occupy unattractive spaces that decline in value, partly through the low status of the new occupants. Services decline to match this, so areas enter a vicious spiral of low income, decaying conditions and population loss. This happened in all four areas in the study.[43] Newcomers sometimes end up dominating, as decline becomes self-perpetuating and others try to leave.
- ***Low-income families need poor neighbourhoods*** for low-cost housing, access to low-paid jobs and basic services such as schools. Families thrown together offer the chance for community formation, even if they have different backgrounds, as their needs are remarkably similar. The inability to access better alternatives makes these areas a lifeline for low-income families. However, the poorest areas can eventually break down if they are not maintained.[44] This leads to future demolition, as several families explained.
- ***Cities function at the city level***, rather than at the community level, yet the families function at the micro-scale, as well as more widely. So they need to disaggregate their operations to the community level. For family survival requires not just community links but the wider city and society as a whole.[45]

To answer our three questions, then:

- Neighbourhood conditions do have a direct impact on family survival, making it difficult for parents to do the best they can for their children.
- Families can counter wider problems by creating support networks that have the potential to help the wider city as well as themselves to survive.
- Cities can help families by valuing their contributions and creating more locally based structures to deliver sensitive local services, hands on instead of hands off.

Cities need families, and particularly low-income families, to fill essential jobs and keep cities functioning and healthy. How we broker the interplay between the family, community, neighbourhood and city will determine our ability to keep modern economies afloat, dependent as they are on vast flows of people and resources around the globe. In the small neighbourhoods where the 24 families in *City survivors* live, these high stakes are being played out.

Notes

[1] Willmot and Power, 2007.

[2] Reader, 2005.

[3] Jacobs, 1970.

[4] ONS, 2005; NOMIS official labour market statistics, www.nomisweb.co.uk

[5] National Advisory Commission on Civil Disorders, 1968; Home Office, 2001.

[6] Wilson, 1987.

[7] DETR, 1999; Rogers and Power, 2000,

[8] Strategy Unit, 2005.

[9] Hills, 2007.

[10] Paskell, 2005.

[11] LSE Cities Programme, Mayor's Conference, Barcelona, February 2004.

[12] Glennerster et al, 1999; ODPM, 2003b.

[13] DoE, 1974-77; Manchester City Council, Pathfinders Seminar, July 2005.

[14] Lupton and Power, 2002; ODPM, 2002.

[15] Reader, 2005.

[16] Briggs, 1968.

[17] UNCHS (UN-Habitat), 2003.

[18] Briggs, 1983; Girardet, 2004.

[19] Young and Lemos, 1997; Lupton and Power, 2004.

[20] Richardson and Mumford, 2002.

[21] GLA, 2004.

[22] Power and Tunstall, 1997.

[23] Whitehead and Kleinman, 1986; Power, 1993; UNCHS (UN-Habitat), 1996.

[24] Burgess et al, 2005; DfES, 2007.

[25] UNHCS (UN-Habitat), 2001.

[26] Home Office, 2001.

[27] Power and Houghton, 2007.

[28] Gehl, 1996; DETR, 1999.

[29] DETR, 1999.

[30] Power, 2004a.

[31] Hills, 2007.

[32] Lupton, 2003a.

[33] Waltham Forest HAT, 1998; Mansfield, 2005: personal communication.

[34] Greenhalgh and Worpole, 1996; SEU, 1999.

[35] Power and Mumford, K. 1999.

[36] Beck, 2005; Berube, 2005.

[37] London Development Research, 2005.

[38] Urban Task Force, 2005.

[39] Layard, 2005.

[40] Paskell, 2004.

[41] Sassen, 1996, 2001.

[42] Power, 2005.

[43] Bowman, 2001; Mumford, 2001.

[44] Wilson, 1996.

[45] Diamond, 2005.

Appendix 1
Methods

Tracking 12 disadvantaged areas

This book is part of a long-term, wide-ranging longitudinal study of 12 highly disadvantaged areas and neighbourhoods, each covering between 14,000 and 31,000 residents. The areas were selected in 1998 based on close analysis of the 1991 Census, the government's Index of Multiple Deprivation and the Breadline Britain Index, which derives a definition of deprivation from national responses, that change over time, on what excludes people by income and social conditions from mainstream society.[1]

We used wards as a proxy for areas, although ward boundaries do not exactly coincide with the neighbourhoods we studied. We first identified the 5% of wards that were most work poor, meaning wards with the highest proportion of households where no one was in work, studying or on a full-time training programme. We then identified the 5% most 'deprived' wards as revealed by the government's Index of Multiple Deprivation. A majority of the 5% identified as work poor were also identified on the Index of Multiple Deprivation. Three per cent of all Census wards were both 'work poor' and 'multiply deprived' by these two definitions, a total of 280 wards. Mapping these wards revealed that all except 41 of them were in 'poverty clusters', that is, adjacent to other high-poverty wards. The 12 areas were selected out of the 280 wards.

The high-poverty wards were concentrated in six of the 12 Office for National Statistics categories of area types with high deprivation. These included London, large cities, industrial areas, mining and port areas, inner city areas, and other. The 12 areas reflect regional and ethnic differences and cover a wide range of characteristics. The 12 areas represent the range of problems affecting disadvantaged areas and are frequently used in other research.[2] The study tracks change over time and shows the impact of government policies on area change, in order to understand area trajectories. A final book will present an overview in 2008.

The families study

Within the 12 areas, four areas were chosen as the focus for an in-depth longitudinal study of 200 families, 50 in each area, in order to understand the impact of urban neighbourhood conditions on family life; and to learn how low-income families cope with the problems that surround them. The aim was to learn from families directly about how area conditions affect families.

Two adjacent East London areas were chosen, which were undergoing similar regeneration and change. Both areas had been hit hard by the decline of industrial and port activity. Two adjacent areas rather than a single area avoided the risk of a major initiative or intervention in a single area distorting the experiences of families in a particular direction, such as demolition causing a majority of the families to move, while one researcher could interview 50 families per area yearly in two adjacent areas.

With matched funding from the Nuffield Foundation, we mounted a parallel study of 100 families in the North, in two disadvantaged neighbourhoods in two Yorkshire cities. They are accessible to each other, allowing a single researcher to interview 50 families in each; both are important regional cities; and both are areas of concentrated disadvantage, undergoing major regeneration and changes of function, due to deindustrialisation and the restructuring of Northern economies, not dissimilar from the East End. Renewed funding for both parts of the study lasted to 2006. The aim was to compare family experiences in two contrasting regions, the North and the South East.

Identifying the sample of families

We found 50 families per area through local routes. We needed to recruit families on the basis of willing participation, since the study involved repeat rounds of interviews. We talked to many local organisations before we contacted the families. We were advised not to recruit through random door knocking since many households did not have children and there were risks in not knowing whom we were approaching. Recruiting in places families visited in the course of their daily lives would encourage families to opt into the study. The aim was to recruit and retain families who wanted to participate voluntarily and share their experiences. We decided against purely random selection, since we wanted to reflect the make-up of the local population as closely as we could in terms of parent status, tenure, ethnic origin and work. With only 50 families per area, we recognised that a random sample might not achieve this.

We used a snowballing method for contacting parents in order to create a purposive sample of families that reflected local population characteristics. Some families were recruited via local support groups and advice organisations. Direct personal contact with families at local access points became a central activity; it included schools, doctors' surgeries, childcare and Sure Start centres, Post Offices, community centres, cafes and shops. When our sample contained enough families with particular characteristics, we then recruited to match other characteristics. We recruited a broad cross-section of families from these generally low-income communities.

A potential drawback of this form of willing and purposive recruitment through channels where parents participate in local life is that it may bias the sample towards active, positive families and away from problematic, withdrawn families.

In practice, we found that virtually all families with children were in contact with local services, no matter how serious their problems. Some bias against families with deep problems may be inevitable, as they may remain hidden, but our sample includes many families in serious difficulty.

We deliberately avoided recruiting families whose lives were overwhelmed with unmanageable difficulties on the grounds that our study would be an added and unfair intrusion on such families; also our study was trying to understand through the families how neighbourhoods affect families, rather than how families with multiple problems survive there. This did not preclude our recruiting many highly disadvantaged families and several of the families we interviewed relied on social workers and other welfare assistance.

Documentation, anonymising and storing data

At the outset of the study, we created a database of the 200 families, recording important information about them. Each interviewee was assigned a code number. In this way, we kept track of all cases across all rounds. These codes were attached to all questions and to all extracted quotes. We kept in a special secure file the actual contact details of all interviewees. We protected families' anonymity in various ways: we recorded all interview material according to the family identifier with a letter for the area and a number for their position in recruitment; we gave each interviewee and other family members pseudonyms; we created broad age bands rather than specific ages for the children, for parents and for their time in the area. We changed certain features of each family, avoiding changing the meaning or significance of their story. In this way we ensured anonymity of individuals while retaining the integrity of the families' experience.

Our archives hold all typed interviews for all rounds, all tables, all quotes, qualitative analysis of open-ended responses and observations. The data will be available to a restricted body of researchers, at the end of the project, in accordance with Economic and Social Research Council (ESRC) guidelines.

Attrition and turnover of families

In basing this study within highly disadvantaged areas of predominantly rented housing, we knew that we were likely to find families in precarious housing, work and personal circumstances. A large majority of the families we interviewed were on low incomes and in categories of employment and tenure where changes and instability were common. We also know from other longitudinal studies that holding onto and tracking families from low-income backgrounds with low educational qualifications is extremely hard, even with resources to attempt this. These factors affected many of the families we identified. Over the eight years of the study we expected to lose a number of families, since on average families move every 11 years, every 14 years for social housing tenants. On this basis, half the families would have moved over seven years. We did not have resources to track more than a small number of families who moved out. By round 5, we retained 63% of families from East London and 74% from the North.

We took steps to minimise the loss of participants by building up a close rapport with the families. Sixty per cent of our original families were still in the study at the end of eight years and over seven repeat rounds of visits. Sending Christmas cards and short newsletters about the project at intervals and phoning families before visiting and fitting in around family schedules helped. We kept interviews to one hour whenever possible, to make it easier for families. But we gave interviewees maximum freedom to express their views and we therefore went on longer if they wanted.

We did not press parents for details when sensitive issues came up, unless volunteered by the families, and we made it clear to them that they did not need to answer questions where they felt awkward. We cut short interviews where family needs arose. A modest gift voucher was offered at the end of each interview as a thank you, without prior notice. Most families said they enjoyed our visits.

Researchers invested considerable efforts to locate and re-interview the families who had not moved. Working parents have very little time; children cause frequent and unexpected changes of plan; our interviews were never top priority, so cancellation or simply not being there made completing some interviews very time consuming. Around one-third of the interviews had to be rescheduled in each round; nonetheless, wherever a family was willing to continue, we rearranged times as often as necessary. Where a family was hard to locate (for example they did not answer the telephone or door) we developed different strategies such as leaving notes with contact numbers and calling and telephoning at different times of the day. We wanted to avoid putting families under unnecessary pressure or interfering with their privacy; so we worked around the problems if they could not stay involved or were particularly busy.

Three life changes particularly affected parents' ability to continue, apart from moving, which was the most common: breaking up with a partner or joining a new partner; having a baby; and getting a new job or starting college; in addition, health and personal events could make someone unwilling to carry on. Dramatic family change and particularly partnership break-up may explain why some families simply disappeared. In spite of such organisational hurdles, we were surprised by the families' generosity, hospitality and enthusiasm for our work. The majority of the families wanted to stay involved, were glad to be asked for their views and hoped it would make a difference.

Where we could locate the families who had moved, we followed them. Some were no longer interested in a study of the neighbourhoods they had left; others simply proved untraceable. Some schools were willing to forward letters to the next school where they knew it, but this indirect method was rarely fruitful. Council housing offices simply did not keep records of where families had moved to; this was the biggest obstacle. No public body was able to disclose follow-on addresses to us. Sometimes neighbours or relatives helped. Up to round 7, we continued to interview about five out-mover families in each area, 20 in total.

Replacing lost families

We decided to replace families we lost with other families recruited in the same way, through local contacts within the area, seeking as close a match as possible to the original sample.

The aim was to keep our total of families per area close to 50 in order to:

- keep the sample representative across the key indicators: ethnic origin; parent status; work status; tenure. These main variables could change significantly with smaller numbers;
- maintain as broad a picture as possible of area conditions by drawing on as representative a sample of views as we could;
- gain wider gain insights into changing conditions.

At each round, we asked the newly recruited families about key topics covered in previous rounds. We developed condensed interview schedules for this, omitting earlier questions that were repeated or that reflected changes between rounds of interviews. This enabled us to compare family views on generic subjects such as schools, crime and neighbours.

The attrition cases we recruited covered shorter timescales. But they reflected family experiences in these areas, against a background of the longitudinal perspective of the majority of the families we interviewed. The additional families lent considerable strength to the study by maintaining a broad spectrum of views on many local issues and also helped us to understand the dynamics of change in the areas by adding new perspectives to those of the majority.

The female bias of the study

We decided to interview the main carer for the children, the 'most present parent', since our focus was on bringing up children in difficult areas. We expected that a majority of our interviewees would be mothers, given the family focus of the study and the dominant role of women in caring for children. In practice, 98% of all interviews were with mothers although in two of the 24 families in this book fathers were actively involved in the interviews. We omitted two cases where the father's role was particularly significant both in the family and the community because it proved too difficult to disguise the family's identity. However, we frequently include their views in this book. In two cases, interviewees were older women (over the age of 50) who were grandparents as well as parents of teenagers at the outset of the study.

We decided that where possible we would interview people in their homes in order to create a relaxed environment, to minimise the inconvenience to families, to avoid childcare problems and to enhance our understanding of family circumstances. In the Northern estate we interviewed a few mothers in a local community centre; and in two East London cases we interviewed mothers in a local school. All our interviewers were female, which helped win the confidence of families. This did not seem to impede access to fathers where they were involved in a carer role. The London study had three main interviewers, plus two part-time, short-term interviewers; the Northern study had two interviewers.

We set out in the Introduction why we believe the female bias of the study provides a relevant and useful perspective on area conditions and family life. Women, and mothers in particular, offer unique insights into neighbourhood conditions and attachment to local communities, because of their survival needs. Through them we are able to explore the small scale at which most families operate in low-income neighbourhoods. However, we maximise the use of fathers' perspectives and recognise that this deserves further study.

The use of questionnaires and quantitative analysis of the evidence

While the study relied mainly on qualitative methods of interviewing and observation, we devised semi-structured questionnaires for each round to allow us to analyse as many answers as possible from 200 responses to a particular question or topic. We tabulated about two-thirds of the answers in all rounds using SPSS. In all this amounted to 84,000 responses from 200 families over seven rounds of interviews recorded in 1,400 questionnaires. This enabled us to show through tables what 200 families said about a large range of current issues, comparing findings across the four areas and between the North and East London. We used figures from these tables to support what families say. We also tabulated the family and area changes between the rounds, based on our repeat questions. We structured some questions on area conditions to make them comparable with wider studies, so we were also able to compare the families' views on area problems with wider surveys.[3]

We also encouraged parents to explain what they thought about some issues in an open-ended way by combining quantitative and qualitative questions: for example 'what school does your child attend?' (name, level, location, church, state and so on) – a factual question where responses can be tabulated; 'how satisfied or dissatisfied are you with your child's progress?' (satisfied/dissatisfied) can also produce tabulated responses; 'can you explain why?' (open-ended) requires more qualitative analysis.

With open-ended questions such as 'What helps you most as a parent?', we analysed responses on the basis of recurring themes that parents themselves identified, for example open spaces, play areas, friendly neighbours, community activities and family. We then grouped parents' responses under these broad themes, thus helping us to identify the patterns of dominant concern across a wide range of families in relation to particular issues. By using some quantitative tools of analysis alongside our large volume of qualitative material we were able to handle the scale of material and draw some broad-based findings from this large and complex study.

Selection and use of quotations

After completing the analysis of the questionnaires using SPSS and qualitative analysis in each round, we identified quotations, family by family, for each open-ended or explanatory response on each topic. These quotations, each carrying the family identifier, were documented under each topic, by area, for each round. Over five rounds, we built up a large stock of quotations covering the main topics shown in Appendix 3. This identified from all four areas relevant quotes on any of the issues we discussed with parents: schools, race, community, parenting, regeneration and so on. It would clearly be arbitrary and unmanageable to use the most memorable, or to hunt through 1,000 questionnaires covering five rounds. Our systematic documentation of quotes for each topic and each round allows us to select relevant quotes from a wide range of quotes on that topic or theme. It forces us to select carefully on the basis of all quotes on that theme or topic. Using a systematic method of extracting quotes, question by question, reduces interviewer bias and creates a database of qualitative feedback that as nearly as possible reflects what families said across the board.

Different parents articulated very different views on particular topics. Some families offered a minimal response; some elaborated more fully on most subjects. This means that useful and revealing quotes tended to come from a more limited range of parents than direct answers to questions that came from everyone. We feel that the combined methods of tabulating all answers, and systematically extracting revealing quotes to illustrate themes, provides an overview of what these families experience and their views on different issues.

Observation in the areas

Interviewers spent a lot of their time in the areas and observed many aspects of local life simply by virtue of being there. Open spaces, shops, schools, doctors' surgeries, community facilities, cafes, children's centres, housing offices, streets, parks, blocks and parking areas were all places where interviewers passed their time in between interviews. It is how they found out about what was going on in the areas. Since the interviewers were actively engaged in what was happening in the areas through their repeated contact with families, it was useful to record their impressions over time systematically. Observations were recorded at the time of each interview on the front sheet of each interview schedule, including what they encountered in the approach to an interviewee's home and once inside. This gave valuable context to the interviews, documenting over time the interviewers' and the interviewees' changing perceptions. It provided a ready way of refreshing memories, grounding the interviews in observed conditions.

These recorded observations provided valuable additional information on neighbourhood conditions and social relations; the interviewers also recorded at each family's interview the evolving context that surrounded each family and was often quite specific to them. This was particularly useful for the stories in *City survivors*, where incidental information, recorded as a by-product of the interviews, often revealed back-up evidence of what the family described. During the interviews, interviewers filled in responses in note form on the questionnaires, recording verbatim as far as possible parents' answers. Questionnaires were then typed up as soon as possible after the interviews. We taped interviews in at least 10 cases per area in each round, and typed into the interview schedule for these cases the much longer answers.

The emerging themes of the study

The early themes for investigation emerged from the original aims of the study and from pilot interviews, to find out how poor area conditions and area change affected families. Further themes emerged round by round from the families themselves as shown in Appendix 3. For example in round 1, so many families commented on the changing ethnic composition of the areas in relation to community that in round 2 we asked about it directly, building on the families' willingness to feed information into our study over time. But we avoided questions of a personal and sensitive nature, for example divorce, separation, domestic violence, childrearing problems, legal status and money matters, until parents brought them up. We felt that intruding into their personal lives would not directly shed light on neighbourhood conditions, but in practice they told us a great deal about the interaction of their personal circumstances and the wider environment.

The relationship of confidence and trust that we built up over time allowed us cumulatively to learn about family lives, offering insights over time that would not have been obvious in a single visit. This applied to the newer attrition cases as well as the original families, since they were aware that they were part of an established study involving many other families in their area. Local support for the study was strong, and we did not start from scratch with each new attrition family each time as there was much common ground between new and original families. In this book, a qualitative approach is adopted, only occasionally using quantitative evidence directly.

Ethical issues

The study raised a number of ethnical considerations. We followed the ethical guidelines set out by the ESRC. We also satisfied the medical research ethical guidelines and gained approval from local medical ethics committees to access families via doctors' surgeries. Similar rules applied to schools. Rules on complete confidentiality, accurate and responsible use of research findings, clear consent, care over the storage of information, accurate recording of evidence and anonymity were all followed carefully. Throughout the study we looked on the families as willing partners and accepted throughout that they had the right to withhold information or end their participation. Occasionally interviewers decided not to record what interviewees said because it seemed too sensitive an issue and too private to them.

The safety of interviewers in areas regarded as risky places for strangers was a concern. We agreed with all interviewers some basic precautions. They let the office know where and when they were going to an interview and rang in before and after each interview. They carried a mobile phone; they dressed inconspicuously; and they made sure they knew in advance where they were going. Being clear about the route to take added to their confidence and this increased their acceptance in the areas.

Interviewers did not go into a home without seeing someone they knew or the interviewee at the door. Interviewers did not go along routes where they felt uneasy to reach a house. Obstacles included a lift that appeared 'threatening'; a deserted street; an empty, poorly lit underpass; a dark, wet evening with no one about. The main worries were on the street during long, dark evenings and we encouraged interviewers to arrange taxis to pick them up directly from the address as they left in winter. The precautions we took gave confidence to the interviewers. Once they became familiar with the areas and knew their way around, they generally felt safe. We had only one potentially serious incident where a group of youths driving recklessly mounted the pavement where an interviewer was walking, seriously frightening her, but then driving off without doing more.

Without exception, families gave a warm welcome and made the interviewers feel comfortable. The fact that contact was in the home put the interviewer–interviewee relationship on a friendly and accepting basis. The cooperative and long-run nature of the study ensured a positive experience.

Detailed case studies of the 24 families

We explain in the Introduction why we adopted a 'life story' approach to this study. We selected the 24 families in *City survivors* based on the matrix of characteristics used in finding 200 broadly representative families from four areas. There were some variations, but we produced an approximate match between the 24 families and the areas as a whole. We only included families who took part in all five rounds. The 24 families represented closely the wider experience of the 200 families, which is shown using quantitative evidence from the tables of 200 families. With only six families per area we could not capture all family types for each area. Within this constraint we chose families who reflected positive and negative experiences of the area, who articulated their views clearly, offering insights into the areas.

The process of preparing the stories was complicated as much family information was buried within long interview schedules comprising around 60 questions in each round. Based on each family's complete interviews and observations, a summary outline round by round of the salient points about the family's background and experiences was produced, repeating this process 24 times. Records from 40 families were examined in this way to identify 24.

This process led to the emergence of six themes, as outlined in the Introduction. We then allocated one family from each area to each of the six themes, for example, four families from the four areas to the neighbourhoods theme, based on the particular relevance of those families' stories to that theme. This process was repeated for all six themes. Each family's five interviews covered all the themes, often overlapping; for example family and parenting; neighbourhoods and communities. But the families' experiences unfolded in ways that illustrated a particular theme more strongly than the others. Using one family from each area made it possible to illustrate each theme reflecting conditions in all areas. At the same time, every family had views on most of the themes and there are many cross-references in the text between stories and themes.

By putting together each family's experience over six years, we were able to develop the life story within the area of each family. By following families over time, their views became much clearer. This story approach showed the evolution of experience within each family while reflecting conditions in each of the four areas, giving us insights into how cities could be organised to help families more. We captured the families' circumstances and views by using their own words wherever possible. We only corrected language where it would otherwise be difficult to understand. We included all they said on the key themes.

The only changes we made in a family's own account were those necessary to anonymise the stories. However, in order to create a coherent story from around 300 responses to five rounds of questions from each family, we had to group their answers according to topics. For example, schools, community or regeneration came up in several rounds. Wherever necessary for understanding, we make clear the sequence of events. But in order to allow the families' own words to dominate, we have not included all questions, topics and rounds, as we felt that this would deflect from the strength of their story. However, we do make clear how parents' views fit with life changes and with area developments. In each chapter, the four stories are linked by explanatory texts and backed by statistical evidence from the wider survey.

The story method in this book seemed to convey most convincingly and in greatest depth the families' direct experiences and views over time. It gave the families a chance to explain in detail how they saw things, underlining the mixture of experiences and views within each family. The direct experience of particular families brought the areas to life. Live stories help readers to understand and identify with what is going on. It makes the best use of long-term, slow-moving changes, coupled with abrupt events; it enables us to see into neighbourhood dynamics through the lens of particular, but very different families, through the events and incidents that they witnessed or were involved in. The life story approach reflects contrasts and similarities across four areas, illustrating vividly the six themes of the book.

Limitations of the study

There are many potential biases in such a study. We have already discussed the dominance of mothers and female interviewers in the sample. The study reflects the 'female' perspectives of the participating interviewers as well as interviewees. Female interviewers clearly had success interviewing women about family matters whereas a male interviewer might have had more problems in some areas the study covered. Gender overrode other factors in this female-oriented study.

We screened interviewers for suitability, asking them to carry out a dummy interview with a local mother who lived near to one of the areas who was willing to work as a 'guinea pig' under the observation of a senior researcher. This helped to screen out off-putting or inadaptable interviewers and select sensitive, careful and adaptable ones. Empathy, listening skills and an interest in children were all extremely important. Alongside this, interviewers needed to be systematic in getting through the questions, accurate and quick in recording responses and motivated to persist in tracking down elusive families. Empathy and listening skills led families to report satisfaction at the chance to talk about their children, the neighbourhood and their direct experiences. Their desire to communicate generally overrode inhibitions and sensitivities. For example, some white families were willing to express sometimes hostile or fearful views about minority ethnic neighbours to minority ethnic interviewers, while some minority ethnic families often openly explained to white interviewers the bitterness they felt.

Another potential bias is our reliance on parent perspectives on family experiences. Some researchers question the legitimacy of reflecting family experience almost exclusively through the eyes of an adult. We occasionally include comments by children as they were sometimes present and contributed their views. But we did not set out to interview children or to interview more than one parent, even though in a number of families both parents did participate. This limitation does not reduce the validity of the views of those we did interview and we believe that the perspective of the most present parents on bringing up children in disadvantaged areas is relevant and timely.

There is a potential bias in the ethnic and class background of our interviewers. Over the course of the study we employed seven interviewers, two in the North, five in London, including two temporary, part-time interviewers. Two of the London interviewers were from a minority ethnic background, one African-Caribbean and the other South Asian. They both felt that their backgrounds helped in creating a relaxed and trusting atmosphere for talking to families from different backgrounds. Inter-ethnic tensions, between people of African and African-Caribbean origin, Sikhs and Muslims and mixed race and others limited this advantage somewhat. One interviewer felt that the more prejudiced white families might be more reluctant to be open to a black interviewer, while the other thought she blended in and encountered no problems with any racial group. One minority ethnic interviewer thought that class background also made a difference.

White interviewers did not have difficulty recruiting or retaining families of different minority ethnic backgrounds and a few of these families said spontaneously that they felt free talking with a white interviewer. But it is likely that some of the views expressed by minority ethnic families to white interviewers were tempered by considerations of courtesy and sensitivity and vice versa.

Different responses might have been elicited with ethnically matched interviewers; in comparable US studies, it is common to match interviewers and interviewees by race.[4] We could not do this, given the variety within each area. In spite of potential barriers, the issue of race relations was raised spontaneously by virtually all families of all races in the three areas with large minority ethnic populations and fast-changing populations, regardless of the interviewers' background. We are therefore confident that we captured with reasonable accuracy people's views on delicate subjects. All the interviewers were selected for their neutral, adaptable and reassuring style, so this did not seem to apply.

Continuity of researchers

The long-term role of the lead researcher has provided continuity and consistency of approach from 1998 to date and has lent stability and continuity to the overall framework of study, with one person responsible for the families research and for the wider areas study throughout. This helped each new interviewer to fit in quickly, providing scope to check on any uncertainties, to clarify problems and to ensure systematic records.

Our documentation methods and storage systems allow interviewers to access the accumulated records of each family at each round prior to interviewing. In an ideal world a single researcher would complete all rounds of the study and would record and analyse consistently all information. Even though this was not possible, we managed to retain the confidence of the families and local organisations and to retain the continuity and consistency of the research method, by following carefully laid-down rules and methods, as outlined here.

Notes

[1] Glennerster et al, 1999.

[2] Lupton, 2003a; Paskell and Power, 2005.

[3] Mumford, 2001; Bowman, 2001.

[4] Wilson and Taub, 2006.

Appendix 2a Summary of characteristics of the 24 families whose stories we tell

(1) Couple status

Married	With partner	Lone parent	Total
12	4	8	24

Note: At least one mother was no longer married in 2005, but had been living with her husband at the last interview.

(2) Numbers of children

One only	Two to three	Four or more	Total
5	14	5	24

Note: In the stories we amend the number, age and sex of children to disguise the identity of the family. We only do this where it does not affect the meaning of the story. The families have an average of two children per family.

(3) Age range of children at round 5 (by family)

Families with babies and toddlers	Families with children aged three to five years	Families with children in primary school	Families with children in secondary school	Families with children in work
5	7	18	11	5

Note: There is some overlap between these categories as most families have several children.

(4) Ethnic status

White	Mixed race	Black	South Asian	Turkish	Total
12	2	6	3	1	24

Notes: White includes Irish; mixed race includes Caribbean/White and South American; South Asian includes Indian and Pakistani; Black includes African-Caribbean in origin, and Black British. These ethnic groups are identified by parents whose stories we include.

(5) Work status in 2003

In work full time	In work part time	Not in work	Total
6	7	11	24

Note: Of those in work, six had taken on jobs since 1998 or moved from part-time to full-time work; none had given up working.

(6) Tenure of families

Owner-occupation	Renting from council	Renting from housing association	Renting from private landlord	Total
7	13	2	2	24

Note: Five of the seven owner-occupiers had exercised the Right-to-Buy.

(7) Mother reports suffering from depression

Yes	No	Maybe	Total
11	8	5	24

Notes: 'Yes' means parents referred to medical treatment for depression. 'No' means parents neither referred to treatment nor gave any hint of depression. 'Maybe' means parents referred to feeling depressed and showed signs of depression in comments about themselves, the area and family problems. Among the 24 families, only mothers reported depression.

Appendix 2b
Information about the 24 families whose stories we tell

Code name	Ethnicity	Partner (at outset)	Age at outset	Paid work (at outset, round 3 and round 5)	Number. of children (at outset)	Age of children (at outset)	Area	Length of time in area	Length of time at address	Wants to move (at outset, round 3 and round 5)	Own home (at outset)	Depression
Angela	White	Partner	20s	No/No/No	5	14, 12, 11, 6, 6	North Outer Estate	All life	3 years	No/Yes/No	Council	Yes
Annie	Black British	Married	30s	PT/No/PT	3	12, 10, 3	Outer London	All life	2½ years	Yes/Yes/not sure	Own – Right-to-Buy	No
Becky	White	Lone	30s	PT/PT/FT	3	9, 6, 4	North Outer Estate	11 months	11 months	No/Yes/Yes	Council	Yes
Cynthia	Black African	Married	30s	PT/PT/PT	2	11, 4	Inner London	13 years	11 years	No/Yes/Yes	Council	No
Delilah	Black African	Partner	30s	No/No/No	4	5, 4, 2, 0	Inner London	9 years	6-7 years	Yes/Yes/Yes	Council	No
Ellie	White	Married	50s	No/No/No	4	17 (+ 3 adult)	Inner London	29 years	29 years	No/No/No	Own – Right-to-Buyy	No

continued . . ./

Code name	Ethnicity	Partner (at outset)	Age at outset	Paid work (at outset, round 3 and round 5)	Number. of children (at outset)	Age of children (at outset)	Area	Length of time in area	Length of time at address	Wants to move (at outset, round 3 and round 5)	Own home (at outset)	Depression
Fatima	Pakistani/ Kashmiri	Married	20s	PT/No/No	2	2, 1	North Inner City	18 years	5 years	Yes/Yes/Yes	Housing association	Yes
Flowella	Black Caribbean	Lone	20s	No/No/Yes	1	7	Outer London	All life	8 years	Yes/Yes/Yes	Council	No
Jane	White	Lone	40s	No/No/No	11	2-19	North Inner City	7 years	4 years	Yes/(Moved)/ No/No	Council	Yes
Joyce	White British	Lone	40s	FT/FT/FT	3	21, 14, 10	Outer London	9 years	4 years	Yes/Yes/ Moved	Council	Maybe
Kali	Sudanese	Lone	30s	No/No/PT	8	16, 15, 13, 12, 9, 5, 3, 2	North Inner City	10 years	8 years	Yes/Yes/Yes	Council	Maybe
Kamal	Kashmiri	Married	40s	No/No/No	2	4, 6 months	North Inner City	30+ years	18 years	Yes/Moved (temp)/No	Own	Yes
Lesley	White British	Partner	30s	No/No/No	3	9, 6, 1	Outer London	All life	21 years	Yes/Yes/Yes	Own – Right-to-Buy	No
Louise	White	Lone	20s	No/PT/PT	2	2, 1	North Outer Estate	16 years	2 years	No/Yes/No	Council	Yes
Luiza	Brazilian (mixed)	Partner	20s	No/FT/PT	1	1	Outer London	1 year	1 year	Yes/No/ Moved	Private renting	Yes

continued . . ./

Code name	Ethnicity	Partner (at outset)	Age at out-set	Paid work (at outset, round 3 and round 5)	Number. of chil-dren (at outset)	Age of children (at out-set)	Area	Length of time in area	Length of time at ad-dress	Wants to move (at out-set, round 3 and round 5)	Own home (at outset)	Depression
Marissa	White	Married	30s	No/PT/PT	2	2, 6 months	North Inner City	4 months	6 weeks	No/No/No	Own	No
Nadia	Irish	Married	30s	PT/PT/No	2	9, 7	Outer London	3 years	3 years	Yes/Yes/ Moved	Housing association	Maybe
Olivia	White	Partner	20s	FT/FT/FT	1	4	North Outer Estate	6 years	4 years	Yes/No/Yes	Council	Maybe
Peter/ Margaret	White	Married	40s	Peter No Margaret PT	2	11,7	North Outer Estate	10 years	10 years	Yes/No/No	Own	No
Phoebe	White	Lone	40s	No/No/No	2	9, 4	North Inner City	12 years	1 year	Yes/Moved/ Yes	Council	Yes
Poonam	Indian	Lone	30s	No/No/No	1	3	North Outer Estate	4 years	4 years	No/No/No	Council	Maybe
Sola	Black Caribbean	Married	40s	FT/FT/FT	4	17 (+ 3 adult)	Inner London	19 years	19 years	Yes/Yes/No	Council	Yes
Yonca	Turkish	Married	40s	No/No/No	1	2	Inner London	9 years	9 years	Yes/Yes/Yes	Council	Yes
Zoe	Mixed race	Lone	30s	No/No/No	1	5	Inner London	10 years	3 years	No/Yes/Yes	Council	Yes

Note: FT = full time; PT = part time.

Appendix 3
Development of themes – round by round

	1 (1998)	2 (1999)	3 (2001)	4 (2002)	5 (2003)
1	Family Ethnic Housing	Update on households/ work/study	✓	✓	✓ New info on partners' work
2	Area changes, like/dislike, length of residence	Area changes – area issues Burrows index	Area changes – plan to move/stay	More changes? Better/worse	Local environment Gentrification Moving
3	Schools	Schools and children's activities	Same/better/ worse Secondary	Secondary school – work preparation Difference – primary/ secondary	Same schools Secondary
4	Health (omitted)		Health – disability/ medicine/ smoke/health services		When last used? Who/what for/ how often? Better/same/ worse
5	Local links/ community	Ethnicity Links with community Belong to groups	Relatives and friends	Community and race relations Barriers/ divisions Bringing people together Who to count on	
6	Image of area				
7	Economic – work/income/ benefits	Jobs – type, trajectories, qualifications		Unofficial work – cash-in-hand	Changes in income/benefits Bank accounts Credit cards Who handles money? Family budget Partner employment? Children's work

continued . . ./

	1 (1998)	2 (1999)	3 (2001)	4 (2002)	5 (2003)
8	Future – hopes, worries, stay in area?				Pressures within area
9		Crime and drugs			Community safety: Police Wardens Local action
10		Services people use			
11		Parks and open spaces			Parks renovation
12			Regeneration programmes		Regeneration – Sure Start and involve other – transport NDC/parks/ projects
13			Trust, security, mutual aid, influence		
14				Political engagement Belonging to groups	
15				Housing changes/ demolition	Right-to-Buy/Owner-occupation
16				Parenting: Difficult Time/enjoy Pressures Gangs/bullying Helps? What safer? Let out	Helping look after children
17					Social exclusion
18					Use of time

Note: ✓ = further development of that theme in later rounds.

Bibliography

Alcock, P., Erskine, A. and May, M. (2003) *The student's companion to social policy*, Oxford: Blackwells.

Allatt, P. (1993) 'Becoming privileged: the role of family processes', in Bates, I. and Riseborough, G. (eds) *Youth and inequality*, Buckingham: Open University Press, pp 139-59.

Barker, K. (2004) *Review of housing supply: Delivering stability: Securing our future housing needs*, Final Report Recommendation, London: HM Treasury.

Bartlett, S. (1999) *Cities for children: Children's rights, poverty and urban management*, London: Earthscan.

Beattie, J. (1964) *Other cultures: Aims, methods and achievements in social anthropology*, London: Routledge.

Beck, H. (2005) *Report from Demolition and Renewal Workshop held at Trafford Hall, 26th July 2005*, London: LSE.

Bell, L. and Ribbins, J. (1994) 'Isolated housewives and complex maternal worlds: The significance of social contacts between women with young children in industrial societies', *Sociological Review*, vol 42, pp 227-62.

Berube, A. (2005) *Narrowing the gap? The trajectory of England's poor neighbourhoods, 1991-2001*, London: CASE/LSE/Brookings Census Briefs No. 2.

Birmingham City Council (2003) *One size doesn't fit all: Community housing and flourishing neighbourhoods*, Birmingham: Birmingham City Council.

Blair, T. (2005) 'Get real on climate change', *The Observer*, 30 October.

Bowman, H. (2001) *Talking to families in Leeds and Sheffield: A report on the first stage of the research*, CASEreport 19, London: CASE, LSE.

Bramley, G. et al (2000) *Low demand housing and unpopular neighbourhoods*, London: Department of the Environment, Transport and the Regions.

Briggs, A. (1968) *Victorian cities*, Harmondsworth: Penguin.

Briggs, A. (1983) *A social history of England*, Harmondsworth: Penguin.

Briggs, S. (1976) *Keep smiling through: Home Front, 1939-45*, London: HarperCollins.

Bruce, J., Lloyd, C. and Leonard, A. (1995) *Families in focus: New perspectives on mothers, fathers and children*, New York: The Population Council.

Burgess, S., Lupton, R. and Wilson, D. (2005) *Parallel lives: Ethnic segregation in schools and neighbourhoods*, CASEpaper 101, London: CASE, LSE.

Cabinet Office (2005) Strategy Unit Report evaluating NRU, Cabinet Office.

Champion, T. (2005) 'Population movement within the UK', in National Statistics, *People and migration*, www.statistics.gov.uk

Cheshire, P. and Sheppard, S. (2004) 'Capitalising the value of free schools: the impact of supply characteristics and uncertainty', *Economic Journal*, vol 114, no 499, pp F397-F424.

Davidson, R. and Power, A. (2007) *Families' and children's experience of sport and informal activity in Olympic areas of the East End: Report to Sport England*, London: LSE.

Dench, G., Gavron, K. and Young, M. (2006) *The new East End: Kinship, race and conflict*, London: Profile Books.

DETR (Department of the Environment, Transport and the Regions) (1999) *Towards an urban renaissance: Final Report of the Urban Task Force*, London: The Stationery Office.

DfES (Department for Education and Skills) (2005) *Youth matters: Youth Green Paper*, London: The Stationery Office.

DfES (2007) *Departmental report 2007*, London: The Stationery Office.

DfT (Department for Transport) (2005) *Home Zones: Challenging the future of our streets*, London: DfT.

Diamond, J. (2005) *Collapse: How societies choose to fail or succeed*, New York: Viking.

DoE (Department of the Environment) (1974-77) *Inner areas studies*, London: HMSO.

Downes, D. (1989) *Crime and the city: Essays in memory of John Barron Mays*, London: Macmillan.

Dunleavy, P., Bastow, S., Beck, H. and Richardson, L. (2007) 'Incentive schemes and civil renewal', in T. Brannan, P. John and G. Stoker, *Re-energizing citizenship: Strategies for civil renewal*, Basingstoke: Palgrave Macmillan.

Economist, The (2004) 'Grandmother's footsteps', 11 March.

Economist, The (2005) 'Part-time workers', 30 June.

Farrington, D. and Loeber, R. (eds) (1998) *Serious and violent juvenile offenders: Risk factors and successful interventions*, London: SAGE Publications.

Finch, J. and Groves, D. (1983) *A labour of love: Women, work and caring*, London and Boston: Routledge and Kegan Paul.

Furstenberg, F.F., Brooks-Gunn, J. and Morgan, S.P. (1987) *Adolescent mothers in later life*, New York, NY: Cambridge University Press.

Garrow, D.J. (1986) *Bearing the cross: Martin Luther King, Jr. and the Southern Christian Leadership Conference, 1955-1968*, New York, NY: W. Morrow.

Gehl, J. (1996) *Life between buildings: Using public space*, Copenhagen: Arkitektens Forlag.

Ghate, D. and Hazel, N. (2002) *Parenting in poor environments: Stress, support and coping*, London: Jessica Kingsley Publishers.

Giddens, A. and Diamond, P. (eds) (2005) *The new egalitarianism*, Cambridge: Polity Press.

Girardet, H. (2004) *Cities people planet: Liveable cities for a sustainable world*, Chichester and Hoboken, NJ: Wiley-Academy.

Gladwell, M. (2000) *The tipping point: How little things can make a big difference*, London: Abacus.

GLA (Greater London Authority) (2004) *The state of London's children report*, London: GLA.

GLA (2005) *DMAG briefing 2005/17: Focus on London's demography*, London: GLA.

Glaser, E., Laibson, D., Scheinkman, J. and Soutter, C. (2000) 'Measuring trust', *Quarterly Journal of Economics*, vol 115, pp 811-46.

Glennerster, H., Lupton, R., Noden, P. and Power, A. (1999) *Poverty, social exclusion and neighbourhood: Studying the area bases of social exclusion*, CASEpaper 22, London: CASE, LSE.

Goldschneider, F.K. and Waite, L.J. (1991) *New families, no families? The transformation of the American home*, Berkeley, CA: University of California Press.

Greenhalgh, L. and Worpole, K. (1996) *The freedom of the city*, London: DEMOS/Comedia.

Groundwork (2005) *Play, participation and potential: Putting young people at the heart of communities*, available at www.groundwork.org.uk/publications-and-resources

Guardian, The (2005) 'In the hood', 13 May.

Hall, P. (1999) Evidence presented to Urban Task Force Report, London: DETR.

Halsey, A.H. with Webb, J. (2000) *Twentieth-century British social trends*, Basingstoke and New York, NY: Macmillan Press and St Martin's Press, p 2.

Healy, P. (2007) Unpublished paper on challenges of planning, Department for Communities and Local Government.

Hill, J., Le Grand, J. and Piachaud, D. (2002) *Understanding social exclusion*, Oxford: Oxford University Press.

Hills, J. (2007) *Ends and means: The future roles of social housing in England*, CASEreport 34, London: CASE, LSE.

HM Treasury (2000) Press notice SR2000/X1, 'Improving the life chances for children and young people', 18 July.

HM Treasury and CASE (1999) *Persistent poverty and lifetime inequality: The evidence*, CASEreport 5, London: CASE, LSE.

Hodge, M. (2007) 'A message to my fellow immigrants', *The Observer*, 20 May.

Holman, B. (2001) *Champions for children: The lives of modern child care pioneers*, Bristol: The Policy Press.

Home Office (2001) *Community cohesion: A report of the Independent Review Team chaired by Ted Cantle* (Cantle Report), London: Home Office.

Hunt, T. (2007) 'Teaching history', *The Observer*, 10 June.

Jacobs, J. (1970) *The economy of cities*, New York, NY: Random House.

King, O. (2007) 'Let's stick together', *Society Guardian*, 6 June.

Kleinman, M. (2004) 'Housing supply and economic growth: a view from London', Paper presented at the European Network for Housing Research (ENHR) conference, 2 July, Cambridge.

Kotlowitz, A. (1992) *There are no children here: The story of two boys growing up in the other America*, New York, NY: Anchor Books.

Lareau, A. (2003) *Unequal childhoods: Class, race, and family life*, Berkeley, CA: University of California Press.

LaRossa, R. (1988) 'Fatherhood and social change', *Family Relations*, vol 37, pp 451-8.

Latchford, P. (2007) *Lozells disturbances summary report*, Birmingham: Black Radley Ltd.

Layard, R. (2005) *Happiness: Lessons from a new science*, London: Allen Lane.

London Development Research (2005) *London's housing capacity on sites of less than half a hectare*, London: LDR.

Lupton, R. (2003a) *Poverty street: Causes and consequences of neighbourhood decline*, Bristol: The Policy Press.

Lupton, R. (2003b) 'Secondary schools in disadvantaged areas: the impact of context on school processes and quality', PhD thesis, University of London.

Lupton, R. and Power, A. (2002) 'Social exclusion and neighbourhoods' in J. Hills, J. Le Grand and D. Piachaud (eds) *Understanding social exclusion*, Oxford: Oxford University Press.

Lupton, R. and Power, A. (2004) *Minority ethnic groups in Britain*, CASE-Brookings Census Briefs, no 2, London: LSE, CASE/The Brookings Institution.

Médecins du Monde, Project: London, www.medecinsdumonde.org.uk/projectlondon/projectlondonspartnerorganisations.asp

Metropolitan Police (2006) 'Evidence on environmental signals and fear of crime', *The Economist*, March.

Miliband, D. (2006) 'Local government as a place maker', Speech given to the Local Government Association, Birmingham, 14 February.

Moser, C. (1993) *Gender planning and development: Theory, practice and training*, London: Routledge.

Moser, C. and Peake, L. (eds) (1987) *Women, human settlements and housing*, London: Tavistock.

Mumford, K. (2001) *Talking to families in East London: A report on the first stage of the research*, London: CASE, LSE.

Mumford, K. and Power, A. (2003) *East Enders: Family and community in East London*, Bristol: The Policy Press.

National Advisory Commission on Civil Disorders (1968) *A report by the Kerner Commission*, Washington, DC: US Government Printing Office.

National Travel Survey (2000-2005) London: ONS.

Newman, O. (1973) *Defensible space*, London: Architectural Press.

Newson, J. and Newson, E. (1968) *Four years old in an urban community*, London: Allen and Unwin.

Observer, The (2005) 'The hoodies, the editor and the fear factor', 25 September.

ODPM (Office of the Deputy Prime Minister) (2000) *Housing Act 2000*, London: The Stationery Office.

ODPM (2002) *Green spaces, better places: The report of the Urban Green Spaces Taskforce*, London: Stationery Office.

ODPM (2003a) *English House Condition Survey*, London: ONS.

ODPM (2003b) *The English Indices of Deprivation 2004*, London: The Stationery Office.

ODPM (2006) *Neighbourhood management – at the turning point? Programme review 2005–06*, London: ODPM.

ONS (Office for National Statistics) (2005) *Social Trends*, London: ONS.

Paskell, C.A. (2004) 'Community action around youth crime, drug-use and anti-social behaviour: who benefits?', PhD thesis, University of London.

Paskell, C.A. (2005) *Statistical profiles of areas in 'Dynamics of 12 low income areas study'*, London: LSE.

Paskell, C.A. and Power, A. (2005) *'The future's changed': Local impacts of housing, environment and regeneration policy since 1997*, CASEreport 29, London: CASE, LSE.

Phillips, M. (2000) 'Bernie Grant: Passionate leftwing MP and tireless anti-racism campaigner', *The Guardian*, 10 April.

Phillips, T. (2005) 'We need a highway code for the multi-ethnic society', Speech given to the Conservative Party Conference Muslim Forum, 3 October.

Power, A. (1987) *Property before people: The management of twentieth-century council housing*, London: Allen and Unwin.

Power, A. (1992) *Empowering residents*, Edinburgh: OECD.

Power, A. (1993) *Hovels to high rise: State housing in Europe since 1850*, London: Routledge.

Power, A. (1997) *Estates on the edge*, London: Macmillan.

Power, A. (2004a) *Neighbourhood management and the future of urban areas*, CASEpaper 77, London: CASE, LSE.

Power, A. (2004b) *Sustainable communities and sustainable development: A review of the Sustainable Communities Plan*, CASEreport 23, London: CASE, LSE/Sustainable Development Commission.

Power, A. (2005) 'Where are the poor? The changing patterns of inequality and the attempts to reduce it', in Giddens, A. and Diamond, P. (eds) *The new egalitarianism*, Cambridge: Polity Press.

Power, A. and Houghton, J. (2007) *Jigsaw cities: Big places, small spaces*, Bristol: The Policy Press.

Power, A. and Mumford, K. (1999) *The slow death of great cities? Urban abandonment or urban renaissance*, York: York Publishing Services.

Power, A. and Tunstall, R. (1997) *Dangerous disorder: Riots and violent disturbances in 13 areas of Britain 1991-92*, York: Joseph Rowntree Foundation.

Power, A. and Willmot, H. (2007) 'SCARP report: Social Capital within the Neighbourhood Study', Unpublished.

Putnam, R.D. (2000) *Bowling alone: The collapse and revival of American community*, New York, NY: Simon and Schuster.

Putnam, R.D., Feldstein, L. and Cohen, D. (2003) *Better together: Restoring the American community*, New York: Simon and Schuster.

Quinton, D. (2004) *Supporting parents: Messages from research*, London: Jessica Kingsley Publishers.

Ramphele, M. (2002) 'Steering by the stars: youth in cities', in Tienda, M. and Wilson, W.J., *Youth in cities: A cross-national perspective*, Cambridge: Cambridge University Press.

Ratcliffe, P. (2001) *Breaking down the barriers: Improving Asian access to social rented housing*, Coventry: Chartered Institute of Housing.

Reader, J. (2005) *Cities*, London: Vintage.

Richardson, E. (2008: forthcoming) *DIY community action: Neighbourhood problems and community self-help*, Bristol: The Policy Press.

Richardson, L. and Mumford, K. (2002) 'Community, neighbourhood and social infrastructure', in Hills, J., Le Grand, J. and Piachaud, D. (eds) *Understanding social exclusion*, Oxford: Oxford University Press.

Ridge, T. (2002) *Childhood poverty and social exclusion*, Bristol: The Policy Press.

Rogers, R. and Power, A. (2000) *Cities for a small country*, London: Faber and Faber.

Rowe, P. (1999) *Civic realism*, Cambridge, MA and London: MIT Press.

Runnymede Trust (2000) *The future of multi-ethnic Britain: The Parekh Report*, London: Profile Books.

Sassen, S. (1996) *The de-facto transnationalizing of immigration policy*, Florence: European University Institute.

Sassen, S. (2001) *Global city: New York, London, Tokyo*, Princeton: Princeton University Press.

Scarman, Lord (1981) *The Brixton disorders 10-12 April 1981: Report of an enquiry by the Rt. Hon. Lord Scarman OBE*, Cmnd, 8427, London: HMSO.

SEU (Social Exclusion Unit) (1998) *Bringing Britain together: A National Strategy for Neighbourhood Renewal*, London: SEU.

SEU (1999) *Policy Action Team 10: Report on Social Exclusion: Arts and sport*, London: Department for Culture, Media and Sport.

SEU (Social Exclusion Unit) (2000) *Young people: Policy Action Team report 12*, London: The Stationery Office.

Silverman, E., Lupton, R. and Fenton, A. (2005) *A good place for children? Attracting and retaining families in inner urban mixed income communities*, York: Joseph Rowntree Foundation/Chartered Institute of Housing.

Sport England (1999) *The value of sport*, London: Sport England.

Sport England (2003) *Young people and sport in England: Trends in participation 1994-2002*, London: Sport England.

Strategy Unit (2005) *Improving the prospects of people living in areas of multiple deprivation in England*, London: Cabinet Office.

Summerfield, C. and Gill, B. (2005) *Social trends 35*, London: Office for National Statistics.

Tablet, The (2006) Editorial, 21 October, www.thetablet.co.uk/issues/1000048/

Thompson, F.M. (ed) (1990) *The Cambridge social history of Britain 1750-1950: Vol 2, People and their environment*, Cambridge: Cambridge University Press.

Trafford Hall (2004) *Young movers*, Chester: Trafford Hall.

UNCHS (United Nations Centre for Human Settlements) (UN-Habitat) (1996) *An urbanizing world: Global report on human settlements*, Oxford: Oxford University Press.

UNCHS (UN-Habitat) (2001) *Cities in a globalizing world: Global report on human settlements 2001*, London: Earthscan Publications.

UNCHS (UN-Habitat) (2003) *Challenge of slums: Global report on human settlements*, London: Earthscan Publications.

Urban Task Force (2005) *Towards a stronger urban renaissance*, London: Urban Task Force.

Utting, D. (1995) 'Family and parenthood: supporting families, preventing breakdown', in *Social Policy Summary 4*, York: Joseph Rowntree Foundation.

Utting, D., Bright, J. and Henricson, C. (1993) *Crime and the family: Improving child-rearing and reducing delinquency*, London: Family Policy Study Centre.

Waldfogel, J. (2006) *What children need*, Cambridge, MA: Harvard University Press.

Walker, D. (2005) BBC Radio 4's Analysis, 'Love thy Neighbour', presenter David Walker, 28 July.

Waltham Forest Housing Action Trust/Evidence in DETR (2000) *Our towns and cities: The future – delivering an urban renaissance*, Urban White Paper, London: The Stationery Office.

Whitehead, C. and Kleinman, M. (1986) *Private rented housing in the 1980s and 1990s*, Cambridge: Granta Editions.

Whyte, W. (1980) *The social life of small urban spaces*, Washington, DC: The Conservation Foundation.

Willmot, H. and Power, A. (2007) *Social capital within neighbourhoods*, London: CASE and Rural Evidence Research Centre.

Wilson, E.O. (1999) *Consilience: The unity of knowledge*, New York, NY: Vintage Books.

Wilson, E.O. (2002) *The future of life*, New York, NY: Alfred A. Knopf.

Wilson, W.J. (1987) *The truly disadvantaged: The inner city, the underclass and public policy*, Chicago, IL: University of Chicago Press.

Wilson, W.J. (1996) *When work disappears: The world of the new urban poor*, New York, NY: Alfred A. Knopf.

Wilson, W.J. and Taub, R. (2006) *There goes the neighborhood: Racial, ethnic, and class tensions in four Chicago neighborhoods and their meaning for America*, New York, NY: Alfred A. Knopf.

Winkler, A.H. (2005) (unpublished) 'Survey of professional working mothers and their family responsibilities', London: CASE, LSE.

Worpole, K. and Knox, K. (2007) *The social value of public spaces*, York: Joseph Rowntree Foundation.

Young, M. and Lemos, G. (1997) *The communities we have lost and can regain*, London: Lemos and Crane.
Young, M. and Willmott, P. (1957) *Family and kinship in East London*, Harmondsworth: Penguin.

Index

F

G

H